Introducing the Liberal Arts

Introducing the Liberal Arts
A Guidebook for English Learners

Edited by

Cherie Brown
Akita International University (retired), Japan

James Reid
Akita International University, Japan

Malcolm Sim
Akita International University, Japan

And

Clay Williams
Akita International University, Japan

United Kingdom – North America – Japan
India – Malaysia – China

Emerald Publishing Limited
Emerald Publishing, Floor 5, Northspring, 21-23 Wellington Street, Leeds LS1 4DL

First edition 2026

Copyright © 2026 by Emerald Publishing Limited.
All rights of reproduction in any form reserved.

Cover photo: iStock

Reprints and permissions service
Contact: www.copyright.com

No part of this book may be reproduced, stored in a retrieval system, transmitted in any form or by any means electronic, mechanical, photocopying, recording or otherwise without either the prior written permission of the publisher or a licence permitting restricted copying issued in the UK by The Copyright Licensing Agency and in the USA by The Copyright Clearance Center. Any opinions expressed in the chapters are those of the authors. Whilst Emerald makes every effort to ensure the quality and accuracy of its content, Emerald makes no representation implied or otherwise, as to the chapters' suitability and application and disclaims any warranties, express or implied, to their use.

British Library Cataloguing in Publication Data
A catalogue record for this book is available from the British Library

ISBN: 978-1-80592-304-6 (Print hardback)
ISBN: 978-1-80592-306-0 (Print paperback)
ISBN: 978-1-80592-303-9 (Ebooks)
ISBN: 978-1-80592-305-3 (Epub)

Typeset by TNQ Tech

CONTENTS

About the Editors .... *ix*

About the Contributors .... *xi*

Teacher's Guide .... *xvii*

SECTION 1: THE HUMANITIES: AN INTRODUCTION

1. History *5*
   William McGovern

2. English Literature *11*
   Laura Kobata

3. Film Studies *17*
   Sean O'Reilly

4. Religious Studies *23*
   Seth Clippard

5. Western Philosophy *29*
   Kyle Michael James Shuttleworth

6. Rhetoric *35*
   Patrick Dougherty

7. Drama for Education *41*
   Naoko Araki

8. Creative Writing *47*
   Joel Friederich

9. Japanese Philosophy *53*
   Kyle Michael James Shuttleworth

10. Art History *59*
    Kuniko Abe

SECTION 2: THE SOCIAL SCIENCES: AN INTRODUCTION

11. Macroeconomics 71
    Wenti Du

12. Sociology 77
    Matthew Ryczek

13. Sociolinguistics 83
    Leigh Bennett

14. Cultural Anthropology 89
    Hisako Omori

15. The Geography of Public Health 95
    Sig Langegger

16. Management Studies 101
    Masahiko Agata

17. Social Anthropology 107
    Julian Manning

18. Linguistics: How Does Language Work? 113
    Clay Williams

19. Development Economics 119
    Hideyuki Nakagawa

20. Marketing 125
    Tomas Nilsson

21. Constitutional Law 131
    Takeshi Akiba

22. Political Science 137
    James Reid

SECTION 3: THE SCIENCES: AN INTRODUCTION

23. Mathematics 151
    Attila Egri-Nagy

24. Biology 157
    Jeanette Dennisson

25. Chemistry 165
    Jeanette Dennisson

26. Physics 177
    Yasushi Nara

27. Geology *185*
    James Reid

28. Programming *193*
    Florent Domenach

29. Environmental Science *199*
    James Reid

30. Statistics *207*
    Eric Yanchenko

31. Zoology *215*
    James Reid

ABOUT THE EDITORS

Cherie Brown is a former Assistant Professor in the English for Academic Purposes (EAP) Program at Akita International University, Japan, and member of THT (Teachers Helping Teachers), a special interest group within the Japan Association of Language Teachers that conducts English as a Foreign Language (EFL) teacher-development programs in Vietnam, Bangladesh, Nepal, and Kyrgyzstan. She is co-author of "Max Vocab" and "Partners in the Classroom," numerous other academic publications, and initiated the "Stories About Ourselves" project promoting the use of culturally relevant reading and critical thinking skills' materials in Bangladeshi EFL classrooms. She holds an MA degree in Applied Linguistics, and her professional interests include EFL materials development, high-frequency vocabulary acquisition, the professional development of teachers in limited-resource settings, and collaborative learning and teaching. She is now enjoying retirement in her home country of New Zealand.

James Reid is the EAP Coordinator and an Assistant Professor at Akita International University. He has published research on student creativity and critical thinking and convenes an academic reading course on Liberal Arts disciplines. In addition to editing this book, he researched and wrote the chapters on Political Science, Geology, Zoology, and Environmental Science.

Malcolm Sim is a Professor and Head of the English for Academic Purposes (EAP) and Foreign Language Education (FLE) programs at Akita International University. His interests lie in the fields of applied linguistics and psychology and how they interact in TESOL contexts. This includes second language acquisition (particularly the role of affective factors), pragmatics, learner autonomy, learner beliefs, English-medium instruction (EMI), teacher education, and curriculum design. He has worked in the area of language education for over 25 years and continues to be intrigued and inspired by the challenges that teachers and students face as each strives to reach their goals.

Clay Williams is a Global Communication and Language Professor at Akita International University, Japan. His research explores reading development, phonological awareness, and cross-linguistic transfer in second language acquisition. He has published widely in international journals and is an active presenter at TESOL and applied linguistics conferences. In this book, he serves not only as one of the editors but also as the author of the chapter Linguistics: How Does Language Work?, which introduces students to the scientific study of language—tracing its historical development, major theories, and the subfields of linguistics. Williams emphasises language as a core aspect of human identity and cognition, inviting readers to reflect on how language shapes our understanding of the world.

ABOUT THE CONTRIBUTORS

Kuniko Abe, PhD is a Select Professor at Akita International University, Japan, with expertise in Art History and visual culture. In this book, she contributed the chapter Art History, which introduces the discipline as both a study of artistic expressi on and a lens into cultural, historical, and social contexts. The chapter outlines major developments in the field, from connoisseurship and stylistic analysis to modern critical approaches and interdisciplinary methods. Abe also highlights how Art History fosters visual literacy and offers diverse career paths, from museum work to conservation and cultural law. The chapter encourages students to see artworks not just as objects of beauty, but as windows into the human experience across time.

Masahiko Agata, BEcon is an Honorary Select Professor at Akita International University. With a background in economics and extensive experience in higher education administration, reflecting a wealth of real business career that ranges from international financing, working in global teams of American and British company and organizations to a school foundation, he played a vital role in shaping Akita International University (AIUs) curriculum and institutional development over a decade. In this book, he contributed the chapter Management Studies, which introduces the evolution of management thinking—from early industrial approaches to modern leadership and organizational strategy. Agata emphasizes the integration of human values, ethics, and liberal arts into management education, highlighting how strategic and responsible leadership can contribute to sustainable, inclusive progress in business and society.

Takeshi Akiba, PhD is a Professor in the School of International Liberal Studies at Waseda University. His research focuses on constitutional law and sociology of law, especially regarding the rights of minorities. In this book, he authored the chapter Constitutional Law, which introduces students to the foundations and contemporary challenges of constitutional governance, focusing especially on Japan. Akiba explains how historical events, political values, and global comparisons shape the interpretation of constitutional principles such as pacifism, equality, and freedom. His chapter encourages readers to think critically about the real-world implications of constitutional law in democratic societies.

Naoko Araki, PhD is a Professor in the EAP Program at Akita International University, Japan. Her research explores the intersection of language education, performance, and intercultural understanding, with a focus on reducing learner anxiety and increasing communicative confidence through drama-based pedagogy. In this book, she contributed the chapter Drama for Education, which introduces readers to the educational potential of process drama. Drawing on classroom practice and global research, the chapter highlights how drama supports language learning, fosters empathy, and creates dynamic, student-centered learning environments across a range of disciplines.

Leigh Bennett, MA is a Lecturer in EAP at Akita International University. In this book, he contributed the chapter Sociolinguistics, which explores the fascinating relationship between language and society. Bennett introduces foundational ideas from pioneers like John Lyle Fischer and William Labov, while also covering key topics such as language variation, style-shifting, language attitudes, and sociolinguistic competence. Through accessible examples and thoughtful questions, the chapter reveals how our speech reflects identity, culture, and context—helping readers understand why language is never neutral and how being aware of these dynamics benefits language learners and global citizens alike.

Seth Clippard, PhD is an independent scholar and former faculty member at Hung Kuang University in Taichung, Taiwan. His academic interests lie in the intersection of religion, philosophy, and cultural theory, focusing on how belief systems shape human understanding and social structures. In Dr. Clippard's chapter on Religious Studies, he introduces the field as an interdisciplinary pursuit that draws from philosophy, history, anthropology, and sociology to explore the nature and impact of religion. The chapter traces the evolution of the academic study of religion from theology to a critical, comparative discipline. It discusses foundational thinkers, the challenge of defining "religion," and the shifting boundaries of religious inquiry. Clippard also highlights the relevance of Religious Studies in today's world, noting its value in fostering empathy, cross-cultural understanding, and analytical thinking. Whether examining sacred texts, rituals, or modern political movements, Religious Studies equips students with the tools to interpret complex social phenomena and engage thoughtfully with diverse worldviews.

Jeanette Dennisson, MS is a Professor at St. Marianna University School of Medicine. Her research background informs her teaching, which helps scientists and healthcare professionals gain the language skills to publish, present, and collaborate internationally. In her Biology chapter, Dennisson presents biology as an inquiry-based science rooted in childhood curiosity. She covers genetics, classification, and evolution, while tracing biology's history from natural history to biotechnology. She also addresses ethical questions around cloning and genetic data, stressing the importance of responsible research. In her Chemistry chapter, she uses everyday examples like baking and cleaning to explain atoms, chemical reactions, and catalysis. She outlines chemistry's evolution from alchemy to spectroscopy and highlights its role in developing medicines, materials, and green technologies. Dennisson encourages students to view science as a dynamic, interdisciplinary process—one that explains life and empowers them to engage ethically with the world's challenges.

Florent Domenach, PhD, is a Professor of Computer Science at Akita International University. With research interests in programming languages, computational logic, and software engineering, he is also active in reforming computer science education for Liberal Arts students. In the chapter Programming, he argues passionately that learning to program is not just about mastering code—it is about learning how to think. Domenach invites readers to see programming as a powerful tool for creativity, logic, and critical agency in the digital age, enabling students to move from passive users of technology to active designers of tomorrow's solutions.

Patrick Dougherty, EdD is Dean of Faculty and Professor at Akita International University, Japan. With a background in EAP and rhetoric, his teaching and research focus on developing students' academic communication skills, critical thinking, and persuasive writing. He has extensive experience in curriculum design and liberal arts education. In this book, he contributed the chapter on Rhetoric, which introduces readers to the classical art of persuasion and explores how rhetorical strategies—such as ethos, pathos, and logos—continue to shape the way we communicate in everyday life, media, and politics. The chapter highlights the practical value of rhetoric, both as a tool for analyzing persuasive messages and as a skill set for expressing ideas more clearly, effectively, and ethically across disciplines.

Wenti Du, PhD is an Associate Professor of Economics in the Global Business Program at Akita International University, Japan, specializing in open economy macroeconomics and financial economics. In this book, she contributed the chapter Macroeconomics, which introduces readers to the big-picture forces that shape economies, from inflation and unemployment to national income and government policy. The chapter traces the history of the field from the Great Depression and the ideas of Keynes and Friedman to modern approaches like New Keynesianism and real business-cycle theory. Du explains how tools like fiscal and monetary policy work in practice and how studying macroeconomics can help individuals make better life and financial decisions. The chapter also explores career paths in economics, finance, government, and international organizations.

Attila Egri-Nagy, PhD is a Professor of Mathematics at Akita International University. He is recognized for his work in algebraic computation, abstract algebra, and artificial intelligence, often exploring how mathematical thinking applies across disciplines. In this book, he authored the chapter Mathematics, which reintroduces the subject not as a set of rigid rules, but as a tool for clear and creative thinking. Emphasizing abstraction and mental modeling, Egri-Nagy invites students to see mathematics as a flexible language for communication when solving real-world problems—especially when integrated with computer programming and a Liberal Arts perspective.

Joel Friederich, MFA is a Professor in the EAP Program at Akita International University in Japan, with an MFA in Creative Writing and Poetry. His work focuses on literary expression in academic contexts and the role of creative writing in liberal arts education. In this book, he contributed the chapter Creative Writing, which traces the historical development of creative writing as a university subject, highlighting its roots in humanism and its emphasis on personal experience. The chapter explores how writing workshops emerged as the core pedagogy of the discipline and argues for the value of creative writing in nurturing voice, imagination, and intellectual freedom in higher education.

Laura Kobata is a Senior Assistant Professor at the Center for Global Education and Research at the University of Fukui, Japan. Her academic work focuses on EMI, academic writing, and intercultural learning. She introduces the subject as a reflection of the human experience and a powerful tool for developing empathy, critical thinking, and global understanding. She explores literature's evolution from ancient religious texts and classical drama to modern novels, digital formats, and diverse global voices, and highlights how literary study deepens our awareness of culture, identity, and communication, inviting us to engage with language, society, and the self. Kobata also emphasizes the practical value of studying literature, noting its relevance in various careers—from education and media to marketing, law, and even medicine. Through this chapter, she invites students to see English Literature not just as a subject, but as a lifelong gateway to human connection and intellectual growth.

Sig Langegger, PhD is an Associate Professor of Geography in the Faculty of International Liberal Arts at Akita International University. His research explores urban space, migration, and the politics of belonging, and his work has been published in international journals in geography and urban studies. In this book, he contributed the chapter The Geography of Public Health, which introduces students to how physical and human geography intersect with public health, sanitation, and city planning. Langegger highlights historical milestones and contemporary challenges in disease prevention, emphasizing how mapping, infrastructure, and social equity shape the health of populations.

Julian Manning, PhD is a Professor of English and Social and Cultural Studies at Nihon University College of Art. Holding a PhD in Social Anthropology, his research focuses on ritual, performance, and identity in Japanese and Southeast Asian contexts. In this book, he contributed the chapter Social Anthropology, which critically explores the meaning and use of the concept of "culture"—from universalist and nationalist ideologies to the modern anthropological view of culture as dynamic, diverse, and historically constructed. Manning challenges essentialist thinking and reveals how anthropology can help us understand human difference with nuance, empathy, and intellectual rigor.

William McGovern, PhD The late William McGovern was an Assistant Professor of History in the Global Studies Program at Akita International University. His academic interests included modern European history, political theory, and historiography, and he was known for his interdisciplinary approach to liberal arts education. In McGovern's chapter on History, he introduces the discipline within the context of International Liberal Arts, highlighting how historians study change over time and how historical methods have evolved—from 19th-century empiricism to postmodern and global perspectives. The chapter addresses major academic debates, the inclusion of marginalized voices, and the growing focus on transnational approaches. It also explores the real-world relevance of historical thinking, emphasizing skills such as critical analysis, research, and communication.

Hideyuki Nakagawa, PhD is a Professor in the Global Business Program at Akita International University. His research explores poverty alleviation, labour markets, and public policy in developing countries, particularly in Southeast Asia. He has conducted extensive fieldwork and evaluation studies on aid effectiveness and randomized controlled trials. In this book, he contributed the chapter Development Economics, introducing students to the causes and consequences of global poverty and inequality. Nakagawa presents real-world case studies from India and Indonesia, highlighting how rigorous research and data-driven decision-making can improve development.

Yasushi Nara, PhD, is a Professor of Theoretical and Nuclear Physics in the Global Connectivity Program at Akita International University. His research spans particle transport models, computational physics, and interdisciplinary applications of physics in higher education. In this book, he authored the chapter Physics, which introduces readers to fundamental scientific questions about the universe, matter, and motion. Drawing from historical discoveries and modern theories like relativity and quantum mechanics, Nara explains how the scientific method, rational thinking, and experimentation have shaped our current understanding of physical reality. His chapter invites students to think deeply about the nature of scientific inquiry and humanity's place in the cosmos.

Tomas Nilsson, PhD is a Senior Lecturer at Linnaeus University in Sweden, specializing in storytelling and rhetoric for organizational purposes. He frequently collaborates on international projects related to leadership, marketing, and tourism. In this book, he authored the chapter Marketing, which introduces students to the core concepts, history, and real-world applications of marketing in today's global and digital world. Nilsson explores the classic 4Ps framework, evolving marketing strategies, and the growing importance of sustainability and branding. He also outlines diverse career paths in the field, making this chapter especially relevant for students interested in creativity, communication, and business innovation.

Hisako Omori, PhD is an Associate Professor at Akita International University. Her research focuses on religion, agency, and power, and she is interested in the category of the person and the unit of an individual in various cultural contexts. In this book, she contributed the chapter Cultural Anthropology, which introduces students to the study of human behavior through the lens of culture, fieldwork, and participant-observation. Omori traces the historical roots of anthropology and its colonial legacy, while highlighting its evolving role in addressing global issues, from public health crises to cultural understanding in modern societies.

Sean O'Reilly, PhD is Professor of Japanese History, Popular Culture, and Cinema at Akita International University, Japan. His research spans cultural history, media studies, and the social impact of visual storytelling. In Dr. O'Reilly's chapter on Film Studies, he introduces the field as a vital discipline that explores how movies shape our thoughts, emotions, and understanding of the world. The chapter traces the development of film studies from its early roots to contemporary concerns, including gender and racial representation, narrative techniques, and the power of cinematic form to influence viewers. It also explains key concepts such as cinematography, editing, sound, and mise-en-scène, helping students become visually literate and critically aware. Emphasizing both enjoyment and analysis, the chapter reveals how studying film deepens our appreciation of cinema while preparing students for careers in media, education, production, and beyond. O'Reilly argues that films are more than entertainment—they are cultural texts that reflect and shape global society.

Matthew Ryczek, MA is a lecturer at Rikkyo University in the Center for Foreign Language Education and Research. In this book, he contributed the chapter Sociology, an engaging introduction to the study of human behavior in society. The chapter explores key sociological theories and thinkers—such as Auguste Comte, Emile Durkheim, and Karl Marx—while explaining the importance of social structures, norms, and the concept of the sociological imagination. With relatable real-world examples and a clear overview of both micro and macro perspectives, Ryczek shows how sociology can help us better understand ourselves, our communities, and the forces shaping the modern world.

Kyle Michael James Shuttleworth, PhD is Assistant Professor of Philosophy at Akita International University, Japan. His research focuses on environmental ethics, comparative philosophy, and the intellectual traditions of East Asia. Professor Shuttleworth contributed two chapters to this book: Western Philosophy and Japanese Philosophy. In Western Philosophy, he introduces students to key branches of philosophical inquiry—metaphysics, epistemology, logic, and ethics—tracing their historical development from Ancient Greece through to contemporary debates in analytic and continental traditions. He highlights how philosophy fosters systematic, critical, and open-minded thinking in response to enduring human questions. In Japanese Philosophy, he explores how Japanese thinkers adopted Western philosophical frameworks to reinterpret Buddhist concepts such as nothingness and non-duality. The chapter highlights the Kyoto School's distinctive contributions and introduces Watsuji Tetsurō's theories of fūdo (climatic and cultural environment) and ethical "betweenness," proposing their relevance to ecological thinking today. Together, these chapters show how philosophical inquiry—across cultures and contexts—remains central to understanding our place in the world.

Eric Yanchenko, PhD is an Assistant Professor of AI and Data Science at Akita International University. His research interests include statistical inference on mesoscale structures in networks, developing priors for scale parameters in Bayesian hierarchical models and Bayesian optimization. In the chapter Statistics, he unpacks the real-world value of statistical thinking—arguing that statistics is far more than numbers and formulas. With applications ranging from weather forecasts to AI, he presents statistics as a vital decision-making tool in the age of data. For Yanchenko, viewing problems through a statistical lens can facilitate clear thinking in a complex world

TEACHER'S GUIDE

Each reading in this volume introduces one of the subject disciplines that may be studied in a Liberal Arts University program of study and describes the relationship of the subject discipline to the study of the liberal arts as a whole. By exploring the various chapters in this volume, readers will learn something about the background of each field of study, along with a rationale for pursuing that subject at the university level.

To assist with readability for the target audience, each reading text has been modified from an original authentic academic text to remove unnecessary idiomatic language or convoluted grammatical constructions. The vocabulary has been analyzed and selected according to its frequency in English, using the online Lextutor vocabulary analysis tool.

Following the vocabulary analysis, the level of difficulty of each reading text was adjusted according to the two well-known high-frequency English vocabulary lists commonly used by English language teachers and researchers today: the General Service Word Lists and the Academic Word List (AWL). Words found in the second 1,000 General Service List of high-frequency words (known as the GSL), and words that appear in the AWL of high-frequency academic words (or AWL), are identified in each reading by means of bold type, helping students notice the words they need to learn within the context of each sentence in which they are found and within the context of the text as a whole.

These high-frequency general and academic English words are the most important words for learners to acquire for everyday English and use in academic life. They should be the highest priority for all teachers and learners of English.

Following each reading text are two lists comprised of the words found in the text that are most important for learners to study and learn, along with a glossary explaining words and phrases that are useful (to help with understanding the text) but not necessary for students to spend time learning. In each case, the first list identifies high-frequency words from the second 1000 GSL, which native speakers of English use in all types of everyday communicative exchanges. In fact, only around 5,000 English words are commonly used by speakers of English on a daily basis. Considering this, it makes sense for teachers to ensure that learners are exposed to these words before being exposed to less frequent words, as these are the words they are most likely to encounter and the words they most need to know.

Professor Paul Nation, a vocabulary researcher and vocabulary expert, reminds us that "The high-frequency words of the language are… so important that considerable time should be spent on them by teachers and learners…" He says that "… the time spent on them is well justified by their frequency, coverage, and range. In general, high-frequency words are so important that anything that teachers and learners can do to make sure they are learned is worth doing." (2001).

The second list found after each reading contains words from the AWL that are commonly found in academic use, regardless of subject discipline. The AWL was created by Prof. Averil Coxhead of Victoria University, Wellington, New Zealand, for the purpose of introducing students of English to the words they most need to know for university study. The AWL contains around 570 word families divided into ten sub-lists according to frequency, with those in sub-list 1 being the most common and those in sub-list 10 being less common (however, it is worth pointing out that all 570 word families are important because the high frequency at which they appear in academic life overall).

The lists of headwords for the AWL can be found here: https://www.victoria.ac.nz/lals/resources/academicwordlist/information/thesublists.

According to Professor Coxhead (n.d.),

> Just over 94% of the words in the AWL occur in 20 or more subject areas. This principle ensures that the words in the AWL are useful for all learners, regardless of their area of study or what combination of subjects they take at the tertiary level.

To successfully use the material in this volume, students and teachers should first be thoroughly familiar with, at the very least, 80% of the first 1,000 English words found on the General Service Lists of high-frequency English words (either the original list by West, M. (1953.) "A General Service List of English Words. London: Longman, Green and Co." which, though out of print, can be found in PDF format at the following URL address https://www.victoria.ac.nz/lals/about/staff/Publications/general-service-list-headwords.pdf or the New General Service List, available from http://www.newgeneralservicelist.org/).

Students should be encouraged to study the words listed for each chapter and to revise them often. Most importantly, they should use these words as much as possible in their own original sentences (through speaking practice or writing activities) to ensure that meaning is retained. They should also be encouraged to check out the meaning of each word and to identify the form of the word they need to use as they put the word to use for themselves. This is because it is the "need" to know a word, the "search" for meaning, and the "evaluation" inherent in the selection of the appropriate form of the word for the moment that ensures the deep processing required for memory-making (Laufer & Hulstijn, 2001).

Practical Suggestions

All teachers, of course, have curriculum guidelines they need to follow. This book, then, is designed to supplement existing programs and is not necessarily designed as a stand-alone course book, although a teacher may choose to use it in this way if they wish. The purpose, as explained earlier, is to provide students who are learning English with English language material that explains the various Liberal Arts disciplines and, at the same time, provides a rationale for pursuing studies in these disciplines at the tertiary level. Rather than working through the entire book chapter by chapter, the authors recommend that teachers select those readings that they believe best suit the needs and interests of their learners. The learners themselves can be involved in this decision if teachers indicate the various topic options to them. By making a careful selection, it is hoped that enough readings will be chosen to provide learners with an insight into future study possibilities in the medium of English at the university level. This can motivate them to consider a broader range of future study options than they may have considered previously. By systematically and thoroughly working through each of the selected readings, learners will begin to build a conceptual framework that will enable them to understand what Liberal Arts studies entail. Simultaneously, due to the material's graded nature and focus on key high-frequency vocabulary, they will develop and review the most critical English vocabulary and broaden their grammatical knowledge.

There are several ways in which a teacher might use the readings in this book. The aim of the authors is not to prescribe how to use this volume but simply to suggest. Teachers should feel free to use the material as they see fit and to experiment with and adapt the suggestions given below, keeping the needs and goals of their own learners in mind.

- Assign the selected reading text as homework. Have your learners note down any vocabulary or phrases they don't understand in their notebooks and bring these to class for the first discussion of the reading text. In class, have learners work in small groups (no larger than four people) to share their notes with the intention of assisting each other in better understanding the material. Alternatively, teachers can prepare a handout of questions for discussion.
- After reading the text and understanding it as much as possible, learners can also work with a partner to create written questions, in English, about the content within the reading text they want clarified. Set a specific number of questions to be created, for example, three or four. Collect their questions. In a later class, they put their questions on display for everyone to see. Divide the class into small groups and tell each group to select four questions they want to discuss. Allow time for each group to discuss each of their selected questions, asking them to make brief notes of their answers and ideas as they go. If any groups finish early, ask

them to choose another discussion question. Towards the latter part of the lesson, have each group randomly select a reporter to report back to the whole class. The reporters should say which questions their group selected and briefly explain the answers or any new insights they came up with in their discussion. The teacher can comment or ask the whole class questions too at this stage.
- After reading the text (either in class or at home), each learner could write a short paragraph in English summarizing two or three key points (remind them to keep this brief, they do not have to explain everything) and then state what they have personally learned from the reading text, using as many of the target vocabulary words as possible. They should also indicate whether, after having read the selected reading text, they would be interested in studying that subject at the university or not, giving reasons for their opinion. This writing can be shared with a partner and followed up with a pair discussion.
- Alternatively, and depending on the level of ability of your learners, assign different reading texts to different learners or pairs of learners. Have them work together, over two or three lessons, to create a poster or mini-presentation that summarizes the key ideas of the reading text they have studied. Their presentation should require them to use some of the new target vocabulary listed after the reading text they studied. They should then present their material to the others in the class. This presentation, which should be around five to eight minutes long, can be delivered to the whole class, or you could arrange a "poster presentation day," dividing your class in half to take turns to present. In this case, half the class presents (two or three times), while the other half of the class rotates around the room and listens to each presentation in turn. After half the lesson time is over (or you could spread this across two lessons), the presenters and listeners exchange places, and the process is repeated. During the presentations, the teacher can visit each presenter or pair of presenters in turn and either assess the presentation or, if you choose not to assess them, make notes for feedback later. In a final lesson, have learners comment to each other in groups or write individually, in English, about something they learned about each discipline area that was represented in each presentation. They should state whether or not the presentation motivated them in any way to study that subject further at the university or not and why.

The above ideas do not constitute an exhaustive list of suggestions but are simply a starting point providing possibilities for teachers to consider. At all times, teachers should monitor their learners' discussions and make notes of any concepts or language that seem to present common problems. Discuss these with the whole class after each of the selected reading texts has been studied and together, enjoy a shared exploration of the world of liberal arts.

References

Coxhead, A. (n.d.). *Academic Word List selection: Principles of selection used in developing the academic word list*. Victoria University of Wellington. https://www.victoria.ac.nz/lals/resources/academicwordlist/information/principles

Laufer, B., & Hulstijn, J. (2001). Incidental vocabulary acquisition in a second language: The construct of task-induced involvement. *Applied Linguist, 22*(1), 1–26.

Nation, I. S. P. (2001). *Learning vocabulary in another language*. Cambridge University Press.

SECTION 1

THE HUMANITIES: AN INTRODUCTION

In this book, we have classified the subjects covered as either humanities, social sciences, or sciences. The humanities include **disciplines** such as literature, philosophy, and history, which **focus** on **interpreting** and analyzing human **culture**, values, and experiences. Unlike the social sciences, which use both **qualitative** and **quantitative*** **methods** to study **societal*** behaviors, the humanities **emphasize subjective*** and **interpretive approaches**. In contrast, the physical sciences—such as physics, chemistry, and biology—**rely** on **empirical** methods to understand the natural world.

It is important to note that certain **disciplines**, including history, linguistics, and anthropology, can be studied as either humanities or social sciences, depending on the research methods used. In this book, we have decided to consider history a humanity due to its interpretive study of past human events and cultures, while classifying linguistics and anthropology as social sciences because they focus on systematic, empirical research of human behavior, language, and societies.

So, what are the humanities, well as the name **implies**, the humanities cover the essential **aspects** of *being human*. We can think of the humanities as a discipline that **seeks** to formally study and **analyse** human beings, their **cultures**, and the various ways they express themselves as a **species***. Put simply, it's the *study of ourselves*. Given the **classical** (and **literal***) **definition** of the **liberal** arts as the "art of freedom," **emphasising** building **intellectual*** **capacity** to be able to reason, argue, and to defend one's **premises*** and thus one's liberty, it is no **coincidence** that we first **delve*** into the essentials of what is **quintessentially*** human. The concept of *studia humanitatis** (i.e., Latin for "studies of humanity"), **comprising** literature, grammar, history, **rhetoric***, **philosophy**, etc., has been at the **core** of education since at least the **Renaissance*** in the 15th century. In order to really understand the world around us, we must first turn our attention inwards to know our own nature (i.e., *nosce te ipsum**, Latin for "know **thyself***").

In this section, we will be examining many of the **classical domains** of the study of humanities. We'll look at literature and film, we'll examine **drama** and **creative** writing, we'll **analyse** religion, history and Art History, and we'll examine **rhetoric** and Philosophy. While this may, at first **glance***, appear to be a **dizzying array*** of disconnected subject matters, they are all central to the **theme** of what is at the **core** of being human. Humans **communicate**, we tell stories, we **create** art and literature. History and religion are at the **core** of culture, **simultaneously*** directing practice and giving a **rationale*** for those **cultural** acts. Literature, **drama**, and art are the most **tangible** expressions of **culture**, and language is the **vehicle** for **culture** and **ultimately** how we **cooperate** as a **species***.

So, let's look at the field of humanities and examine the question of what it is to be human!

Vocabulary

Words From the Second 1,000 General Service High Frequency Word List

argue	examining
attention	film
century	formal
defend	grammar
discipline	liberty
educate	practise
essential	

Words From the Academic Word List (AWL)

interpretive	domain
analyse	drama
approaches	emphasize
aspect	empirical
capacity	imply
classic	liberal
coincide	methods
communicate	philosophy
comprise	rely
concept	section
contrast	seek
cooperate	theme
core	ultimately
create	vehicle
culture	focus
define	qualitative

Glossary

Delve (verb): Investigate deeply

Dizzying array (noun): An overwhelmingly large number of something

Glance (verb/noun): Look at briefly

Intellectual (adjective/noun): Relating to the power to know

Literal (adjective): Conforming to the simplest or plainest meaning of a word

Nosce te ipsum (phrase): Latin expression meaning "know yourself"

Premises (noun): The idea that an argument is based upon

Quantitative (adjective): Refers to anything that is measurable or expressible in numerical terms, often involving quantities or amounts

Quintessential (adjective): The purest or most typical of a category

Renaissance (noun): A period from the 14th to 17th centuries in Europe which revived classical learning and wisdom

Rhetoric (noun): The art of using language effectively to persuade

Simultaneously (adverb): Happening at the same time

Societal (adjective): Refers to anything related to society or its organization, structures, and functioning.

Species (noun): A group of closely related organisms

Studia humanitatis (phrase): Latin expression meaning "studies of humanity"

Subjective (adjective): Refers to something based on personal feelings, opinions, or perspectives rather than external facts or objective reality

Tangible (adjective): Something real or concrete; touchable

Thyself (pronoun): An older word for "yourself" (singular)

Ultimately (adverb): In the end; at the end

CHAPTER 1

HISTORY

William McGovern
Akita International University, Japan

Introduction

In this chapter, we will consider the subject of History as it fits within the field of **International Liberal** Arts studies. History is one of the oldest and most well-studied fields of all time. This interest in History comes from the common human need to understand our past. Although the basic ideas and ways that **historians*** study history have changed greatly over time, the desire to understand our history has not changed.

History, as a subject of study, includes both **academic** points of view of **scholars*** and popular (nonacademic) points of view of ordinary people. As a subject of study, History has a large influence on the way **individuals**, groups, and nations understand themselves. History and the way we view it produce shared experiences, memories, and a sense of belonging to a particular group of people. These ideas and beliefs help to shape how people view themselves, their **communities**, and the world around them.

The ways historians study and use our knowledge of the past help us to increase our understanding of what has happened in earlier times and of what is happening now, in the present.

Introduction to History

The word "History" means both (1) past events and (2) the study of the past. As an academic field, History centers on the second point. History covers all forms of human experience, from **culture** and social life to the **economy**, deep (or **intellectual***) human thought and politics. Historians study many **aspects** of human existence, from the ancient world to the present day, as well as anywhere in the world where human beings can be found living.

At its heart, history seeks to understand change over time — how and why events, individuals, groups, **institutions**, nations, and the world developed in certain ways. Historians use many different **methods** and **theories**. These methods and theories are often also used by other academics working in different fields of study to understand changes that occur over time and the causes of these changes. Historians **aim** not only to understand the past but also to understand how the past influences the present.

The History of History

History is one of the oldest and most respected academic fields. Although some historical accounts date back thousands of years, the modern academic base of history has developed over recent **centuries.**

From the earliest beginnings of modern science and a **period** known as "**The Enlightenment***" (also known as "The Age of Reason"), scholars began to accept that knowledge of the world and human society should be based on events that can be observed.

During the 19th century, many historians began to follow the ideas of the **German*** scholar Leopold von Ranke. Ranke is generally understood to be the person who began the modern study of History. He said that historians should try to understand the past as it actually happened. He also said that historians should not make judgements of the events and the people who took part in those events. Because of this view, Ranke trained his students to first go to **"primary" sources** — that is, **documents** that were produced at the same time in history where the events the students are learning about took place. Ranke believed doing this was more useful than studying later sources of **information** that were written a long time after those events. For **empiricists***, as historians who follow Ranke's ideas are sometimes called, our understanding of history should be based upon **objective** study and historical proof.

These ideas remain important in the academic study of history. However, many historians have since questioned whether full scientific objectivity is actually possible. Because of these questions, historians developed a number of different methods and theories to try to understand the past from new points of view. They have tried to understand the lives of people who had less of a voice in the historical record. For example, beginning around the middle of the 20th century, social historians moved away from political history toward the study of ordinary people.

Over time, social historians began to give more **attention** to the way economic and social forces cause historical change. To do this, they tried to understand the experiences of **peasants***, working-class people, women, and people belonging to different **racial*** and **ethnic** groups. Other scholars were interested in how people living in parts of the world, such as Africa and South Asia, tried to fight back against colonization.

Scholars coming after Ranke have also recognized that primary sources are almost always incomplete. These sources often **reflect** the ideas and beliefs of a small number of well-**educated** people. This group of people in a society is often called "the **elite***."

Recently, a growing number of academics, known as **cultural** historians, have moved away from studying the lives of certain **categories*** of people to understanding those categories themselves and how they are formed. Instead of thinking only about the experiences of women or racial **minorities**, for example, cultural historians have begun to study how the categories of **gender** and race themselves were built and **challenged**.

The different ways of studying history often cross over into each other. For example, historians might use methods and theories from social, cultural, and gender history together as they try to understand and get a complete picture of the past.

Current Debates in History

Recently, new ways to study the past have been developed. These theories and methods come from new ways of thinking about earlier historical **models**. For example, **postmodern*** historians (sometimes called **post-structuralist*** historians) disagreed with the idea that it is possible to understand the past without our present experience, knowledge and beliefs shaping our thinking. In other words, they believe it is impossible to be completely **objective*** about the past.

Many postmodern scholars suggested that any primary source, or **text**, contained **multiple** and sometimes **opposed** meanings. When someone tried to read such a source, their thinking was shaped by their own **biases** and understandings of the ideas in the text. In other words, any understanding of the sources would be shaped by the **subjective*** opinion belonging to the reader.

Other newer ways of studying history have come from the fact that many scholars are not happy with the common way that history is studied. Many historians think that scholars think of their area of study only within the idea of a nation-state or events in particular places. These historians **argue** that doing this causes us to forget that there are larger forces at work. They believe this may lead us to put too much importance on Western states, Western people, and Western institutions.

Historians who argue this way favor studying history from a bigger point of view, that is, from a **global** point of view, and they stress global **connections** and the fact that these change over time. They are also interested in the development of **globalization.** Some other scholars, known as **transnational*** historians, are more interested in how communities form, in institutions, and in the economic forces that connect people and institutions in two or more nation-states.

History in Modern International Liberal Arts

Although the **exact** meaning of liberal arts is questioned, the idea of liberal arts can be found several centuries ago (or maybe far longer). To begin, the idea was mostly found in the study of **logic** (the study of the ways in which people think and reason). Over time, Western universities added other fields, such as history and literature, as well as scientific fields, such as **mathematics*** and **physical** sciences. The 19th century saw the beginning and growth of numerous academic subjects. This growth included subjects within the social and physical sciences, as well as increasing specialization among scholars, students, and universities.

However, during the 20th century, the popularity of liberal arts education has grown, both at smaller liberal arts colleges and some universities. A liberal arts education tries to help students to follow their interests and to study a wide range of subjects. As a field of study, history takes theories and methods from many other fields, such as **anthropology***, literature, political science, **psychology**, and **sociology***. In addition, a growing number of historians tend to include global or transnational forces (forces that cross national **boundaries**).

Real-World Applications of History

The study of history has a number of **practical** applications. Many history students go on to work in universities, **museums***, and historical **sites**. However, studying history also prepares students to find other kinds of **careers*** too. Many of the **skills** taught in history classes—such as **critical** thinking, **research**, writing, how to build and support academic arguments, and **communication**—are useful in many different careers. Examples of these include education, the **media**, public **administration** and **policy**, the foreign service, business, politics, and law.

History also has many other real-world applications, though these might not be **immediately** clear to us. One of the reasons most modern nation-states provide primary and secondary school students with an education in history is because it builds and strengthens a shared sense of national **identity**, values, and the **responsibilities** of **citizenship***. History is also useful for understanding the wider world. As part of international liberal arts, studying history will give you a deeper knowledge of different cultures, nations, and global systems. This can be useful when you meet or work with people from around the world. Studying history will also help you to be better at **analyzing** world events and the people and institutions that take part in them.

Adapted from a text by the late Professor William McGovern, PhD
Who was Assistant Professor History, Global Studies Program.
Akita International University.
Japan.

Vocabulary

Words from the Second 1000 General Service List

aim	boundaries
argue/arguments	centuries connect connections
attention	critical

discipline
during
educated education
exact
immediately
information
international
models
multiple

opposed
practical
preservation
refers
reflect
responsibilities
skills
ten

Words from the Academic Word List

academic
administration
analyze
area
aspects
biases
categories
challenged
communication
communities
constructed
cultural/culture
debates
documents
economic economy
emphasize
ethnic
gender
global globalization
identity

individuals
institutions
liberal
logic
media
methods
minorities
objective objectivity
period
physical
policy
primary
psychology
range
research
seeks
sites
source
text
theories

Glossary

It is not necessary for learners to memorize these words.

Anthropology (noun): The academic study of humans and human behavior and societies in the past and present.
Career (noun): Often understood as one's profession or job pathway.
Categories (plural noun): Groupings of people, ideas or things according to qualities or characteristics that they have in common.
Citizenship (noun): The state of being recognized as a legal member of a certain country or nation.
Empiricists (plural noun): The name given to scholars who stress the importance of objectivity and scientific and historical evidence to support ideas and beliefs.
The Elite (noun phrase): Used to describe a small group of people who are privileged above other people because of high status, advanced education or extreme wealth.
The Enlightenment (noun): A Western 17th- and 18th-century intellectual and philosophical movement that stressed rational thinking as the way to understand the world and freedom of thought.
German (adjective): Used to describe the people and language of the country of Germany.

Historians (noun): The name given to academic scholars who study History.

Intellectual (adjective): Used to describe educated/academic ways of thinking

Mathematics (noun): A subject that covers learning about topics such as quantity, structure, space and change, usually through the use of numbers and symbols.

Museum (noun): A place where important cultural, historical, scientific and artistic items are stored and may be studied. Museums are usually open to members of the public.

Objective (adjective): Used to describe an observation or interpretation that is not influenced by individual biases, opinions or points of view.

Peasant (noun): A small landowner or agricultural laborer usually of low socioeconomic status.

Post-modern/post-structuralist (noun phrases): The names given to a philosophical movement that began around the middle of the 20th century. This movement influenced many fields such as philosophy, economics, the arts and architecture and criticized the ideas of earlier philosophical movements, including modernism.

Racial (adjective): Used to describe people on the basis of their race or ethnicity.

Sociology (noun): The academic study of human social relationships and institutions.

Scholars (noun plural): The name given to people who work in the field of academic study. University professors, researchers and students in institutions of higher learning are often referred to as scholars.

Subjective (adjective): Used to describe an observation or interpretation that is influenced by individual biases, interpretations, beliefs and opinions.

Transnational (adjective): Used to describe human activity or ideas that move from country to country, cross national boundaries.

CHAPTER 2

ENGLISH LITERATURE

Laura Kobata
University of Fukui, Japan

Introduction

Have you ever passed the time on a long train or **bus** ride by watching a stranger nearby and trying to **imagine** the story of his or her life? Have you ever found yourself telling the story of your daily life to yourself as you went through your day? As human beings, we naturally try to find and **create** meaning in the events and actions of others around us. We often think of our own life experiences as **chapters** in the greater story of our life. Every experience offers us a chance to learn something new about the world, about others, and, **ultimately,** about ourselves. In our daily lives, the events we observe and **participate** in are like "**texts**" which we "read."

In literature—**novels*** short stories, plays, **poetry, essays***—we get to see someone else's (the writer's) view of the world. Sometimes this view is **fantastical***, like the **magical*** world of Hogwarts, the "School of **Witchcraft and Wizardry***" in the Harry Potter novels by J.K. Rowling. However, along with our **delight** in a world where magic is possible and **pet owls*** are common, we also find **connections** to real human experience.

In the world of Hogwarts, "dementors" are magical **beasts** that take away the will of a human to live by **sucking** all the happiness out of a person's life. Readers can easily connect these magical beasts with the real-life experience of **depression** and hopelessness. Anyone who has ever suffered from depression will recognize that these "dementors" are not just characters in a fantasy but in fact, are used to show us a very real part of human experience, the sad and difficult side of life. As we understand this, the magical world becomes part of our world.

Writers use the written word to **communicate** messages to their readers for a number of purposes—to describe what they see, to **instruct** and **improve** moral knowledge, to **warn**, to call to action, and, of course, to **entertain**. Perhaps part of being human is this love of telling stories. Literature, with all its great **diversity** of time, place, **origins**, purpose, **method**, and **messages**, offers us a valuable **tool** for answering the question of what it means to be human. The study of English literature is, therefore, a study not only of the written word but also of our human condition.

History

The origins of literature go far back into human history. Some of our oldest texts are the ancient texts of many of the world religions. The first **dramas** may have come from the Egyptians and go back as far as 3,000 **BCE**, while our modern ideas of drama come from long ago in ancient Greece. Ancient Greek playwrights like Aeschylus (525-426 BCE), Sophocles (496-406 BCE), and Euripides (c.480-406 BCE) wrote plays that people still read today.

Researchers are still undecided about which text in the world should be regarded as the "first novel." For many people, the answer lies in the history of Japanese literature with the novel, "The Tale of Genji" (Genji Monogatari), written by Murasaki Shikibu, a Japanese **lady-in-waiting*** at the **Imperial court*** in Heian times (794-1185 **CE**).

English literature as a field of study, however, is much more recent. Before the 1800s, in the West, a "person of letters" (that is, someone who was well-**educated**) was someone who had read the **classics**—the dramas, histories, poetry, **philosophy**, religious writings, and stories starting from the Ancient Greeks and Romans. It was not until the early 19th **century** that university departments of English Literature began to exist in the form we see in universities today. For many years, people thought that a person needed to know about the classic texts from the time of the ancient Greeks up until the 19th century if they were to be considered an educated person. It was not until quite recently that a study of English literature and the chance to make English literature the main field of study began. However, ever since the beginning of English literature departments at Universities, English Literature, as a field of study, has been popular with students worldwide.

Modern-Day Positioning

To begin, English literature studies **focused** on the *Western canon** (a particular group of Western texts considered to be examples of the best of their kind), and students read the works of **classical** Greek **theater***; the works of Shakespeare; **poets** such as Shelley and Keats; and novelists Hardy, Tolstoy, Dostoevsky, Joyce, and so on. Today, the canon has been **challenged** and is seen as ever-**evolving,** with many university courses now including more texts from a wider spread of writers. Many English literature departments offer courses in World Literature as well as in **Ethnic** and **Minority** Literature, such as Women's Literature, **LGBTQ*** Literature, African-American Literature, Japanese-American Literature, and Native-American Indian Literature.

Other **genres*** (types or kinds of literature) besides the novel and essay are more widely recognized as well, for example, **creative non-fiction***, science **fiction***, **detective** fiction, true **crime**, travel literature, **graphic*** novels, comics (manga) and many more. The forms of texts have also changed and grown in number in this **digital*** age. The way we live our modern lives means that, for many people, free time is hard to find. Many people are always on the move from the time they get up and go to work to the moment they return home and are **tired** at the end of a long day. Websites and **apps*** such as "audible.com," offer readers **audio recordings*** of novels. Having literature in this form means that people can listen to a book as they travel to and from work or while they make **dinner**. Such audio texts have become popular with many people.

The Internet has also opened up new opportunities for people to **publish** their work themselves. Now many writers publish essays, poetry, and stories **online** in blogs, **e-zines***, podcasts, tweets, and social **networks** like Facebook. In fact, the "**instapoet***" Rupi Kaur, who began by publishing her poetry on Instagram, ended up at the top of the '**New York Times Best Seller List***' with the first poems she published at the age of 24.

An example of the **dynamic** changes taking place in the field of literature is that the winner of the famous **Nobel Prize*** in Literature in 2016 was Bob Dylan, a famous American singer-songwriter. The words of Dylan's songs—set to rock, folk, and blues music—have influenced **generations** of listeners. The **controversial** naming of Dylan as the 2016 winner of the Nobel Prize caused a great deal of **public** discussion because he is known as a master songwriter, but is not widely recognized as a **formal** "poet." However, the fact that such an honor was given to a popular musician proves that indeed, as Bob Dylan himself might say, "**The Times They Are a-Changing***."

Benefits

Recently there have been many articles and studies **published** about the **benefits** of reading. These studies say that the number one benefit of reading literature is that it helps people to develop a greater **capacity** for **empathy***. For many young people, today's **connected** world seems to be opening up new opportunities and helping us to see the world in new ways. At the same time, the growing use of digital tools has lessened the time people meet face-to-face each day. To develop empathy, we need to know how others experience life. Researchers who have studied this believe that reading a novel increases one's ability to understand what others think and feel. This is because when we read, we learn how other people see and experience the world around them, and we see life from a point of view that is not our own.

The act of reading literature also increases our capacity to think in a more **critical** way. Reading and studying literature helps a reader to think about different relationships. We, the readers, relate not only to the *characters* in a novel but to the *writer* of the novel as well. Thus, when we read a text, we need to think about it on more than one level.

The first level is our **emotional*** response to the text. What is it telling us? How is it challenging or **confirming** our life experiences and views? At another level, we have to look deeply into the text itself and ask a number of other important questions. How has the writer used special writing methods (called **rhetorical devices***) to shape our thinking? How does the use of this kind of language **affect** us as readers? What is being said directly? And what is being **implied**? That is, what **information** in the text helps us to **infer** the things that a writer *doesn't* actually say that show us the bigger picture about what is happening? As we build our understanding of a text, yet another level we need to think about includes the political, historical, and social influences. How do these influences help us to understand the people in the story, and how does our world connect to these ideas? What important messages, **arguments** and ideas are presented in the text?

As we have seen above, reading and studying literature is one of the best exercises in gaining and developing critical thinking **skills**. It means the reader has to take part in the story in an active way. Now you can see that reading and studying literature is far from just taking in words with one's eyes or being "entertained" by a great story. Students of literature need to think deeply and critically about what they read.

You may now be starting to understand how important it is for a student of Literature to be a careful reader. A book without a reader is just words on paper; a book with a thoughtful reader becomes a wonderful experience. Taking a course in English Literature at a **Liberal Arts*** university will open up this field of study fully for you in new ways you may not have ever imagined.

Employment Opportunities

Becoming a more **empathetic*** person and a stronger critical thinker can really help you, not only in daily life but also in most types of work. In today's world, studying English Literature can also help you understand other cultures and other ways of thinking, but it can also be useful to you when working with other people within your own **culture**.

Perhaps the first employment opportunity that comes to mind for those who study English literature is that of researching and teaching English literature at a university. Other opportunities include teaching children and young people at all school levels, being a librarian, and teaching English as a foreign language. Of course, if you love words and are creative, you could become a writer and write novels yourself or become a poet. Most highly successful writers are known to have strong and **regular** reading **habits**. In fact, they would say that reading is as important to their lives as eating and sleeping!

There are also many other fields of work for which a knowledge of English literature is needed: **digital copywriter***; film critic, **journalist***; **copy-editor*** or **proofreader***; **web content manager***; **advertising copywriter***; **scriptwriter*** and **editor***. In addition, English Literature is seen as highly valuable in other fields, such as **anthropology*, sociology***, **psychology**, marketing, and social work. Studying English literature can even help you get into law school or **medical** school! You never know; by studying English Literature, a whole new and exciting future life direction might open up to you.

Adapted from a text by Laura Kobata,
Senior Assistant Professor,
Center for Global Education and Research.
University of Fukui, Japan.

Vocabulary

Words from the second 1000 General Service High-Frequency Word List

arguments
beasts
bus
century
connect/connections
crime
critical
delight
dinner
discussion
educated
entertain
formal
habit
imagine

improve
information
messages
origins
pet
poem/poet/poetry
regular
sad
skills
sucking
tired
traditional
tool
warn

Words From the Academic Word List

affect
benefits
challenged/challenging
chapters
classic/classical
communicate
create/creative
culture
depression
detective
diversity
drama
dynamic
capacity
controversial
ethnic
evolving
focused

generations
implied
infer
medical
method
minority
networks
participate
period
philosophy
publish
psychology
researcher
response
text
traditional
instruct
ultimately

Glossary

It is not necessary for learners to memorize these words and expressions.

Advertising copywriter (noun): Advertising copywriters write texts that help sell goods and services.
Anthropology (noun): the study of human societies and cultures and their development.
Apps (noun): An app, which is short for "application," is a type of software that can be installed and run on a computer, tablet, smartphone or other electronic devices.

Audio recordings *(noun phrase)*: Sound events (e.g. songs or spoken language) that are stored on a tape, or by digital means that can be listened to again later

BCE/CE: Acronyms used to describe two large periods of time in history. BCE Before (the) Common (or Current) Era (previously called BC (or Before Christ). CE (the) Common Era (previously called AD)

Copy-editor (noun): A person who revises written material to improve readability and fitness and makes sure the text is free of grammatical and factual errors

Digital (adjective): A way of storing information, usually for use by some kind of computer or electronic machine, using 1 and 0 as a form of electronic code.

Digital copywriter (noun): A digital copywriter produces the written content for webpages.

Editor (noun): a person who is in charge of and determines the final content of a newspaper, magazine, or multi-author book.

Emotions/emotional (noun/adjective): Feelings (eg, sadness, joy, anger, fear)

Empathy/empathetic (noun/adjective): The ability to share and understand someone else's feelings or experiences.

Essay (noun): A piece of writing on a particular subject. Essays are often given to students as a part of their coursework

Ethnic (adjective): Relating to a particular place or people (Source: ethnic (n.d.). in *Cambridge dictionary*. Retrieved from https://dictionary.cambridge.org/dictionary/english/ethnic?qEthnic).

Ezine (noun): Electronic magazine (see also 'magazine', below)

Fantasy/fantastical (noun/adjective): An imaginary story or idea in which the events and characters are very different from those found in the real world.

Fiction/non-fiction (noun): Fiction written works that are not actual but come from a writer's imagination. Non-fiction written works that describe actual events, real people and facts.

Film critic (noun): A film critic is a person who evaluates and analyzes a film and writes a review of it. In the USA, film critics are also known as movie critics.

Genre (noun): A word from the French language but used in English to describe a style or kind of written text, music or film that involves a particular set of characteristics. Used especially in the arts.

Graphic novel (noun phrase): A book in which the story is told by means of pictures.

Imperial Court (noun phrase): The home and members of the royal household, the officials and staff of an Emperor and/or Empress

Instapoet (noun): A young emerging poet who often self-publishes on social media like Instagram. This recently formed word is made by joining the first part of the word 'Instagram' with the word 'poet'

Journalist (noun): A person who writes for newspapers, magazines, or news websites or prepares news to be broadcast

Lady-in-waiting (noun): Woman working as a servant/helper to a Queen or Empress

Liberal Arts (noun phrase): "Liberal arts is a field of study based on rational thinking, and it includes the areas of humanities, social and physical sciences, and mathematics. A liberal arts education emphasizes the development of critical thinking … the ability to solve complex problems, and an understanding of ethics and morality, as well as a desire to continue to learn." Retrieved from https://www.thoughtco.com/liberal-arts-definition-4585053

LGBTQ: Acronym for people who identify their sexual orientation as Lesbian, Gay, Bi-sexual, Transgender, Queer or Questioning.

Magic/magical (noun/adjective): Special power that can make unusual or impossible things happen

Magazine (noun): A kind of thin book made of paper with large pages. Magazines are published regularly, eg. every month. They often contain many colourful photos and short articles of interest. Famous examples are 'Vogue' fashion magazine and 'Time' magazine

New York Times Best Seller List (noun phrase): A list of books that reach the top in sales for a particular period of time in the US It is considered one of the most important and respected of such lists.

Nobel Prize (noun phrase): Any of the six international prizes that are given each year to people who make important discoveries or progress in chemistry, physics, medicine, literature, peace, and economics (Nobel Prize. (n.d.). In *Cambridge Dictionary*. Retrieved from https://dictionary.cambridge.org/dictionary/english/nobel-prize

Novel/Novelist (nouns): A novel is a long story, usually in book form, about imaginary characters and events. A novelist is a person who writes a novel.

Online (adjective): On the Internet
Owl (noun): A type of bird with big eyes that hunts at night
Proofreader (noun): A person whose job is to check the text before it is printed or put online.
Rhetorical Device (noun phrase): One of a group of writing methods used by writers to persuade, inform, explain or otherwise give information.
Sociology (noun): The study of the development, structure, and functioning of human society.
Scriptwriter (noun): A person who writes a script for a play, film, or broadcast.
Theater (noun—spelt 'theatre' in British English): A place where live plays are performed by real people
The Times They Are a-Changing: Title of a song originally written and performed by Bob Dylan. It was the title track on his 1964 album by the same name.
Web content manager (noun): A person who oversees the **content** presented on websites.
Western canon (noun phrase): The texts (novels, essays, poems etc) that are generally agreed upon as being the best of their kind and worth studying.
Witchcraft/wizardry (nouns): Magic actions performed by people with special powers. Witches (female) and wizards (male)
The Times They Are a-Changing (noun): Title of a song originally written and performed by Bob Dylan. It was the title track on his 1964 album by the same name.
Rhetorical devices (noun plural): Use of language that helps an author or speaker achieve a particular purpose (usually *persuasion*, since rhetoric is typically defined as the art of persuasion). But "rhetorical device" is an extremely broad term and can include techniques for generating emotion, beauty, and spiritual significance as well as persuasion (Source: rhetorical device (n.d.) *Literary Terms*. Retrieved from https://literaryterms.net/rhetorical-device/).

CHAPTER 3

FILM STUDIES

Sean O'Reilly
Akita International University, Japan

Introduction

You may have seen many **movies*** before, so you might think there is no need to study this **topic** at all. However, the truth is that movies are very important to study because they are so good at **manipulating** the feelings and even the thoughts and beliefs of the **audience**.

Of all the movies you have seen in your life, a few may have made you **jump** in surprise. The surprise you feel is called a **visceral*** reaction. A visceral reaction is when your body reacts or moves because of something strange that you saw. That is, *you* think it is strange, even though it may not be strange at all.

Why would moving **images** on a two-**dimensional screen** make us **afraid** or **angry**? What is it that makes us so interested in the story we see on screen? Doubtless, some of the movies you have seen made you laugh out **loud.** Maybe some movies made you cry. Sometimes, the same movie even made you do both. While it is easy to understand why certain movies make us laugh, do you really understand why **films** are so good at moving **audiences** to tears or to **screams**? By studying movies **academically**, we can better understand this emotional manipulation and guard ourselves against it without losing any of the enjoyment of watching films.

History of Film Studies

Clearly, Film Studies is a very important field of study. When did it begin, and why is it called Film Studies? Believe it or not, while there were courses to teach people how to make movies, there was no **formal** academic discipline **devoted** to the study of movies at the start of the age of **cinema**.

Classes in Film Studies at universities first **emerged** in The United States. These classes also came from the **theoretically** advanced work of film **critics** in **Europe, especially** in **France**.

The field of Film Studies grew for two other reasons: the rise of **feminism** and a growing interest in popular culture, and with these, the idea and popularity of Film Studies spread **quickly** throughout the world.

Meanwhile, before the **digital*** age, movies were recorded on **strips** (or lengths) of **plastic** film. That is why this field of study is called Film Studies. It is also why the length of a movie used to be given in **footage***. The fact that strips of film were used is also why a **transition** from one **angle** or scene to another is called a "*cut.*" This is because the filmmakers would cut the film strip when making changes (also called **editing**). These days, because the way we make movies has changed, we do not really have to keep using the word film anymore.

The term "*Cinema Studies*" is also good since it shows we are speaking about the sorts of movies and experiences people have in actual cinemas. However, **labeling** this subject "Cinema Studies" would **exclude** the home movie experience. Nowadays, many of us watch movies at home **via** streaming services. Perhaps that is why the term Film Studies **persists**, **despite** being outdated.

REAL-WORLD Applications

One **aim** of the field of Film Studies is to **identify** the **key features** of movies so we can understand how they manipulate us into thinking and feeling a certain way about their subjects. Having this understanding is important in the real world. For example, most people **derive** their understanding of history **primarily** from movies rather than books since movies change our feelings more than dry **textbooks**.

Because of this, we are more likely to remember the ideas in a movie than the ideas in a book. If these movies give the audience a **false** view of history, millions of people could be badly tricked and may end up believing things that are not true. To become **aware** of this and other dangers, we need to study the *form* of movies and learn how movies can and do manipulate us. There are four basic **elements** we need to study when learning about movies.

1. Cinematography*
2. Editing*
3. Mise-en-scène*
4. Sound

Two of these seem difficult to understand, while the other two are easy, so let's start with the easiest two first.

Sound is the easiest to understand since it covers everything an audience can hear; sound effects, the music within the story, for example, when a character is singing **inside** a scene, and also sound outside the story, such as background music that is added in later.

Editing is also **straightforward**. A movie **editor** takes all the **available** film **footage***, whether that is digital or **analog***, and **splices*** (or joins) it together in a certain order to tell a story. Much more footage is recorded by the **cameras** than is finally used. This usually means a lot of footage gets cut from the **final version** of a movie an audience gets to see.

What about the two more difficult terms? You may know the words "photograph" or "photography." Well, cinematography is a bit like that because it also involves cameras and **images.** Cinematography means everything about the camera and includes all the decisions filmmakers must make. Things like where to place the camera for a scene, how far away it will be from the actors, how high and at what angle the camera should be, how brightly or **darkly** the scene will be lit, and more.

You might have heard the term "close up" before. It is a cinematographic term. If the camera is placed so close to the person that only the person's face is shown on screen, and if that actor's face fills up most of the camera **frame**, then the person using the camera is taking a "close up."

On the other hand, can you think how an action scene will **impact** you if it is filmed in "long shot," that is, with the camera far away rather than in "close up?" In general, the closer we (that is the cameras) are to the action the more we feel we are right there!

In this way, the scene becomes very powerful.

What if the camera is placed into what is called a "low-angle shot?" In this kind of shot, the camera is placed *below* a figure and angled up towards an actor's face. Can you see how this would be different in its effects? For example, how does it seem to you, as a part of the audience, when the camera is placed *above* a character, looking *down* on him or her, or when the camera is taking an angle shot? These cinematographic **techniques** help the audience to know straight away who in the movie is a **hero***, who is a **villain***, who is feeling powerful, and who is **weak**. Unless we study how and how much, these techniques **affect** the audience, we will continue to be **manipulated** by the power of the cinema.

Finally, what does "*mise-en-scène*" mean? This term comes from the French language. It means "placed in the scene" and **refers** to everything we see in a scene or shot. This includes **props***, **costumes***, backgrounds, the actors themselves, their **choreographed*** (or planned) movements within the space, and more.

When filmmakers move or **adjust** the things we see, it can have powerful effects on the audience. Sometimes, filmmakers will use one certain color very often within a movie. A good example of this is the science **fiction*** film "The Matrix." In this movie, all the backgrounds, props, and costumes within the **fake*** world of the Matrix were a **dull** green. Using one color in this way helps the audience to recognize some **fundamental** quality of the world being shown.

Important Issues in Film Studies

Exciting controversies in the field of Film Studies are many. For example, which films, filmmakers, and actors receive most of the **awards***? In recent years, the people in **Hollywood** who give out the most important awards, the **Academy Awards** or **Oscars***, have been **accused** of systematic **racism***.

A very basic form of **evidence** for the idea that the film world is **racist*** is the fact that, for almost the whole history of the Oscars, **virtually** all the awards have gone to white people. But that is just one example only. The real problem might simply be that even today, it remains much more difficult to become a successful actor or filmmaker in Hollywood if you are not a white person.

What about **sexism** in the world of film? Have you noticed that many movies seem to **privilege*** their male characters, whether hero or villain? They are the ones who *do* things, while **female** characters do less, and are seen less often, and are given less to say. In fact, since Hollywood began, there has been a remarkably **consistent ratio** of male to female main characters in movies.

Can you guess what the difference is? If you guessed an equal ratio of 1:1 (one male main role per female main role), think again! It's actually 2:1, and it hasn't **varied** almost at all in over 120 years of film history.

Commentators such as the noted **feminist*** film **theorist** Laura Mulvey, have **argued**, in fact, that the camera itself is both **gendered*** and **sexualized*** and has a sort of "male *gaze.**" What does this mean? It means the usually male filmmakers are showing female characters mostly as *objects* for both the male characters and the audience to **consume** with their eyes.

Obviously, since many people in the audience are women, this male gaze causes problems. If you are a woman, will you **identify** with the male hero and gaze on the female character as an object, or will you identify with the female character and allow yourself to be gazed at in that **objectifying*** way? This theory is as controversial as it is influential, and it is just one of the many interesting topics waiting for you to think about in Film Studies.

Film Studies has much to offer almost anyone on earth. This is because almost everyone has watched, or will watch, movies. That means they have been influenced by those movies, but very few people have ever thought of movies as something to study academically. We **usually** don't spend time thinking deeply about how movies manipulate an audience. We don't often consider whether movies have more male characters, or if those male characters are more active, and more numerous than female characters on **screen**. We don't usually stop to ask why some movies make us feel a certain way. Yet as **global** citizens we will continue to **encounter** movies, and other closely related **technologies***, like **online videos***.

If you enjoy movies and these things interest you, consider studying Film Studies to learn more about how they already affect you. But don't worry. If you think that learning about movies in an academic way will **ruin** the experience, remember, studying the cinema makes watching movies even more **fun** since it gives you deeper **insights, enabling** you to **appreciate** movies on a much deeper level.

Employment Opportunities

It goes without saying that "**visual literacy***" is a very valuable and important skill, and would be useful to study even if it did not directly lead to a practical career. Fortunately, though, film studies, and the visual literacy it teaches students, is strongly connected with a wide variety of jobs. These jobs include Filmmaker, the person who directs or produces films or TV programs; **Editor,** the person who puts the various scenes together into a cohesive finished product; Director of Photography, the person behind the movie camera setting-up the shots; Producer, the person who provides funding and supervision for movie and TV **projects**; **Professional** Critic, a writer who reviews movies and/or TV programs for a **publication**, usually a newspaper or journal; and Screenwriter, a writer who writes the screenplay for a movie or TV show. Of course, a graduate of Film Studies may also go on to be an Actor or a Stunt Performer.

But mastery of film studies is indirectly useful in other careers as well, such as Advertising, since movies or TV shows depend on endorsement deals seen in "product placement". Or Marketing, as those making expensive films or TV programs often spend nearly as much money on marketing as they did making the movie or program. Photography is another career option because many of the visual analysis skills learned in film studies, for example controlling the lighting and adjusting the angle of the camera, are also useful in taking still photos. Finally, teaching and researching at the university level is an option for people with an academic interest in film.

As you can see, the academic study of movies has a great deal to offer. It helps us develop critical thinking and analytical skills, gives us insight into how gender and race are viewed by society and can lead to interesting career choices. And as they say in the movie business, "That's a wrap!"

Adapted from a text by Sean O'Reilly PhD
Professor of Japanese History, Popular Culture and Cinema.
Akita International University.
Japan.

Vocabulary

Words From the Second 1000 High-Frequency General Service Word List

accused	guess
afraid	inside
aim	jump
angle	key
angry	lot
argued	loud
audience	male
bit	meanwhile
camera	photograph photography
critics	quickly
dull	refers
especially	ruin
exciting	screen
false	straight
female	strip
film	tricked
formal	weak
frame	worry
fun	

Words From the Academic Word List

academically academy	appreciate available
adjust	aware
affect	brief

consistent
consume controversies/controversial
culture
derive
despite
devoted
dimensional
editing/editor
elements
emerged
enabling evidence
exclude
features
final/finally
fundamental
global
identify
images
impact
insights

involves
issues
labeling
manipulate
persists
primarily
ratio
reaction
resources
sexism
statistics
straightforward
techniques theoretically/theory/theorist
topic
transition
varied
version
via
virtually
visual

Glossary

Adjectives (noun plural): The grammatical name for a class of words used to describe nouns (people, animals, places, things, events, situations, feelings etc.)
Analog (adjective): In this case, physical film material made of plastic (i.e. not digital)
Awards (noun plural): Prizes for excellence
Choreographed (adjective): Planned movements or sequences of events
Cinema/cinematographic/cinematography (noun/adjective/noun): Relating to movie theatres and the movies
Costumes (noun plural): Special clothing designed for and worn by actors
Darkly (adverb): In a dark or gloomy manner. Opposite of brightly
Digital (adjective): In electronic form, can be used by computers
Europe (noun): Area of the world to the north of Africa and west of the Middle East.
Fake (adjective): Not real, false
Feminism/feminist (noun/adjective or noun): A person who supports and works towards improving the rights of women
Fiction (noun): A story that does not relate true events. Imaginary story.
Footage (noun): A scene or series of scenes from a movie (originally referred to a length of plastic film)
France/French (noun/adjective): The name of a European country and its people and language
Gaze (verb): To look at closely for a long time
Gendered (adjective): Biased towards a particular gender or sex
Hero (noun): A person who is admired for his achievements and abilities (female = heroine)
Hollywood (noun): A famous place in the city of Los Angeles in the USA where films are produced
Movie (noun): A moving picture, usually lasting for an extended period of time, that tells a story. Sometimes called a film.
Objectifying (verb in gerund form): To think of someone as if they are an object or thing rather than as a human being.
Online (adjective): Connected to a computer network
Oscars (noun): The name of a special movie award ceremony

Plastic (adjective/noun): An artificial material made by humans that can be molded or shaped into many forms.

Privilege (noun): Special rights or benefits available only to certain people

Props (noun plural): Objects used in a movie scene to create a certain sense of time and place.

Racism/racist (noun/adjective): Believing, and acting on the belief, that one group of people is better than other groups, based on their physical appearance (e.g. skin color)

Screams (noun, plural): Loud cries of fear

Sexualized (adjective): Focused on the sexual qualities of someone, usually without considering that person's other qualities (e.g. their character, intelligence and personal abilities)

Splices (verb): To edit a length of film by cutting and rejoining it

Technologies (noun plural): Various practical materials and equipment that enable us to do tasks more quickly. Nowadays, this often refers to computers and complex machines.

Textbooks (noun plural): School books used to teach learners about different subject areas

Videos (noun plural): Visual material with moving images that may or may not have sound added

Villain (noun): A bad person (opposite to a hero)

Visceral (adjective): Coming from the emotions or from an automatic physical response, not from the mind

Visual literacy (noun phrase): Is the ability to read, write and create visual images

CHAPTER 4

RELIGIOUS STUDIES

Seth Clippard
Hung Kuang University Taichung, Taiwan

Introduction

You may have heard the **adage*** that the two things you should never **discuss** at the dinner table are politics and religion. While this might make for a **quiet** yet boring evening, the very idea of not discussing religion would strike a religious studies student as a **wasted** opportunity. Religion is one of the most widely discussed, **argued** over, and **impassioned* topics** in societies throughout the world. And because it is, the field of Religious Studies offers an extensive opportunity for continuous intellectual **engagement***.

Religion, or Religious Studies (as it is more often called), is not a common subject at most universities and nearly **unheard*** of outside of Western universities. Part of the reason is that the field has not been around as long as more **traditional** fields (e.g., **philosophy**, history, biology, chemistry, etc.). But more importantly, religion itself is not considered a standard **area** of **academic** study. Some **subfields*** in religious studies are **akin*** to the **humanities***, **whereas** other subfields are more based in the **social sciences***. People will learn about their own religious traditions, generally to better understand how to **fulfill*** their religious **commitments** more completely. Some people may take a passing interest in other religions as a result of traveling or **sheer*** curiosity. In the United States, many people still a**ssume** that a Religious Studies student plans to become a minister or **theologian***. The **typical** question **posed** to Religious Studies **majors*** (and the one which Religious Studies departments must always address) is: What can you do with a degree in religion? **Aside** from applying to **graduate school***, the short answer is nothing. But the more **honest** answer is anything.

University students typically do not choose to major in Religious Studies to be anything; they are interested in learning about something. Perhaps that something is a different way of seeing the world, a **worldview***, and this might include the **customs** and beliefs of a group of people in a **specific** part of the world (What do Indian, Chinese or Arabic peoples believe). Or perhaps it is to better understand the history of ideas throughout a tradition or across traditions (What does God mean to Christians, Jews, and Muslims). In some cases (mine, for example), the **root** cause was **indecision***: not able to choose between History, Philosophy, Literature, and **Anthropology***, I chose a major in which I could study all of these! Whatever the reason, a desire to learn about humans and human societies lies at the heart of the **impetus*** to choose to study religion.

A Short History of the Field

The academic field of Religion or Religious Studies is said to have begun with the German **philologist*** Max Müller (1823–1900). Before his time, the study of religion was **equivalent** to theology. Theology comes from the Greek *theologia*, meaning accounts of the gods or God. It traditionally **refers** to Christian or Jewish **understandings*** or beliefs about God and philosophical attempts to **articulate*** the nature of God and God's **creation**. Seen thus, **theology*** is done by **believers*** of a tradition to help understand the meaning and purpose of human life. Theology and courses on Theology are still commonly taught today, but what we call Religious Studies is mostly seen as a related but separate field of study.

What Max Müller **initiated** was a **program** of scientific **inquiry** based on the other sciences that arose in the 18th and 19th **centuries**. Thus, the term first used for Religious Studies was "the science of religion" (German, *Religionswissenshaft*). The **goal** was to gather all the data about "religion" that could be gained from observation (**initially,** this only referred to reading religious **texts**). Then, this data could be classified into topics such as **myths***, **rituals***, beliefs, gods, and the like. This **enterprise*** was **aided** by the colonial **projects** being **undertaken** by European powers such as England, Germany, the Netherlands, Spain, and France. **Scholars*** from these countries were able to travel to Egypt, India, China, Greece, Iran, and the Middle East, or at least learn to read the **classical** languages of these **civilizations***, which opened up their **textual** history.

The **project** of classifying belief systems continued throughout the 20th century, **bolstered*** by the popularity of Darwin's **theory** of **evolution*** as a **model** for ranking religions along a **spectrum*** from **primitive***/immature to modern/**mature**. This **period** of development of the field **relied** mostly on **methods** from history, philosophy, literature, and philology (the study of languages). This stage of the scientific study of religion gave rise to subfields like **Comparative Mythology***/Religion, the History of Religions, and the **Phenomenology*** of Religion. In these areas, scholars **focus** on **theorizing** about religion, **seeking** to **identify aspects** of religious **practice** and religious **structures** (related to but separate from other societal structures such as **economic**, political, or **familial***) upon which theories of religion can be **refined** or developed. **Examining** theories of religion is a **significant** aspect of the academic study of religion, the goal of which is to **encourage** students to think **critically** about religion. The **emphasis** on language study to master the literature of the particular tradition a scholar is focused on brought Religious Studies into the realm of Area Studies. Research on religious traditions of China, India, Iran, and Greece meant that scholars had to devote time to become proficient in many languages, including Chinese, Sanskrit, Pali, Urdu, Arabic, Persian, Greek, Latin, Japanese, Hindi, Tibetan, and Mongolian. Today, there are many English **translations** of works of religious literature that would never have been available without the effort of religious studies scholars.

By the 20th century, religion had become the subject of other newer fields of study, such as psychology, anthropology, and sociology. **Luminaries*** such as Karl Marx, Sigmund Freud, and Max Weber all made significant contributions to how religion is discussed and thought about. In recent decades, scholars from even more diverse fields have taken up the study of religion: biology, physics, cultural theory, and economics, to name a few. What these scholars all seem to agree on is that what we call religion **constitutes** a significant personal and social force, in addition to being just plain interesting.

The Problem of Definition

One of the most challenging aspects of Religious Studies is simply defining the scope of the field. Essentially, what are people studying when they study religion? Introductory courses in Religious Studies focus for several weeks on what religion means, and this is true at both the undergraduate and graduate level. It is hard to **imagine** a first-year graduate level. Much of the problem comes from the lack of any clear definition of religion itself. Many academic fields are **bound** by the limits of the object of inquiry: Biology—the study of the natural world; Literature—the study of written works; or Anthropology—the study of humans and human society. One could simply say, Religious Studies is the study of religion," but what is religion?

The word "religion" comes from the Greek root religio or religare. The root -liga is related to the word "ligament"—something that **ties** or **binds**. In this sense, religion is something that binds—binds people to God, or a divine or **sacred** power, or binds people in a community together. This etymology reflects the interpretation that sociologists tend to use, roughly that religion is "a unified system of beliefs and practices relative to sacred things" that bind members of a society or community together (Émile Durkheim/sociology). However, scholars from other sub-fields have claimed religion is an individual's feelings and experience understood in reference to the divine (William James/psychology), "a system of symbols" (Clifford Geertz/anthropology), or a human being's "ultimate concern" (Paul Tillich/theology). From a comparative perspective, religion is sometimes defined by how other cultures define what western scholars identify as "religion" in those cultures. Religion then becomes equivalent to "law" (Hinduism/dharma), the "way" (Daoism/dao), the "**path**" (Buddhism/marga), or the teachings (Confucianism/jiao). These are in addition to common notions in the West of faith, **obedience**, and ritual.

This variety of definitions of religion illustrates that when scholars seek to identify what is and is not religion, they must make choices. To say that everything is religion would be too broad, and of course, to say that nothing is religion would **entirely** invalidate the object of inquiry. Therefore, the field as it stands now is one that first seeks to qualify the object of inquiry by identifying what is properly religious and putting forth a method for how the inquiry will proceed. The only drawback to this approach is that it assumes that the phenomena that have been identified are, in fact, related to religion.

Real-World Applications of Religious Studies

As mentioned above, a degree in religious studies prepares one for nothing in particular, and yet Religious Studies majors are some of the most sought after by employers. Religious Studies majors not only have a strong desire to uncover the motivations and belief systems that animate human life, but they are also adept at navigating sensitive and **complicated** issues in an articulate, thoughtful, and **balanced** manner. Religious Studies majors tend to be fair and effective communicators, having been trained to see multiple sides of issues that deal directly with day-to-day human life. Other fields certainly **aim** to train their students to develop **excellent** communication, listening, and analytical **skills,** but religious studies adds to that **list** empathy, tolerance, and problem-**solving** skills. Finally, Religious Studies majors develop these skills all while switching between philosophy, history, anthropology, and sociology. One might say Religious Studies is the first interdepartmental field of study.

Because of their understanding of cultures and languages, scholars of religion have become important in commenting on current issues such as Islamic fundamentalism, the economic effects of European colonialism, feminism in developing countries, and the rise of nationalism in China, India, and elsewhere. Religious studies scholars continue to **push** the limits of interdisciplinary research, bringing together history, sociology, media studies, culture studies, and critical theory to shed light on the significance of current events.

People who graduate with degrees in religious studies are sought after by non-profits and corporations **alike** for their ability to grasp and communicate clearly complex ideas to a diverse **audience**.

Seth Clippard, PhD
Independent Scholar.
formerly of Hung Kuang University.
Taichung, Taiwan.

Vocabulary

Words From the second 1000 General Service High Frequency Word List

aim	binds/bound
alike	complicated
audience	comparative
aside	customs
balanced	curiosity

critically
discuss
excellent
entirely
encourage
examining
honest
imagine
inquiry
list
model
obedience
path

practice
program
push
refers
root
sacred
skills
solving
ties
typical
translations
wasted

Words From the Academic Word List (AWL)

academic
analytical
area
aspect
assume
available
challenging
classical
commenting
community
complex
constitutes
contributions
cultural
data
decades
definition
devote
diverse
economic
emphasis
empirical
equivalent
evolve
finally
focus
goal
identify
illustrate
individual
initiate

interpretation
issue
major
mature
media
methods
motivations
notions
period
philosophy
phenomena
posed
project
psychology
refined
rely
research
scope
seek
significant
specific
structures
symbols
textual
theory
topic
traditional
ultimate
undertaken
unified
whereas

Glossary

Adage (noun): A short, memorable saying that expresses a traditional wisdom or truth.

Akin (adjective): Similar or related in nature; having a common origin or quality.

Anthropology (noun): The scientific study of human societies, cultures, and their development.

Articulate (adjective): Expressing thoughts or ideas clearly and effectively in speech or writing.

Believers (noun): People who have faith or hold strong convictions in a particular religion or belief system.

Bolstered (verb): Strengthened or supported, often by adding evidence or reinforcement.

Civilizations (noun): Complex societies with developed cultural, economic, and political systems.

Enterprise (noun): A project, endeavor, or business venture, often involving risk and innovation.

Familial (adjective): Relating to family or characteristic of a family.

Fulfill (verb): To satisfy or meet a requirement, expectation, or goal.

Graduate School (noun): An advanced educational institution where students pursue higher-level degrees (Master's or Ph.D.).

Humanities (noun): Academic disciplines that study human culture, including literature, history, philosophy, art, and languages.

Impassioned (adjective): Full of strong emotions, enthusiasm, or fervor.

Impetus (noun): The driving force or motivation behind a particular action or change.

Indecision (noun): The state of being unable to make a decision or reach a conclusion.

Intellectual Engagement (noun): Active involvement and deep thought in academic or intellectual pursuits.

Mythology (noun): The collection of myths and legends of a particular culture or religious tradition.

Myths (noun): Traditional stories or narratives that explain the beliefs, practices, or natural phenomena of a culture.

Phenomenology (noun): An approach in philosophy that focuses on the first-person experience of consciousness and phenomena.

Philologist (noun): A scholar who studies language, particularly its historical development and structure.

Primitive (adjective): Relating to an early or basic stage of development in human history.

Religious Studies majors (noun): Students who are pursuing a degree in the academic study of religion and its various aspects.

Rituals (noun): Formal and often symbolic actions or ceremonies performed for religious or cultural purposes.

Scholars (noun): Individuals who engage in academic study and research, often in pursuit of new knowledge.

Sheer (adjective): Complete or absolute; used to emphasize the scale or intensity of something.

Spectrum (noun): A wide range or variety of something.

Subfields (noun): Specialized areas within a larger academic discipline or field of study.

Theologian (noun): A scholar or expert in the study of theology, which deals with the nature of deities, religious beliefs, and divine matters.

Theology (noun): The study of the nature of the divine, religious beliefs, and the practice of religion.

Understandings (noun): Knowledge or comprehension of a subject or situation.

Unheard (adjective): Not previously heard or known; not given attention or consideration.

Worldview (noun): A person's overall perspective and way of understanding the world and life.

CHAPTER 5

WESTERN PHILOSOPHY

Kyle Michael James Shuttleworth
Akita International University, Japan

Introduction

Do you ever find yourself thinking about deep and **complex** questions? For example, have you ever thought about the nature of reality, or the meaning of life? Or have you considered why certain things are said to be right whilst other things are wrong? These are **philosophical** questions, which most people **shy*** away from because they are difficult to answer.

Nevertheless, the Ancient Greek **philosopher**, Socrates (469–399 BC) claimed "philosophy begins in wonder". In this regard, all that is **required** to **engage*** with philosophy is to be open-minded and a willingness to **explore** ideas beyond their **initial** appearance. It is the **process** of questioning, rather than the **goal** of arriving at any **specific** answer which is important for philosophy. For this reason, people who seek a **singular***, **definitive** answer may be **frustrated*** by philosophy because philosophical **inquiry** often raises more questions than it answers.

Philosophy is an incredibly **vast*** and **intricate*** field which has been termed the "mother of all **disciplines**", because all other subjects **ultimately stem** from philosophy. And all other academic disciplines' **foundational*** beliefs and values (e.g., politics, psychology, science) are grounded on philosophical **propositions***. Academic philosophy, like music, has a variety of different **genres***, or **categories**, which deal with **distinct** questions or problems. These categories deal with a wide **range** of **topics**, from abstract issues, such as why there is something rather than nothing, to applied problems, including how we ought to live our lives.

There are four main philosophical areas of **enquiry**: (i) **Metaphysics**—which deals with the nature of reality—**seeks** to determine the **origin** of existence, and asks "what does it mean to be?"; (ii) **Epistemology**—the study of knowledge—**involves** questioning not only what we can know, but also how we know, and whether we can **obtain** true knowledge; (iii) Logic—which **seeks** to **articulate*** the **structure** of thought—attempts to **reveal** the structure of human thought processes by **analysing arguments** and reasoning; and (iv) **Ethics**—which **focuses** on good and bad, and right and wrong—asks what it means to live a good life, what is justice, and how one ought to act.

A Brief History

Western philosophy, as we know it, **originated** in Ancient Greece around the 3rd **century** BC, roughly 2500 years ago. **Literally*** meaning "love" "(*philo*) [of] "wisdom" (*sophia*), [Western] philosophy is **defined** by its **rational approach** to the **acquisition** of knowledge. The first Greek philosopher is believed to have been Thales of Miletus (c.624–c.546 BC), whom claimed everything is water. The reason why Thales is considered a philosopher, rather than a natural scientist, is because he proposed a **unifying principle** to explain the origin of existence.

In the Ancient Greek world, philosophy reached its **peak*** with Plato (c.428–347 BC), who **composed dialogues*** **featuring** his teacher, Socrates. The metaphysical foundation of Plato's thought was based on the idea that reality does not exist outside of our minds. In his account, what we experience are mere "forms", or representations of **absolute ideals**. In his **Analogy** of the **Cave**, Plato claims our experience of the world is **analogous** to the **projection** of shadows on a wall, which are **mistaken** for reality itself. According to Alfred North Whitehead, Western philosophy "**consists** of a **series** of **footnotes*** to Plato", meaning Plato's writings provided the **blueprint*** for all future philosophical **discussion**.

Plato's student, Aristotle (384–322 BC), also developed a **complex**, and perhaps even more **comprehensive** philosophical system. **Contrary** to Plato, whose position is known as **idealism***, Aristotle **advocated** a position of **empiricism**, which claimed knowledge can be **achieved** through the senses. In his metaphysical **theory**, Aristotle claimed that there must be a first cause, which was not caused by anything else. To explain such a **phenomenon**, he proposed the idea of an "**unmoved mover***", which **created motion** in the **universe**. From his **empirical approach**, and attempt to **categorise** all **lifeforms*** into **genus*** and **species***, Aristotle became recognized as the father of modern science.

In the ancient western world, philosophy was not simply an **academic** study, but a way of life. The two most famous schools, which **flourished*** through Ancient Greece into the Roman Empire, were **Epicureanism*** and **Stoicism***. Epicurus (341–270 BC), the founder of Epicureanism, taught that the purpose of philosophy was to **obtain** happiness through pleasure and the **absence** of **pain**. He famously claimed that death is not to be feared, since when we are, death is not, and when death is, we are not. Stoicism, which was founded by Zeno of Citium (c334–c262 BC), was based on the idea that virtue is the only good, and that one suffered due to emotions which one should **seek** to control. The **stoics practiced psychological** control and the **endurance*** of hardship to **ensure** they would be able to tolerate the **worst misfortune***. Stoicism became so influential that even the Roman Emperor Marcus Aurelius practiced Stoicism and **composed** his own written record.

Many Ancient Greek ideas, **especially** those of Plato and Aristotle, were later adopted by **Christian** thinkers, who applied them to explain **fundamental theological*** beliefs and values. St. Augustine of Hippo (354–430), for example, **augmented** Plato's metaphysical theory of the forms to explain the Christian understanding of God as the **source** of **absolute** truth and goodness. This **trend**, of marrying pre-modern philosophy to Christian theology in the Middle Ages, became known as "**Scholastic*** philosophy". Perhaps the most **eminent** thinker of this time, St. Thomas Aquinas (1225–1274) adopted Aristotle's "unmoved mover" argument to explain the **concept** of the Christian God. Aquinas also adopted Aristotle's **theory** of being, and developed **ontological*** proofs to provide logical evidence for God's existence.

In the early modern **era***, questions of how we **acquire** knowledge of the world came to the **fore***. The French philosopher René Descartes (1596–1650) **advocated** a **rationalist*** approach, arguing that knowledge can only be found inside of us. An **opposing** theory was advocated by the Scottish **Enlightenment*** thinker David Hume (1711–1776), who took a position of **empiricism***, claiming that all knowledge is achieved through the senses. The Prussian **prodigy*** Immanuel Kant (1724–1804) claimed Hume awoke him from his "**dogmatic*** **slumber***", meaning, until this point he had **uncritically*** accepted **rationalism**. Kant **subsequently** sought to **synthesise*** rationalism and empiricism, which would result in his ground-breaking ideas that **challenged** and divided the **trajectory*** of philosophical thought.

Since Kant, Western philosophy has been marked by a general division into two **distinct traditions**: **Analytic** philosophy and **Continental** philosophy. Analytic philosophy traces its origin to G.E. Moore (1873–1958) and Bertrand Russell (1872–1970) in Cambridge, who **emphasised** the importance of **analysing concepts**. In this tradition, as can be **derived** from the name, **focus** is placed on the analysis of language, **logic**, knowledge, minds, and thought itself. The analytic approach focuses on gaining clarity, modelling itself on the rigorous approach of the scientific method. Topics in analytic philosophy include **epistemology***, logic, metaphysics (philosophy of language, philosophy of mind), moral theory (applied and normative), and philosophy of science.

Continental philosophy, on the other hand, takes its name from the **style** of philosophy which was being practiced on the European continent, of which G.W.F. Hegel (1770–1831) and Friedrich Nietzsche (1844–1900) are prime examples. Rather than **rigorously*** analysing single **concepts** or ideas, continental philosophers **engage** in philosophical **inquiry** for the purpose of answering larger questions. Here, the focus is on understanding the relationship between philosophy and life, culture and society, and time and history as of philosophical importance. Topics in continental philosophy include **aesthetics** (philosophy of art and literature), critical theory, **deconstructionism***, **existentialism***, gender studies, philosophy of history, **poststructuralism***, and political philosophy.

Possible Future Directions

Although philosophy deals with problems which have existed since the **dawn*** of human **civilisation**, the **emergence** of new social and **technological** developments has created new philosophical problems. Perhaps the most pressing philosophical problem of our time is that of the **environmental crisis***—since if our life support system **ceases** to exist, then nothing else will matter.

In the emerging field of environmental **ethics**, a **major focus** is on the problem of **anthropocentrism**, which means "human centred". Anthropocentrism more **specifically refers** to the human **bias** which values and **treats** human beings as more important than non-human beings. Environmental scientists have attributed the **primary** cause of our **climate*** crisis to anthropocentric **attitudes** in human society. For example, the view of nature as a mere **resource** to be **utilised** by human beings has led to **deforestation***, **depriving*** **innumerable*** lifeforms of a **habitat***.

One philosophical **response** to this problem can be seen in the Deep **Ecology*** movement. As **opposed** to "shallow" ecology, which only **seeks** to **preserve** the environment for human ends, Deep Ecologists argue that we should protect non-human lifeforms because they possess **intrinsic** value. This **approach** is also important for **evaluating** our relationship and **obligations*** to the natural world, since existing ethical theories have thus far only **focused** on human relations to other humans.

With the increasing reliance on technology in **contemporary** society, becoming the **lynchpin*** of social interaction, philosophers have questioned the ways in which technology **challenges** existing social practices. Technology, **despite** its many **positive** applications, has created a lot of **unforeseen*** ethical problems. One **intended** purpose of artificial intelligence was to **fulfil*** undesirable **roles**, such as **labour tasks**, which humans do not wish to do, and to make our lives easier.

However, through the **process** of deep learning, it has become questioned whether AI could also develop **consciousness**, and if so, should such AI should also have rights? Another question concerns **design ethics**—that is, should the designer be held **responsible** for **unintended*** consequences of their designs? For example, if an **autonomous*** vehicle accidently kills a **pedestrian***, who is to **blame**? The designer or the owner of the car?

Why Study Philosophy?

As mentioned in the introduction, philosophy is perhaps the most **intellectually*** challenging academic subject, since it **requires** us to think down to the foundations of our beliefs and values. According to Agnes Heller, "philosophy is the **literary genre*** for the **mentally courageous**", meaning that it takes strength of mind to **engage** in **sustained** consideration of deep and **complex** problems. What is the **benefit** of such an intellectual **undertaking** though?

In terms of our own personal and intellectual development, there are three main benefits to studying philosophy. Firstly, the study of philosophy helps us to think more systematically. Philosophical **inquiries** either begin from or **aim** towards arriving at a foundational idea which will explain all other **aspects** under consideration. By understanding this **process** and applying it to our own thoughts and values, it can **enable** us to order our beliefs and ideas, by determining that which is most **fundamental** or important in our own lives.

Secondly, the study of philosophy enables us to become more **objective** in our thinking. When a philosopher develops their own position, it is necessary to consider and analyse **rival** positions. Reading philosophical texts enables us to understand and **appreciate** why other people hold such positions, even when we may disagree with them. Studying such texts, and attempting to understand why others arrive at certain **conclusions** causes us to become more open-minded and even enables us to **overcome** any **bias** or **prejudices** which we may hold.

Thirdly, the study of philosophy can help us to develop **critical** thinking **skills**. In order to **engage** in philosophical analysis, it is necessary to subject beliefs and values to **criticism** in order to **reveal** whether they are **accurate** and **valid**.

Recently, there has been a spread of **fake*** news, deep fakes, and other **spurious*** forms of information on the internet. Since the internet has become the main **source** of information for many people, the application of such systematic scepticism to claims from **unreliable** sources can help us to **assess** the truth of such claims and **avoid deception**.

Adapted from a text by Dr. Kyle Michael James Shuttleworth.
Assistant Professor of Philosophy.
Akita International University.
Japan.

Vocabulary

Words From the 2nd 1000 General Service High Frequency Word List

absence	Absolute	aim	argue
Arguing	argument	arguments	artificial
Avoid	blame	cave	century
Civilisation	composed	consciousness	courageous
Critical	deception	disciplines	discussion
Enquiry	especially	explore	ideals
Information	inquiries	inquiry	inside
Intended	lot	mistaken	modelling
Motion	opposed	opposing	origin
Originated	overcome	pain	practices
Prejudices	preserve	refers	responsible
Rival	skills	stem	Treats
Universe	Worst		

Words From the Academic Word List

abstract	academic	accurate	achieved
Acquire	acquisition	advocated	analogous
Analogy	analyse	analysis	Analytic
Appreciate	approach	areas	Aspects
Assess	attitudes	attributed	Benefit
Benefits	bias	brief	categories
Categorise	ceases	challenge	Clarity
Complex	comprehensive	concept	conclusions
consequences	consists	contemporary	Contrary
Created	culture	defined	definitive
Derived	design	designer	Despite
Distinct	emergence	emerging	emphasised
Empirical	empiricism	enable	ensure

environment	environmental	ethical	ethics
Evaluating	evidence	featuring	focus
Foundation	founded	founder	fundamental
Gender	goal	initial	intelligence
Interaction	intrinsic	involves	issues
Labour	logic	logical	major
Mentally	method	nevertheless	objective
Obtain	phenomenon	philosopher	philosophical
Philosophy	positive	primary	prime
Principle	process	projection	psychological
Psychology	range	rational	rationalism
Reliance	required	resource	response
Reveal	roles	seek	series
Sought	source	specific	specifically
Structure	style	subsequently	sustained
Tasks	technological	technology	texts
Theory	topics	traces	tradition
Trend	ultimately	undertaking	unifying
Unreliable	utilised	valid	vehicle

Glossary

It is not necessary for learners to memorize these words and expressions.

Artificial Intelligence (AI) (Noun phrase): A term used to describe the ability of computers to perform difficult tasks that normally only humans can do, such as thinking, problem solving and learning. Sometimes called machine intelligence.
Articulate (verb): Explain; put into words
Autonomous (adjective): Free from control; automatic
Blueprint (noun): A design plan for making something
Ceases (verb): Stops
Climate (noun): World weather patterns
Dawn (noun): The beginning (lit. sunrise)
Deconstructionism (noun): A type of criticism that seeks to expose underlying contradictions
Deforestation (noun): Disappearing forests
Depriving (verb): Taking something away
Dialogues (noun): Conversations between two participants
Dogmatic (adjective): Making assertions that have not been examined critically
Ecology (noun): The study of the relationship between organisms and their environment
Empiricism (noun): The view that knowledge can only be gained through sensory experience
Endurance (noun): The act of withstanding hardship or stress
Engage with (verb): Become involved with/participate in
Enlightenment (noun): 18th century philosophical movement which rejected traditional social, religious, and political ideals
Epicureanism (noun): Philosophy which promotes the pursuit of sensual pleasure
Epistemology (noun): Philosophy examining the nature of knowledge itself, how it is acquired, etc.

Era (noun): Time period
Existentialism (noun): Philosophy emphasizing the individualism of human experience
Fake (adjective): False
Flourish (verb): Prosper
Footnotes (noun): Note or citation at the bottom of a page
Fore (adjective): In front
Foundational (adjective): Fundamental; what everything else is based upon
Frustrated (verb): To prevent someone from accomplishing what they want
Fulfil (verb): To carry out or bring to completion
Genres (noun): Type
Genus (noun): Biological classification for living organisms
Habitat (noun): The environment in which a specific organism lives
Idealism (noun): Envisioning things in an ideal form, often without regard to practical ends
Innumerable (adjective): Uncountable; a very large number
Intellectually (adverb): Pertaining to logic, reason, and learning
Intricate (adjective): Assembled in a complicated manner
Lifeforms (noun): A living thing
Literally (adverb): Something in reality
Literary genre (noun): A type of literature
Lynchpin (noun): Something critical for stability/security
Misfortune (noun): Bad luck
Obligation (noun): Responsibility
Ontological (adjective): Pertaining to the philosophical study of the nature of being
Peak (noun): The topmost point
Pedestrian (noun): Someone traveling on foot
Poststructuralism (noun): A branch of philosophy that questions the objectivity of the tenets of structuralism
Prodigy (noun): Someone with exceptional talents and abilities
Propositions (noun): Plans/proposals
Rationalist (noun): Someone who follows the philosophical branch of rationalism which asserts that reason is the only source of knowledge
Rigorously (adverb): Following strict standards
Scholastic (adjective): Academic; pertaining to studies/school
Shy away (verb): Avoid
Singular (adjective): Only one
Slumber (noun): Sleep
Species (noun): Biological classification of a type of organism
Spurious (adjective): Not trustworthy
Stoicism (noun): Philosophy which elevates human virtue through the practice of self-control
Synthesise (verb): To bring together; unite
Theological (adjective): The study of the nature of God
Trajectory (noun): Direction
Uncritically (adverb): Not subject to examination
Unforeseen (adjective): Something not predicted
Unintended (adjective): Not deliberate; unplanned
Vast (adjective): Stretching far in all directions

CHAPTER 6

RHETORIC

Patrick Dougherty
Akita International University, Japan

Introduction: What Is Rhetoric?

We are surrounded by rhetoric. We both **practice** rhetoric and have rhetoric **focused** on us. For example, the last time you tried to **convince** your **parents** to buy you something, a new **smart phone**, for example, you used rhetoric in your effort to convince them. The last time a friend tried to **persuade** you to join a school **club**, or watch a movie instead of go to the **mall***, you had rhetoric used on you. So what is "rhetoric" **exactly**?

According to the Greek **philosopher** Aristotle (384–322 BC), rhetoric is "the **faculty*** of observing in any given case the **available** means of **persuasion**." Rhetoric **refers** to two things. First, it is the art of **analyzing** the language choices that a writer or speaker might make in a certain situation so that the **text** or the speech is meaningful for the **audience** and effective at gaining the audience's support. Secondly, rhetoric **involves** understanding why the **features** of a speech or text make it successful or unsuccessful in **appealing*** to an audience. **Fundamentally**, rhetoric is the ability to use language effectively to make others think or act the way that you want them to think or act. If you use language to persuade people, then you are using rhetoric.

A History of Rhetoric

As long as we have had public speaking, we have had rhetoric. But, if we need to speak about the start of the science of rhetoric, we need to go back to the fifth **century** BCE in Greece, to **Athens*** **specifically**, and the start of **democracy***. The word "democracy" comes to us from the Greek word *dēmokratia* and this word is made up of two words that show us **exactly** what the Greeks meant by democracy. The two words are *dēmos*, which means the **entire** group of citizens, and *kratos*, which meant rule. **Essentially**, democracy means that the citizens ruled the country for themselves. In the democracy of the ancient Greeks the spoken word was of great importance. Many people could not read or write, but almost all could listen. All free **adult males** could **participate** in the **Athenian*** assembly, or their **governing** body. They participated by proposing, **arguing** for, or arguing against, the **establishment** of laws, **government policies**, or courses of action. They participated by making speeches of **persuasion**. To succeed in government required an ability to make speeches that, as Aristotle said, "...make the audience well-**disposed** towards ourselves and ill-disposed to our **opponent***." Which means that listeners will believe that the speaker's ideas were better than those of his opponents.

Aristotle studied the art of persuasion and explained what he learned in the first known book on public speaking. He called this book *The Rhetoric*. In it he explained that rhetoric was the ability to "…discover in any particular case all of the **available** means of persuasion." You, as a person who **practices** rhetoric, or a *rhetorician*, must understand three things in order to develop a winning **argument**. You must know your subject, you must understand your audience, and you must choose the best way to persuade the audience to take your side. You do this, according to Aristotle, by choosing one, or a **mixture** of, three persuasive **techniques**, or what Aristotle called, *appeals*. They are **Ethos***, **Logos***, and *Pathos**.

The Appeals and Their Applications in the Real World

The first appeal, *Ethos*, asks the audience to trust the speaker's character or **expertise**. You attempt to get the audience on your side by showing them that you have a good and **trustworthy*** character, or that you are an **expert** on the **topic** being **discussed**, or that you and the audience have a shared set of values. To explain the last case, you show the audience that, since you have much in common and already agree on most things, that they should agree with you on this topic, too. An example might be that one of your friends is thinking of joining a school club. You try to **convince** her to join the art club because you have been in the club for a year and you know that it has helped to **improve** your drawing. You **remind** your friend that she, like you, really liked drawing in **elementary*** school. Joining the art club would give her a chance to **indulge*** her love of **creating** art and will help her **improve** her drawing. In **response** to your appeal, she decides to join the art club.

The second appeal is *Logos*. Logos deals with **logic** and facts. You would show the audience that your idea is the best by using **information**, numbers, and **evidence**. Perhaps one of your friends is trying to decide which smart phone to buy. You think the best type of phone for your friend is the one that you recently bought. You explain to your friend all the **benefits** of the phone you have, perhaps pointing out that the **battery*** lasts a long time or that it is built well and will **rarely** break down. You might point out that its **features** are nearly **similar** to those in more expensive phones, for example. In response to your knowledgeable appeal, he decides to buy the same type of phone that you have **purchased**.

The **final** appeal is what Aristotle called *Pathos*. Pathos draws on the audience's **emotions*** to make them **sympathetic** to the speaker's argument. For example, if you were **collecting** money for a **charity*** that helps homeless people, you might show your audience, in this case your parents, a picture of a homeless man or woman, and you might tell them the story of a homeless person, explaining how they are cold in the winter and **hungry** often. You might then ask your parents to think about their own lives, about their homes and possessions, and ask them how their lives would be different if, for some reason, all of those things, through no **fault** of their own, disappeared. In response to your appeal, and feeling as sorry for the homeless your parents donate money to the charity.

Rhetoricians of Note

There have been many famous **rhetoricians*** throughout history. If you think of a famous speech, the chances are that the speaker was famous for his or her ability to persuade. Abraham Lincoln was a noted public speaker and one of his most famous speeches was also one of his shortest, being only 271 words long and taking only about two minutes to **recite***. That would be his *Gettysburg* Address* of November 19, 1863. The speech was **intended** to **remind** and **encourage** the nation to continue the struggle of the US Civil War, reminding everyone who would hear or read the speech of the war's central purpose, which was to **secure** freedom for all American regardless of their race. An example from more recent history is Martin Luther King. He used pathos in one of his most famous speeches, his 1963 speech at the Lincoln Memorial in Washington D.C., known as his *I Have a Dream* speech. It was given in the middle of the US **Civil** Rights movement. In it he used **images** of white and black children growing up together in **harmony***, and the image of his own children being judged not by their race but by their character.

To Those Who Are Thinking of Studying Rhetoric

Studying rhetoric can help you in two **primary** ways. First, it will help you understand what type of arguments, or reasons, a person is using to get you to agree with him or her, and it will help you determine whether those arguments are **valid** and those reasons are sound. Second, it will help you decide how you will put together your own arguments, or reasons, when you yourself are trying to convince other people to agree with you. Let's **examine** these two points in more detail.

First, let's **review** how the study of rhetoric can help you be a better, more **aware**, audience for rhetoric. If you think about it, we are always surrounded by speakers, **advertisements**, and political **campaigns*** that want us to believe them, buy their products, or vote for their **candidates***. Appeals for our support come to us **via** every **conceivable media**. As an audience, as students, as **consumers**, as members of a society, having the ability to **analyze** spoken and written appeals will **improve** your ability to **interpret** and understand what your teachers are explaining to you or having you read. It will improve your ability to make good decisions about what to purchase or how to spend your money. **Finally**, when you are able to vote and take part in the political **process**, it will give you the **skills** to understand political arguments and make better decisions about voting.

In addition, as a **practitioner** of rhetoric, or one who uses language to persuade others, you can use the study of rhetoric to help you **sharpen** your **intellectual*** and **communicative** skills. Studying rhetoric will help you write more effective **compositions***, speeches, and presentations. **Additionally***, the study of rhetoric will make you a more persuasive **individual**. You will be able to organize your thinking and use effective language to convince people that what you are in favor of is what they should be in favor of, and this in cases as simple as which movie you want to see at the **cinema*** to more **complex** situations such as convincing your audience to support a politician you think should be elected to office.

Related Areas of Study

Over time, rhetoric **evolved** to have a **multidisciplinary*** **scope** that includes all **academic disciplines** in which a **critical awareness** of the **tools** of persuasion, and the **principles** of **logic** that give us the ability to **argue** and **debate** truthfully, skillfully, and effectively, are necessary. Today, rhetorical studies extends across many **areas** of **education** and training. Rhetoric is important when you study advertising, business, **communication**, history, **media** studies, **philosophy**, political science, **psychology**, **sociology***, and **linguistics***. Indeed, any area of study that includes examining the use of speech, texts, or even **images**, to persuade will **require** that you understand rhetoric. Rhetoric surrounds us.

Adapted from a text by Patrick Dougherty EdD
Dean of Faculty, Professor
Akita International University
Japan

Vocabulary

Words From the 2nd 1000 General Service High Frequency Word List

advertise	disciplines
argue	discussed
audience	education
birthday	encourage
century	entire
club	essentially
collecting	exactly
critical	examine

fault
govern
hungry
improve
information
intended
males
mixture
parents
persuade

phone
practice
rarely
refers
remind
review
sharpen
skill
sympathetic
tool

Words From the Academic Word List (AWL)

academic
adult
analyze
area
assembly
available
aware
benefits
civil
communication
complex
conceivable
consumers
convince
creating
debate
disposed
establishment
evidence
evolved
expert
features

final/finally
focused
fundamentally
image
individual
interpret
involves
logic
media
participate
philosopher
policies
practitioner
primary
principles
process
psychology
purchase
require
response
scope
secure

Glossary

Additionally (adverb): One more thing…
Appeal (verb): To make a request in a way that gets sympathy
Athens/Athenians (noun): The capital city of Greece/the people of the city of Athens
Battery (noun): A device for storing energy
Campaign (noun): A series of actions to bring about a desired result, especially in elections
Candidates (noun): Someone trying to be chosen for something
Charity (noun): An institution that gives financial relief to the poor and needy
Cinema (noun): Movie theater
Composition (noun): A piece of writing
Democracy (noun): Government by the people
Elementary (adjective): The first level of public schooling

Emotion (noun): Sentiments/feelings
Ethos (noun): Appeal to morality
Faculty (noun): Ability
Gettysburg (noun): A place in the USA where a famous battle was fought during the Civil War
Harmony (noun): Internal calm
Indulge (verb): Yield to a desire
Intellectual (adjective): Given to thought and study
Linguistics (noun): The study of the system of human language
Logos (noun): Appeal to logic, reason, and facts
Mall (noun): A commercial area with many different stores in the same complex
Multidisciplinary (adjective): Crossing across more than one subject of study
Opponent (noun): Enemy/someone who takes the opposite position
Pathos (noun): Appeal to emotion and sympathy
Recite (verb): To repeat from memory
Rhetoricians (noun): Someone skilled at the effective practice of rhetoric
Sociology (noun): The study of society, institutions, and relationships
Trustworthy (adjective): Dependable; someone that can be trusted

CHAPTER 7

DRAMA FOR EDUCATION

Naoko Araki
Akita International University Japan

Introduction

Simply put, **Drama** is **performing** arts. It includes **traditional performances**, such as *Kabuki** and opera*, and modern performances on stage and in **movies**. Still, often when people hear the word "Drama", they would mostly consider only TV dramas or **soap operas***. Drama for *Liberal* Arts refers to an educational *perspective*, "Drama in **Education**".

Drama in Education is used for teaching and learning purposes in countries including England, Canada, Australia, and New Zealand. These countries recognise Drama as a *fundamental aspect* of learning within the field of "Arts Education" along with **Dance**, Music, and **Visual** Arts (such as Painting, Drawing, **Photography**, and *Filmmaking**). *In contrast,* in Japan, only Music and Visual Arts are offered as Arts Education in the national **programs** of studies for schools, while Dance is part of **Physical** Education (PE). Drama is seen more as an after-school **club** activity where a group of students who are interested in performance may *voluntarily* join the activities, such as acting exercises and/or when schools put on a stage play for an end-of-year event.

It is *significant* to note that the fundamental **concepts** of Drama in Education have also been *widespread* beyond Commonwealth countries and implemented in educational **curricula*** in **areas** of Asia, Africa, Europe, and South America. Drama in Education is becoming available to many more students recently as its *benefits* have been acknowledged and *researched* by educators, practitioners, and their **colleagues**. One of the benefits of its success is *flexibility* as a teaching **approach** within other **academic** subjects, such as history, moral education, social studies, literature, and language learning. In fact, it is seen to be *so* useful that universities in Australia offer Drama Education classes in their Education courses for all students who are studying to become teachers in the future. Even Science students taking Education courses often take part in Drama-Science classes to experience the **impact** of Science on people's lives or how the development of Science *affects* their feelings and relationships (White et al., 2021). Drama for Education is particularly efficient at *investigating* people's **motivations** and reasoning by considering **multiple** *perspectives*.

The *interdisciplinary** way of applying Drama for teaching and learning purposes helps students gain a deeper understanding of **crucial** aspects of **complex issues** in society. In particular, research *evidence revealed* that the use of Drama for additional language learning and **intercultural communication*** accommodates students' *linguistic** and social needs. It also *demonstrates* such an approach *motivates* their learning and **challenges** the *biases* they might hold.

In Drama for English language learning, for example, students use the *target* language (English) in their own ways rather than simply following set words in textbooks. The drama approach sets language learners free from the *constraint* of textbook-teacher-centred learning. The drama perspective gives language learners more control in their use of language so that they can ***devote*** themselves to ***authentic* scenarios*** of daily life. This means that they can find out more about possible ways of using both **verbal*** (words) and **nonverbal*** (actions) *elements* to send and receive **messages** effectively. This is an artistic way of learning, going from "*heart*" to "*art*", in which students can discover and express more of themselves and others through working together within a safe, freeing, less controlled learning **environment**.

Drama in Modern Learning Settings

The idea of using Drama in education first started in England before spreading elsewhere, to places such as North America, Australia, and New Zealand. The effectiveness of Drama in education has been studied ***worldwide****, and its value in education is now well-recognized within schools and beyond.

One interesting example is seen in the famous Louvre ***Museum**** in France. There, some ***curators****, dress up as ***Roman statues**** and take groups of schoolchildren around the museum. The children become more aware of history and art because they see curators changing into ancient statues, becoming **alive**, and speaking to them about famous art pieces in the museum.

Another example *displaying* a way of using Drama in Education *corresponds* with an old *prison* in Melbourne, Australia, which was turned into a museum called the *Old Melbourne* **Gaol***. Visitors can join in a tour and experience for themselves how the prisoners lived in **the old days***. The visitors are asked to wear **clothes** that prisoners in the old days used to wear, while the museum curators there act as prison **guards** and judges. As they walk through the prison, they experience the difficult living conditions of the prisoners by acting as if they are prisoners. As seen in these examples, the use of Drama is effective. As a ***consequence***, ***participants*** of these ***embodied**** activities at the ***venues**** develop ***empathy**** and understand someone else's life by having them directly experience a ***brief*** part of that life for themselves.

Many people might consider drama for **professional** actors and people in theatre groups who want to study the field of Drama. However, its effect on Education, such as making history come alive (E.g. the curators you read about earlier, who play the part of ancient Roman statues) or learning about a lack of fairness in the system of law in society (when acting as prisoners in the "Old Melbourne Gaol"), has such a strong effect on people that everyone can learn from those kinds of experiences.

As seen in the above examples of *incorporating* drama for learning outside school ***settings****, the findings of recent studies in Drama in Education demonstrate similar positive outcomes in school settings, ***motivating*** learners to be more interested in their learning. One of the ***unique*** ways in which Drama is used, called "**Process Drama***", has become known for its effectiveness in learning. "Process Drama" ***constantly*** looks at the way Drama is ***constructed*** by the participants rather than only *focusing* on the stage **performance** at the end of the learning process. Process Drama ***appreciates*** *what* they learn and *how* they ***acquire***.

In this process, learners share ideas by actively ***contributing*** themselves to discussions. They **imagine** the characters' feelings and actions, and they also think about why they act as they do. The characters and ***scenarios*** are always in a meaningful setting, which is related to ***controversial*** issues such as family and ***community conflicts***, **immigration**, and **discrimination** against other people who are in some way different.

In "Process Drama", learners take on the role of a character in a drama and plan and act out a significant scene by expressing the character with body movements and using different expressions on their faces. This is an embodied learning. Studies show that this way of learning through Drama builds students' interest in their learning and leads them to a wider and deeper understanding of human life and experience.

Studying Drama at a Liberal Arts University

All students, with or without any ***previous*** experience in acting or drama education, can ***access*** classes with drama ***approaches***. Students are expected to use their ***imagination*** and creativity and to participate more actively in group discussions in their **classes**, using open space as a space for physical expression. The drama course ***typically consists*** of several *workshops** with a focus on themes. Each workshop may start with a controversial article, a *thought-provoking** photo or *illustration**, a current affair, a picture book, a story, or a song. Below is one example of how drama is used for communication and English language learning, using an English song as a starting point.

Typically, students learn English through songs in their high school English language classes. First, they may learn the words of the song. They may look up the meanings of unknown words in a **dictionary** as they study the song. After that, they **practice** *pronunciation*,* and then they may be asked to sing the song together in class.

A Drama-based language and communication class in a **Liberal** Arts university, however, will usually continue beyond simply learning and singing a song together. Once the basic understanding of the ideas in the song is shared in class, the Drama-based language class asks students to consider relationships and background *settings** more deeply and *critically*. For example, they may **discuss** in small groups the main characters' names, their *emotions**, and the complex situations described in the song.

An English language and communication class, for example, may use a song by the famous *British* pop** group of the 1960s, "The Beatles," as these songs are popular for English language learning in Japanese schools. One of their songs, called "*She's leaving home*", can be used to start the workshop. This song is about a young girl leaving home with her **boyfriend*** without telling her **parents**. She leaves a short note on the table for them. Based on the story that the song tells, students work together to *imagine* and decide all the missing details. They may think of answers to questions such as: What is written on the note? Why is she leaving? What is her relationship with her parents like? What kind of relationship does she have with her boyfriend? How did they meet each other? What do her parents do when they find that she has gone? What kind of person is she? Was she happy in her family? What would make a young person want to leave home? What kind of student was she at school? What might happen to her a few years after she leaves home? Will she make things right with her parents in the future? Questions like these help students begin to form a clear idea of the whole situation.

Based on the *amicable** decisions students made as a class, they start *discussing* the details they need to help them retell the story through drama. They may decide the necessary details such as possible names, ages, and the **community** where the main characters might be living; in this case, the girl, her boyfriend, and her parents. After sharing each group's ideas with everyone in the class, the whole class will come together to make the last decisions on the details for each character and their relationships within the family and the community.

In the next step, students work in **pairs** to come up with possible **sentences** or words that could be written in the note that the girl left on the table. Using what students wrote from the girl's point of view, they are then asked to take her parents' point of view by acting out a short scene of the parents as they read the note and find out that their daughter has left home. Students do not work from a prepared *script**. Instead, they share their ideas and decide together what each character will say and do and how to show their feelings in an *improvised** scene. After that, they will **practice** the scene they have planned and made. The *rehearsal** process shapes and *finalises* the details paying *attention* to the choice of words and body language.

The language used in the scene does not come from school books or scripts that are read out loud or memorized. Instead, students have to carefully construct and demonstrate ideas for their scripts using their imagination. This can help students to understand human problems, such as difficulties in discussing family issues, *articulating** their thoughts and ideas, and expressing their emotions in family relationships, for example, by making them see various perspectives of a situation and family conflict.

This process also helps with language learning by giving the agency, or control, back to students themselves. It also develops their spontaneity and confidence in communication and decreases anxiety in using the target language (Araki & Raphael, 2018). While the students decide on the language they need, the teacher still has important work to do. The teacher will support the group discussions and suggest nuanced words and sentences students could use in a meaningful scenario if the group needs help. They are active in their own decision-making and can try out their ideas in a learning setting where they feel they have more control over those decisions. In the greater freedom of such a setting, they experience the English language becoming "alive" and real. In this way, "*Process Drama*" in language and communication classes offers many *teachable moments** to build the students' communication and language **skills** to a much higher level. By going through this, learners find that they, themselves, change and grow compassion because they experience "life" from the point of view of others by being *"in someone else's shoes"*.

Possible Future Directions

Drama, and Drama in Education, in particular, offers a chance for shared and active learning for all who take part. While Drama in Education has already spread to many countries around the world, educators in Japan have only recently started to recognize that it is also useful for teaching the English language, Japanese literature, moral education, and other fields of study.

Learners who are interested in becoming educators, those who wish to be part of *"the fine arts"**, or those interested in "helping" careers (such as **nurses** and doctors, lawyers and social workers, and more), learn through Drama to understand how *other* people experience the world, and how *they* think, feel and act in different situations. This will be of the greatest help as they build a successful future working life.

Adapted from a text by Naoko Araki PhD
Professor, EAP Program
Akita International University
Japan

Vocabulary

Words From the 2nd 1000 General Service High Frequency Word List

alive	nurse
clothes	pairs
club	parents
dance	performance
dictionary	photography
discuss	practice
education/educators	prison
guards	program
imagine	sentences
message	skills

Words From the Academic Word List (AWL)

discrimination	physical
drama	process
communication	professional
community	traditional
immigration	visual
liberal	

Glossary

Boyfriend (noun): Male person with whom someone is in a romantic relationship

Curator (noun): Person who manages collections in a museum

Gaol (noun): Old spelling of jail (a prison)

Intercultural communication (noun phrase): "Inter-" means "between" and cultural means from a culture, so **intercultural communication** refers to the way people relate to each other between different cultures.

Kabuki (noun): A form of traditional Japanese drama with highly stylized song, mime, and dance performed by male actors.

Movies (noun): Short for moving pictures or films.
Museum (noun): a special public building where important works of art and items of cultural importance are kept and displayed.
Nonverbal (adjective): relating to the use of actions, NOT words.
Opera (noun): A drama set to music accompanied by an orchestra.
Process Drama (noun phrase): The name given to a way of teaching Drama where the teacher and the students work together both in and out of the roles they are playing. The Drama is made up as it goes, with no set script. The purpose is to solve problems and think critically about ideas that they meet along the way.
Roman (adjective): Person or thing from Rome, Italy.
Script (noun): A piece of writing from which someone reads directly or which someone memorizes exactly
Soap Opera (noun phrase): An ongoing set of dramatic TV or radio programs dealing with people and everyday situations. They often show on romantic relationships.
Statue (noun): A 3-D work of art, often made of stone or metal, often taking the form of a human or an animal. Statues are often made of famous people or animals. A famous statue in Japan is the statue of *Hachikō* outside Shibuya Station in Tokyo.
Teachable moments (noun phrase): This idea describes unplanned times in a teaching and learning situation when a teacher has a spontaneous opportunity to explain or teach something.
The old days (idiom): In the past. In history. Usually, meaning a long time ago, not the recent past.
The fine arts (noun phrase): Traditionally these are painting, sculpture, music, architecture, creative writing and poetry, and the performing arts including dance and drama).
To be in someone else's shoes (idiom): Describes being able to see and understand life from another person's point of view.
Verbal (adjective): relating to the use of words.

References

Araki, N., & Raphael, J. (2018). Firing the imagination: Process drama as pedagogy for 'melting' EAP speaking anxiety and increasing Japanese University Students' confidence in speaking. In R. Ruegg, & C. Williams, (Eds.), *Teaching English for Academic Purposes (EAP) in Japan. English language education*, Vol. 14. Springer, pp. 41–58. https://doi.org/10.1007/978-981-10-8264-1_3

White, J. P., Raphael, J., & van Cuylenburg, K. (2021). *Science and drama: Contemporary and creative approaches to teaching and learning.* Springer. https://doi.org/10.1007/978-3-030-84401-1

CHAPTER 8

CREATIVE WRITING

Joel Friederich
Akita International University, Japan

Introduction: The Value of Creative Writing

*A **creative** writing class may be one of the last places you can go where your life still matters*
(Hugo, 1979, p. 65).[1]

This **sentence** was written by the American **poet** Richard Hugo in a small book of essays, *The **Triggering** Town*, which explained his ideas about how to teach and learn creative writing. Hugo was a professor at the University of Montana in the United States in the 1960s and 70s. He was director of the university's creative writing **program** for many of those years, helping **establish** and grow that program into one of the strongest in the U.S. Hugo's poetry was very well-known for the way it **captured*** the lost and **lonely** feeling of small rural communities in the Pacific Northwest **region** of the United States. His teaching at the University of Montana and his writing about teaching creative writing in *The Triggering Town* became very influential for how a generation of writers and university teachers thought about creative writing. Fellow writers, students, and **colleagues treasured** the **honesty** and **directness*** of his writing, and his teaching of creative writing was the **inspiration*** for many of his students also to become professors of creative writing at universities. Today, many of Richard Hugo's students and others who he inspired are now reaching the height of their own careers as writers, professors, and directors of creative writing at universities.

Hugo wrote the sentence above in an essay called "In Defense of Creative-Writing Classes." When he wrote this essay, in the 1970s, creative writing classes in American universities' English departments were becoming increasingly popular, with student **enrollments*** rising **dramatically** while interest in more **traditional** English courses, such as **Shakespeare*** or **classical** literature, was **decreasing**. As creative writing became more popular in universities, other professors in college English departments, traditional **scholars*** of literature, began to question the value of creative writing because its popularity seemed to be taking away from their own fields of study. They questioned whether creative writing was popular because it was simply more **entertaining** for students than learning to **analyze** and **interpret** traditional literature written by the great **authors** of the past.

---

[1]Hugo, Richard (1979, reissued 1992). The Triggering Town: Lectures and Essays on Poetry and Writing. WW Norton.

In his essay, Hugo wanted to **respond** to this **conflict** between scholars of literature and creative writing teachers in university English departments.

Knowledge and Experience: Scholarship versus Creativity

Hugo described a difference between scholarly and creative **approaches** to learning. This difference, he wrote, lies "in the way the mind **reacts** to different forms of knowledge" (p. 58). Much of Hugo's essay described how scholars and creative writers differ in their approach to knowledge and learning. A scholarly or academic approach to knowledge tries to reach "**final** truths," Hugo said, while creative writers are focused more on "possibilities" (p. 56). According to Hugo, **academic** scholars "**distrust*** their responses. They feel that if a response can't be **defended intellectually***, it lacks **validity**" (p. 62). In Hugo's view, it was a **mistake** for universities to approach knowledge only through scholarly **research** to **achieve objective** truths that can be defended intellectually. He believed that this academic approach to knowledge and learning was too **narrow** that it **ignored** the importance of **subjective*** human experiences.

In short, Hugo **argued**, a university **curriculum*** **dedicated*** only to a scholarly approach to knowledge often teaches students that their subjective experiences do not matter. Hugo argued that creative writing courses bring **balance** to college **education** by allowing students to include their own experiences as part of their learning by teaching that studying one's own life and **imagination** also results in new knowledge. "It may have been the most important **lesson** I ever learned, maybe the most important lesson one can teach. You are someone, and you have a right to your life," Hugo wrote (p. 64).

Even with so many **decades** passing since the **publication** in 1979 of "In Defense of Creative-Writing Classes," Hugo's essay remains a powerful description of the **role** creative writing plays in university education, **insisting*** that we must not allow academic study to **exclude** personal experience:

> When we are told in **dozens** of **insidious*** ways that our lives don't matter, we may be forced to insist, often far too **loudly**, that they do. A creative writing class may be one of the last places you can go where your life still matters (p. 65).

A History of Creative Writing

An important part of Hugo's "In Defense of Creative-Writing Classes" **context** is the history of creative writing in the curriculum. Unlike other traditional subjects studied in the **liberal** arts for many **centuries,** creative writing was only recently introduced in college course offerings. In his essay, Hugo noted that **composing** poetry had been **required** for younger students in high and elementary schools for 400 years before the 19th century, though this tradition died out in the 1800s (p. 53). However, colleges and universities did not begin to offer any study in creative writing until much more recently. In "The Rise of Creative Writing," Myers (1993) proposed that creative writing courses were first developed in American universities between 1880 and 1940 "as an effort to **reform*** the study of literature" (p. 278).

The larger background of dramatic changes in higher education **worldwide*** in the 19th century is important for understanding how college creative writing courses began "as an effort to reform literature," as Myers described. Early in the 19th century, the German university system **emphasised** scholarly research, **focusing** on an **empirical** or scientific approach to gaining new knowledge (Menand et al., 2017). The new German **model** of the modern research university was adopted worldwide in the 19th century. For example, in 1876, when John's Hopkins University was **founded** in the United States, almost all **faculty*** members of the new university had studied in Germany (Menand et al., 2017). The scientific model for gaining new knowledge through empirical research became the focus of the modern university system, "the **ideal** of systematic, **rigorous***, scientific knowledge" (Myers, 1993, p. 280).

The same model of empirical research was also applied to the study of literature in the 19th century. The highest level of literary study, which at that time was called **philology***, focused on objective analysis of the **grammar** and **linguistic*** elements of ancient literature, along with **examining** historical data about literary texts. According to Myers, the ideal in this approach to literary study and research was not **humanism*** but a more scientific type of objectivity (p. 281).

Creative writing classes first began to be offered near the end of the 19th century in the United States as a **reaction** against this new scientific approach in universities. That is, college creative writing began to return humanism and subjective personal experience to the study of literature because the system of modern research universities had left it out. According to Myers, creative writing classes **aimed** to **restore** the idea of literature as "a living thing, as if people **intended** to write more of it" (p. 279).

The first creative writing classes were offered early in the 1880s at Harvard University in the U.S. and **quickly** became very popular, with over 150 students enrolling in 1885 (Dale, 2011). Creative writing "was **formulated** at Harvard in the last two decades of the 19th century out of the belief that the ideal end of the study of literature is the making of literature," according to Myers (p. 283). The writing courses introduced at Harvard then were called "Composition" rather than "Creative Writing," these courses also marked the first time that academic writing and essays were taught in college, along with writing poems, stories, and plays. These classes were different from the **previous** literature courses because, according to Myers, they established "that literature could be used in the university for some purpose other than philological research" (p. 284), that is, to inspire and **guide** students to create their own new literature through **self**-expression.

The most important teacher of creative writing at Harvard was Barrett Wendell (1855–1921), who wrote the first writing textbooks and whose teaching **methods** spread quickly to writing classes in other American universities. In one textbook he **authored**, titled *English Composition*, Wendell wrote that his classes aimed to teach students to pay **attention** to their own **unique** experiences. "It is the perception of what makes one moment different from another that marks the **sympathetic** character of the artist," Wendell wrote (as **cited** in Myers, p. 286). Just as Richard Hugo described much later, the **goal** of the first creative writing classes at Harvard was for students to **explore** their unique personal experiences in the reading and writing of literature.

In the first two decades of the 20th Century, composition classes in U.S. universities changed from Wendell's original design. They became more focused on academic writing. These early composition courses were becoming the same academic writing courses, often called "Composition 1" and "Composition 2," still taken by **undergraduates*** today. They no longer focused as much on self-expression or creative writing. As a result, by the early 1920s the first courses called "creative writing" began to be offered at a school **connected** to Columbia University in New York City. These classes could focus **specifically** on literary self-expression instead of the academic writing that was then being taught in college composition (Myers, 1993). In two books he **published**, Hugh Mearns, the teacher who developed these classes at Columbia, described "personal growth" as the goal of his creative writing classes. Mearns' ideas were strongly influenced by the well-known educational **philosophy** of Thomas Dewey, who believed learning should take a student-centered approach to develop each **individual** as a whole person. Mearns wrote that creative writing classes should "touch some of the secret sources of [students'] lives, to discover and to bring out the power that they possessed but, through **timidity*** or **ignorance**, could not use" (as cited in Myers p. 289). According to Mearns, the purpose of a creative writing class should be to develop each student's whole personality through self-expression.

Mearns' books became well-known. His ideas about creative writing classes as a method for students to find personal growth were highly influential in American universities. By the 1930s, there were nearly 50 universities in the United States where creative writing was included in the curriculum, in some cases as part of composition courses, in other cases as classes specifically titled "creative writing."

The Iowa Writers' Workshop and the Workshop Method

However, as Myers pointed out, these **diverse** courses experimenting separately with creative writing at different colleges did not yet mark the beginning of creative writing as a recognized "academic discipline." At that time, creative writing was not recognised officially; it was not yet part of any academic department, such as English. Students could not take a **series** of creative writing courses as a **major** or receive a degree in creative writing.

This changed when creative writing as a **formal** academic **discipline** was introduced at the University of Iowa as an official reform in the study of literature. From 1930–1944, Norman Foerster, the director of the new School of Letters at the University of Iowa, **sought** to leave behind the 19th-century methods of studying literature. Foerster wanted the School of Letters to focus on humanism in the study of literature and writing. Offering a full program of courses in creative writing was a strong part of that humanism. Starting in the 1930s in Iowa's School of Letters, students could choose creative writing as a major field of study and take **various** creative writing classes.

The Iowa Writers' Workshop (https://writersworkshop.uiowa.edu) was formed within the School of Letters at the University of Iowa in 1936, and throughout the 20th century, this program became the **global** leader in creative writing at the university level. There were two major **contributions** of The Iowa Writers Workshop to the development of creative writing as a field of study in universities around the world: First, **establishing** "the workshop method" of teaching as the dominant **pedagogy*** for college creative writing classes, and second, establishing the Master of Fine Arts (MFA) **graduate degree*** as a highly recognized **professional credential*** in the field of creative writing.

The workshop method developed at the University of Iowa became the standard of **practice** for teaching creative writing at all levels and remains so today. The writing workshop classroom does not focus on the **instructor** as a **lecturer** or presenter of new knowledge. Instead, the writing workshop classroom **treats** all **participants**, students and instructors **alike**, equally as working writers **seeking** to **refine** the literary quality of their self-expression. Participants in a writing workshop generally sit facing each other around a **seminar*** table or in a circle. As all participants join in to **discuss** their ideas for **revising** each piece of writing, authors merely listen without participating. Authors only listen because the poems or stories being discussed should "stand on their own **merits***" without any explanation or defence from the author. The focus of the writing workshop is not on understanding **theories** of literature or **analyzing** and **interpreting** great literature of the past. Creative writing workshops are dedicated to the active practice ("**praxis***") of making literature rather than **passive reception*** of knowledge about literature. Each creative writing workshop aims to create new literature by writers helping each other reach their full **potential** in self-expression.

The Benefits of Studying Creative Writing

The creative writing program that began at Iowa and the workshop method have been adopted extensively at universities in countries where English is the native language. With professional writers and instructors **emerging** from graduate degree programs such as the Master of Fine Arts, new creative writing programs have been led by professors trained to meet ever-growing student interest in developing their own creativity through writing poetry, **fiction***, plays, and other forms of literature. The **spark*** that started the growth of college creative writing classes was a desire to include humanism and each student's personal expressions and experiences in university education. Today, college students continue to desire a place, as Richard Hugo wrote, "where their lives still matter."

Adapted from a text by Joel Friederich, MFA (Creative Writing/Poetry)
Associate Professor, English for Academic Purposes
Akita International University, Akita, Japan

Vocabulary

Words From the Second 1000 General Service High-Frequency Word List

alike	discipline
aimed	discuss
argued	dozens
attention	education
balance	entertaining
centuries	examine
composing	explore
composition	formal
connected	grammar
decreasing	guide
defended	honesty

ideal
imagination
intended
lesson
lonely
loudly
mistake
model
narrow
poet

practice
program
quickly
self
sentence
sympathetic
titled
treasured
treats

Words From the Academic Word List (AWL)

academic
achieve
analyzing
analyze
approaches
authored
authors
classical
cited
colleagues
conflict
context
contributions
creative
decades
diverse
dramatically
emerging
emphasized
empirical
establish
establishing
exclude
final
focusing
formulated
founded
global
goal
ignored
ignorance
individual
instructor
interpreting
interpret

lecturer
liberal
methods
objective
participants
passive
philosophy
potential
precision
previous
professional
publication
published
reaction
reacting
region
refine
research
required
respond
responding
restore
revising
role
series
sought
specifically
theories
traditional
triggering
unique
uniformity
validity
various

Glossary

Captured (verb): Taken into possession or control, often by force.
Credential (noun): A qualification, achievement, or aspect of a person's background used to indicate their suitability for something.
Curriculum (noun): The subjects comprising a course of study in a school or college.
Dedicated (adjective): Devoted to a task or purpose.
Directness (noun): The quality of being straightforward and candid.
Distrust (noun): Lack of trust or confidence in someone or something.
Enrollments (noun plural): The act of registering or being registered for a course or institution.
Faculty (noun): A group of teachers or professors in an educational institution.
Fiction (noun): Literature created from the imagination, not presented as fact.
Graduate Degree (noun): An advanced academic degree earned after completing a bachelor's degree.
Humanism (noun): A system of thought that centers on humans and their values, capacities, and worth.
Insidious (adjective): Proceeding in a subtle way but with harmful effects.
Insisting (verb): Demanding something forcefully, not accepting refusal.
Inspiration (noun): The process of being mentally stimulated to do or feel something, especially something creative.
Inspire (verb): To fill someone with the urge or ability to do or feel something, especially something creative.
Intellectually (adverb): In a way that relates to the intellect or mental ability.
Linguistic (adjective): Relating to language or linguistics.
Merits (noun): The quality of being particularly good or worthy.
Pedagogy (noun): The method and practice of teaching, especially as an academic subject or theoretical concept.
Philology (noun): The study of language in written historical sources; it is a combination of literary studies, history, and linguistics.
Praxis (noun): Practice, as distinguished from theory; application of a theory or skill.
Reception (noun): The way in which a person or group of people react to something.
Reform (verb): Make changes in something, typically a social, political, or economic institution or practice, in order to improve it.
Rigorous (adjective): Extremely thorough and careful.
Scholars (noun plural): A specialist in a particular branch of study, especially the humanities; a distinguished academic.
Seminar (noun): A conference or other meeting for discussion or training.
Shakespeare (noun): William Shakespeare, a famous English playwright, poet, and actor, widely regarded as the greatest writer in the English language.
Spark (verb): To inspire or start something, often a creative or imaginative process.
Subjective (adjective): Based on or influenced by personal feelings, tastes, or opinions.
Timidity (noun): Lack of courage or confidence.
Undergraduates (noun plural): Students at a college or university who have not yet earned a degree.
Worldwide (adjective): Extending or reaching throughout the world.

References

Dale, J. (2011, May 25). The rise and rise of creative writing. *The Conversation.* https://theconversation.com/the-rise-and-rise-of-creative-writing-730

Hugo, R. (1979, reissued 1992). *The triggering town: Lectures and essays on poetry and writing.* W. W. Norton.

Menand, L., Reitter, P., & Wellmon, C. (Eds.). (2017). *The rise of the Research University.* Univ of Chicago Press.

Myers, D. G. (1993). The rise of creative writing. *Journal of the History of Ideas, 54*(2), 277–297. https://www.jstor.org/stable/2709983

CHAPTER 9

JAPANESE PHILOSOPHY

Kyle Michael James Shuttleworth
Akita International University, Japan

Introduction

Have you ever wondered whether there is a **distinctly** Japanese **philosophical tradition**? If so, do you know what is distinct about Japanese philosophical thought? If not, what do you think may be **unique** about a philosophical approach which **originated** in Japan?

In general, "philosophy" **refers** to the set of systems and beliefs that we as **individuals**, **communities**, or **cultures adhere*** to. In an **academic context**, philosophy **refers** more **specifically** to the study of **metaphysics*** (questions of being), **epistemology*** (study of knowledge), **logic** (**structure** of thought), and **ethics** (what it means to live well). And although the **foundation** of academic philosophy originated in Ancient Greece, these categories of thought not only came to underpin every other academic field in Western arts, sciences, and **humanities**, but also spread throughout the world.

Various Eastern philosophies—such as **Buddhism***, **Confucianism***, and **Daoism***—are said to have existed in Japan from as early as the *Asuka* **period**, as a **consequence** of cultural exchange with China and Korea. However, Western philosophy did not arrive in Japan until the late *Edo* **era***. What is now considered "Japanese philosophy" did not **emerge** as an independent, or **rival**, tradition to any of the above-mentioned **approaches**. Rather, "Japanese philosophy" was **established** through the **amalgamation*** of existing philosophies. More specifically, Japanese **intellectuals*** adopted the **framework** and **methodological** approach of Western philosophy. This form of **rational enquiry** was then applied to explain **key metaphysical***, **epistemological**, **logical**, and **ethical** concepts **inherent** in **Buddhist** thought.

Western philosophy is often termed the "philosophy of being", because the **metaphysical** foundation of such thought **aimed** at **revealing** the **underlying principle** at the **source** of all existence. Asian philosophies, such as Buddhism and Daoism, on the other hand, are **referred** to as philosophies of nothing, because they claim that being **originated** from **nothingness**. Although the concept of nothingness may seem like an **abstract** and **mystical*** idea to Western philosophers, Japanese intellectuals **sought** to use the philosophical **apparatus*** of Western philosophy to **illustrate** that true reality can only be **revealed** through the **concept** of **absolute nothingness**.

History

As mentioned above, Buddhist, Confucian, and Daoist philosophical thought existed in Japan from as early as the fifth **century**. These intellectual approaches provided systems of thought which greatly shaped Japanese culture and society in terms of religion, ethics, and politics. For example, *O-bon* is a Buddhist **festival***, Japan's **feudal*** structure was based on the Confucian **concept** of **loyalty** between subject and **sovereign***, and *setsubun* has its origin in Daoism. These intellectual traditions also provided the **foundation** for the **education** of the **aristocracy*** and *samurai*, who were required to memorise and **comprehend*** such Chinese classical works of literature as *Analects*, *Mengzi*, *Daodejing*, and *Zhuangzi*. The education of Japanese intellectuals continued in this way until the late Edo era, when Japan was forced to **abandon** its **policy** of national **isolation**.

When Japan's **borders** opened, Western arts, sciences, and **humanities** began to **flood** into Japan. These ideas and **intellectual** approaches were taken up with great **enthusiasm***, with the **aim** of raising the level of Japanese **civilisation** to that of Western nations. It was at this time when Western philosophy was first introduced to Japan, although its **alternative approach** to the existing systems of thought **posed** a problem for **scholars*** who sought new **terminology*** to **define** this **rational** approach. Nishi Amane (1829–1897) **coined*** the term *tetsugaku* [哲学], which was applied specifically to **denote** Western philosophical thought. **Advocates** of Western learning, such as Fukuzawa Yukichi (1835–1901), **espoused*** Western philosophy as the means to both social and **individual** freedom and development. And whilst Fukuzawa was Japanese and developed his own philosophy, he did not **establish** a **uniquely** Japanese system of thought.

What has come to be known as "Japanese" philosophy was first developed by Nishida Kitarō (1870–1945). Nishida had studied and possessed a **keen*** interest in Buddhist thought, but at Tokyo Imperial University he learned about Western philosophers, such as Kant and Hegel, from Prof. Raphael von Koeber (1848–1923). After **graduation***, Nishida began writing **essays*** which **utilised** the **methodological framework** of Western philosophy in order to **articulate*** the Buddhist concepts of **non-duality*** and nothingness. These essays, which were later published as *An Inquiry into the Good* [禅の研究;] (1911), led to Nishida taking up a **professorship*** at Kyoto Imperial University. Nishida's colleagues and students at Kyoto, such as Tanabe Hajime (1885–1962) and Nishitani Keiji (1900–1990), **responded** to, and developed his approach further, which came to be known as the Kyoto School [京都学派]. This represented the first uniquely Japanese approach to philosophy.

People of Note

Another Japanese philosopher of note, whom Nishida **invited** to Kyoto Imperial University, was Watsuji Tetsurō (1889–1960). Watsuji was born in Himeji, into a family of **physicians***, but decided to study philosophy whilst at Tokyo First Higher School. He then entered Tokyo Imperial University, where he also learned from Prof. Koeber, and wrote his graduation thesis on Schopenhauer in English. After graduation, Watsuji **published** books on Nietzsche (1913) and Kierkegaard (1915), but turned his **attention** towards culture, history and religion. Soon after taking up his position teaching in ethics at Kyoto Imperial University in 1925, Watsuji received a **scholarship*** from the Japanese **Ministry** of Education in 1927 to travelled to Germany in order to **research** the history of moral **ideology**. Upon his return to Japan, Watsuji developed one of his most **original** ideas.

From travelling around the world, Watsuji observed differences in cultures and sought to **connect** these to the surrounding **climate***, **geography***, and **topography***. Watsuji then proposed the **concept** of *fūdo* [風土] as a **fundamental factor** in the **structure** of human existence. The most important point for Watsuji is that we realise our own existence through *fūdo*. Offering the example of the cold, Watsuji notes that when we feel the cold it is not an **objective** cold that we **encounter**, but rather we experience ourselves as cold. Namely, through **climatic*** **phenomenon**, such as the cold, we gain awareness of our own existence. *Fūdo* also **enables** us to realise the **dual*** nature of human existence, that we are both **spatial** (located) and **temporal** (historical). That is, we possess a shared history according to where we exist, which will have influenced t**raditional architecture***, **clothing**, and **regional** food.

A further important **contribution** to philosophy by Watsuji was advanced in his **magnum opus***, *Ethics* [倫理学;] (1937). Here, Watsuji begins by **criticising*** Western philosophical approaches to ethics which begin from the **standpoint*** of **individual consciousness** alone. Through **linguistic deconstruction*** of the words for ethics [倫理] and human being [人間存在], Watsuji **illustrates** that humans cannot be reduced to either individual or social beings. Due to this dual structure of human existence, Watsuji claims that any **ethical theory** must **preserve** these two **aspects**. He further **argues** that all ethical actions take place in a certain form of **"betweenness"** [間柄], which determines whether an action is **appropriate**. For example, the form of love and **affection*** expressed in the relation between husband and wife, would not be appropriate between a man and a woman who just met on a train, because an **established** form of betweenness does not exist between them.

Possible Future Directions

Philosophy, by its very nature, is **abstract** and **theoretical**, and as such, it provides the **foundation** for various other academic subjects and fields of study. One important **emerging** field of study is **environmental** science. However, one **issue** in this field concerns how we can exist in an **ethical** relationship with nature, rather than simply seeing nature as a **resource** to be **exploited** for human gain. The **perspective** that only human beings possess **intrinsic** value, whilst nonhuman beings only possess **instrumental** value has been seen as a contributing factor to our current **environmental crisis***. That is, **deforestation*** can be understood to be a **consequence** of only thinking about trees in terms of their **raw** material, and the production of **goods*** from this resource for human beings. This **attitude** has become known as the problem of **anthropocentrism***, which **refers** to the belief that human beings are **superior*** to nonhuman beings.

In order to **overcome** the problem of anthropocentrism, and **mitigate*** the environmental crisis, it is necessary to change how we think about and act towards our natural **environment**. In **response** to this problem, Western philosophers have attempted to use ethical theories to illustrate why the **instrumental treatment** of nature is wrong. However, one problem with existing ethical theories is that they only deal with human relations. That is, existing ethical approaches can only tell us how we should act in relation to other human beings. **Contemporary** philosophers, such as Peter Singer (1946~), have attempted to extended **utilitarianism*** to **emphasise** the importance of animal life, but what about **non-sentient*** beings such as **insects** and plants? How is it possible to **encourage** an ethical relationship with life-forms with whom we are unable to directly **communicate**?

Although traditional ethical theories focus on the relationships between human beings, I believe that Watsuji's account of the **role** of *fūdo* in human existence can help us **rethink** our relationship to the natural world. That is, by illustrating how the natural world forms human cultures and traditions, recognition of this fact can help us understand that humans do not exist in **isolation** from nature. This causes us to further reflect upon human **reliance** upon our environment, and to help us **reorientate*** how we think about the natural world - as something upon which we depend for our existence, rather than something to be **exploited** for our own gain. From this **perspective**, we can also extend Watsuji's **ethical theory** of **betweenness** to nonhuman beings. That is, by understanding ourselves as a member of an **ecosystem***, rather than the masters of it, we can start to think about how we might exist in relation to the natural world and **restore ecological*** **balance** to our life system.

Adapted from a text by Dr. Kyle Michael James Shuttleworth
Assistant Professor of Philosophy
Akita International University

Vocabulary

Words From the Second 1000 General Service List

absolute	aim	argue	attention
balance	borders	century	civilisation
clothing	connect	consciousness	education

encourage	enquiry	flood	inquiry
insects	instrumental	international	invited
key	loyalty	origin	overcome
preserve	raw	referred	refers
reflect	rival	treatment	

Words From the Academic Word List

abandon	abstract	academic	adapted
advocates	alternative	approach	appropriate
aspects	assistant	attitude	awareness
categories	classical	colleagues	communicate
communities	concept	consequence	contemporary
context	contributing	contribution	cultural/culture
define	denote	distinct	emerge
emphasise	enables	encounter	environment
establish	ethical/ethics	exploited	factor
focus	foundation	framework	fundamental
ideology	illustrate	individual	inherent
intrinsic	isolation	issue	located
logic/logical	methodological	ministry	objective
period	perspective	phenomenon	philosopher/philosophical
philosophy	policy	posed	principle
published	rational	regional	reliance
required	research	resource	responded/response
restore	revealed	role	sought
source	specifically	structure	text
theoretical/theory	thesis	tradition/traditional	underlying
unique/uniquely	utilised		

Glossary

It Is Not Necessary for Learners to Memorise These Words
Adhere (verb): To stick to or be devoted to something.
Affection (noun): A tender emotion; fondness
Amalgamation (noun): A combination of separate things into a single whole.
Anthropocentrism (noun): Evaluating strictly according to human values.
Apparatus (noun): A device for a particular purpose.
Architecture (noun): The art/science of designing buildings and structures
Aristocracy (noun): Nobility; a hereditary ruling class

Articulate (verb): Expressed in clear language
Buddhism (noun): A religion based upon the teachings of the Buddha.
Climate (noun): The weather conditions within a particular location
Climatic (adjective): Relating to climate
Coined (verb—past tense): To create a new word or phrase
Comprehend (verb): Understand
Confucianism (noun): The system of morality taught by Confucious
Crisis (noun): A crucial situation where some change is necessary
Criticizing (verb—gerund): Pointing out the negative features of something
Daoism (noun): A Chinese religious/philosophical tradition emphasizing harmony with the *Tao* ("way")
Deconstruction (noun): A philosophical movement which questioned traditional assumptions
Deforestation (noun): The gradual reduction of the number of trees in an area
Dual (adjective): Having two (of something)
Ecological (adjective): Pertaining to how people exist within their environment
Ecosystem (noun): the interaction of organisms within an environment
Enthusiasm (noun): excitement or interest (in something)
Epistemology (noun): The branch of philosophy which investigates the nature of knowledge
Era (noun): A period of time
Espoused (verb—past tense): To advocate; to speak for
Essays (noun—plural): A short, written composition on a particular topic
Festival (noun): A celebration
Feudal (adjective): Pertaining to the system wherein social relationships are defined by land ownership
Geography (noun): The study of global and regional lands and their features
Goods (noun—plural): Things produced, traded, and consumed
Graduation (noun): The conferral of a diploma/degree at the end of a period of study
Intellectuals (noun—plural): Those members of society who engage in reflection, research, and criticism about said society
Keen (adjective): Well developed; sharpened
Magnum opus (noun): An artist's greatest work; masterpiece
Metaphysical (adjective): Pertaining to metaphysics (see below)
Metaphysics (noun): The branch of philosophy which investigates the nature of reality itself
Mitigate (verb): To relieve or make less severe a problem
Mystical (adjective): Pertaining to belief in or direct experience with transcendent reality and/or spiritual forces
Non-duality (noun): Having only one side; Pertaining to a philosophical tradition which argues against separation in existence (e.g., self vs. others; body vs. mind; etc.)
Non-sentient (adjective): Not having the capacity to form thought or to be self-aware
Physicians (noun—plural): Medical doctors
Professorship (noun): The office or position of being a professor
Reorientate (verb): to cause to face a different direction
Scholars (noun—plural): A learned person—usually a teacher or student
Scholarship (noun): Financial assistance for studying
Sovereign (adjective): Someone who exercises supreme authority
Standpoint (noun): The position or viewpoint from which decisions are made
Superior (adjective): Better than
Terminology (noun): The vocabulary used in a particular field of study
Topography (noun): The detailed, precise study of a region's geographic features
Utilitarianism (noun): An ethical theory which asserts that all societal action should be directed at that which achieves the greatest happiness for the largest number of people

CHAPTER 10

ART HISTORY

Kuniko Abe
Akita International University, Japan

Introduction

What is art? This question may provoke* a long and impassioned* debate without satisfying answers. However we can say Art is a descriptive term and also an **evaluative concept**. Art is also an **aesthetic*** object. Art refers to artworks (or **artifacts***), **processes**, **skills** and effects of **visual** representations artists produce. You may **appreciate** the visual quality of an artwork without knowing the **circumstances** of its **creation**. Art **appreciation** does not **require** knowledge of the historical **context** of a work. However, Art History does.

What is art history? Art History is the historical study of art carried out in **higher education institutions** such as universities. It is usually taught as an **academic discipline** at **undergraduate*** and **postgraduate*** levels.

Art History tells you about the **evolution** of art from the **prehistoric*** **cave** painting at **Lascaux*** to today's new **media** art or **environmental** art. It is a rich story of human **creative** work **assessed** for their artistic **legacies***.

The first study of art history **aims** to get an **overall perspective** and then a more in-depth look at it as understanding progresses. **Areas** of study include **architecture***, **sculpture***, painting, print-making and **decorative*** **design**.

Traditional objectives* of Art History are to gain the knowledge and **skills** to describe, **categorize*** and place any artworks in relation to the **established canon***. European academies determined this canon throughout the past **centuries**. The **discipline** has **aimed** to **acquire** *connoisseurship*** and **methodologies** for understanding art. However **exploring** how art looks is part of a wider **interpretive framework**, because there are different **methodological approaches** to Art History.

Modern **critical approaches** to Art History have provoked more **investigation** of art in its context since "The way we see things is **affected** by what we know or what we believe" (John Berger, *Ways of Seeing*, 1972). Today's Art History is based on the **hypotheses** of many **scholarly inquiries** for understanding the relationship between artworks and society and **dominant** social conditions such as **Socialism***, **Marxism***, **Communism***, and **Capitalism***, as well as Literature, **Philosophy, and Psychology**. It is important to understand the **significant** historical events, thoughts, and **technologies** that shaped the art world within the world at large. Today, this is the **core** of the discipline. Thus, you are invited to **explore** the intersections* of art and different disciplines to place artworks in their contexts.

Learning How to Understand Art

Art History is **principally designed** to **foster*** an **appreciation** and understanding of **historically*** important artworks. These works are from all **periods during** the past 30,000 years: from Prehistoric, Ancient Greek and Roman, **Medieval***, **Renaissance***, **Baroque***, Neo-classical, and Modern to **Contemporary**. The history of art is long, **diverse** and **complex**. Artworks should be studied in **chronological*** order according to the **civilizations*** and different contexts producing them. You will **encounter** Renaissance-era giants like Michelangelo and Leonardo da Vinci, as well as French impressionist painters like Claude Monet, and Vincent van Gogh. Their artworks should be **examined** not as **isolated** objects but with regard to their **messages** or meanings in the society that produced them. Art Historians learn art **theory** and aesthetics, **iconography***, artistic **techniques**, and the **issues** of **patronage***, **function**, and context.

Inquiries About Artworks: Essential Study Fields

Your **inquiries** about each artwork are based on the following **essential** questions: (1) when was it made? (2) where was it made? (3) who made it?

This is carried out through **visual analysis** of artistic form. It is called **formal analysis**. You will **focus** on the following **visual elements** as **clues***: Form and **Composition**, Material and **Technique**, Line, Color, **Texture***, Space, **Perspective**, **Foreshortening***, **Proportion** and **Scale**.

When you can **refine** your methods for answering these **essential** questions with **evidence**, you will be known as a *connoisseur*.

To understand, explain and **interpret** the changes in **style**, you will study histories of style. What is style? In Art History, the term style refers to a **distinctive** and **recognizable pattern** of form. Style is used to characterize both **individual** mark-making (like Leonard da Vinci's, and Pablo Picasso's styles) and **collective, social patterning** (like Renaissance, Baroque, and Impressionist styles).

The second type of visual analysis is called stylistic **analysis,** with **context** and historical **relevance** in relation to the artist, the broader **culture** or an even more **generalized*** sense of the spirit of the time (*zeitgeist**). Once you have learned about a **specific** style, you may ask, for example, for the Gothic architectural style, what was the technique to build the Gothic churches, and how have these constructions influenced later period architecture, and whether this style is being **revived***.

Art **historians** separate subjects of **traditional pictorial*** art into the following **categories**: religious, historical, **mythological***, **genre** (daily life), **portraiture***, landscape, and still life (an **arrangement** of **inanimate*** objects). Other than these **categories**, there are a variety of individual **themes** and **motifs***. Yet some **contemporary** artworks, like **abstract** paintings, have no subject. Iconography, a branch of Art History, brings the **specific** study of subject and content in art, including symbols like Christian **symbols**, and **personifications*** of ideas. Studying subject matter and iconography can lead to determining much about the artworks' period and **provenance***.

The **role** of **patrons*** in making art is another important key of art historical **inquiry** since patrons who **commissioned** and paid artists to make individual works might have determined the content and shaped the form of artworks.

Art can be **analyzed** through **psychological theories**, like Freud's theories of **visual perception**. There are many theories on **visual images**: art and **illusion***, sense of order, image and eye, the power of images, the role of images in **ritual***, and magic and **superstition***.

Art historians also study the "**collections**" and the "**taste,**" as well as the "art market." Studies about **techniques** and **practical aspects** of art making are necessary for understanding art, such as materials and techniques of **sculpture*** and painting, **woodcut***, **engraving***, **etching**, drawing, and building techniques like those of **Romanesque*** and **Gothic*** churches.

The History of "Art History"

Art History as an **academic discipline** begins in the 16th **century** with Giorgio Vasari's *The Lives of the Artists* (1550–1568), the world's first **biography*** of artists. Vasari, a painter and **architect***, chronicled the work of Italian artists, describing and ranking their styles and patrons and their personalities and **behaviours**. Vasari considered the development of art to be **qualitative**, reaching a **peak*** of **perfection** in the work of Michelangelo and Raphael.

During the ***Enlightenment****, Art History became an **empirical** and **rational discipline**, affected by rising interest in **Antiquity*** caused by the recent **excavations*** of the **ruins** of Pompeii and Herculaneum. Together with **classical Greco-Roman*** ruins, these **sites** were visited by many young **travelers** on the ***Grand Tour****. Europeans began to **examine**, **compare** and classify many **artifacts*** of these ruins. In this context, German antiquarian Johan Joachim Winckelmann **founded** modern art history by introducing a scientific **methodology** to the study of artifacts. In his book *Reflections on the Painting and Sculpture of the Greeks* (1765), he **established** the Greek **cultural ideal** by claiming that Art is **linked** with the ideas and values of its **period**. Winckelmann founded a German language-based tradition in Art History, which remained **dominant** into the 20th century.

Heinrich Wölfflin, a Swiss scholar, created a new method for studying art through **aesthetic comparison** and **contrast** in his **major** work, "Principles of Art History" (1915). This work is **academically** regarded as a **foundation** of **comparative visual analysis**. Wölfflin's method examines how Renaissance and Baroque art use different techniques: **linear***(clear lines and shapes) versus **painterly***(softer, more blended forms). He also discusses **mimetic*** and **naturalistic*** art. Mimetic art **replicates*** real-life appearances closely. Often associated with the Renaissance period, it focuses on **accurate depiction*** of the subject, using **precise** lines and detailed representations. Naturalistic art, on the other hand, tries to capture the natural world but allows for more stylistic freedom. This is often seen in Baroque art, where artists used more expressive techniques, including the "painterly" style, to show movement and emotion. By contrasting these approaches, Wölfflin provided a framework for understanding the evolution and characteristics of different art styles, making it easier to analyze and compare artworks from various periods.

Art History is thus a discipline made by European **thinkers**, drawn on *idealist philosophy*. The study of art and its **visual interpretation** was based on particular **assumptions** concerning value and meaning. Art is valued as a **universal** and **humanistic*** expression within nature and the world. These thinkers established an academic **orthodoxy*** with largely shared assumptions and values.

The **ethical core** of the **overall** character of 19th and early 20th-century art history was *connoisseurship*. It is a concern for formal analysis (How the object looks) and **identifying** its date, **authorship** and **provenance** to establish claims to **authenticity***. It is thus the judgment gained through long experience with artworks. *Connoisseurship* explores the "quality" of the art under consideration and how it relates to other "**pictorial traditions** to which it belongs." *Connoisseurship* has emphasized the importance of chronologically ordering works of art and their proper **attribution**—identifying an **original** work from a copy or fake.

Challenges and Problems in Art History Today and in Future

A **range** of critical **theory** was born in the 1960s, from **structuralism*** to **anthropology***, **psychoanalysis***, **feminism***, Marxism and **postcolonial critiques***. Art History had an important **reorientation, homogenizing*** the **plurality*** which **typified*** the work and approaches. This resulted in a greater **awareness** of the **materiality*** of art and visual culture as **commodity** and objects within broader social, **economic** and **psychoanalytic frameworks**. Meanwhile, art historians **acknowledged** the philosophical tradition of art history, even if they were critical of its assumptions and **premises***. We see the **definition** of art by Ades (*Reviewing Art History*, 1986): "It is taken that art is not **hermetic*** and **autonomous***, but **bound** up with social and **economic** movements of the time, as well as conditioned by both artistic tradition and aesthetic **ideology**."

Today's Art History **intersects*** with that of other disciplines, not only in the humanities but also in the social and natural sciences. In the future Art History will become more **interdisciplinary*** than ever. Methodologies of literary **criticism***, **philosophy, sociology, and gender** studies are **frequently** used in art history **research**. Art historians work with other specialists in **multidisciplinary*** inquiries. **Chemists*** date artwork based on the **composition** of the materials used, X-ray **technicians*** can work out if a painting is a **forgery***. While digital technologies are used for art making.

Employment Opportunities for Art Historians

There is a wide **range** of **careers** for Art Historians as specialists and **experts** in the art field and beyond. Jobs **vary** from **curation*** and **conservation*** in museums, to art dealing in **galleries*** and buying and selling art in **auction*** houses, art-related **publishing**, and producing art programs on radio/television or other **media**. Some possible careers are as follows:

1. **Curator**: working for museums, libraries, arts organizations, **corporate** art **collections**, private **foundations** or personal collections, as well as educational **institutions** and public spaces.
2. Art **Conservator/Restorer**: **specializing*** in the **preservation**, care, and **restoration** of artworks, working closely with conservation scientists to work with the **chemical components** of the restoration and preservation process.
3. Architectural Conservator: specializing in the preservation, care, and restoration of architectural works, ranging from historic buildings to large **sculptures** in **outdoor settings.** Architectural conservators often study chemistry and gain a **certification** in conservation techniques.
4. Art **Authenticator**: specializing in a particular artist or style, authenticates the "provenance" of a work by **tracing** the **path** of ownership as far back as possible.
5. **Auctioneer***: sell a piece of art, providing a description of the piece and **handling auctions.** Auctioneers often research particular art pieces to gain knowledge about the artwork itself.
6. Art Publishing/Art Producing professionals—work in **graphic design**, writing, and **editing** and are employed by Art Book publishing houses and film/video producing houses.

Other careers include arts **administrator, archivist***, museum education officer, journalist, teacher or **lecturer**, organizer of artistic **exhibitions** or events and **antiques*** dealer.

You can find some **nontraditional** carriers related to **Economics, Finance, Insurance**, or Law as follows:

Art Economist: An academic and practical study of the modern art **economy** through a **macroeconomic*** and **microeconomic*** lens can lead art historians in real-world settings as an art economist, since fine art can be **purchased** as an **investment**.

Art Lawyer: An art history master's degree, and a Juris Doctor (JD) degree and **expertise** in **contract** law allow art historians to become experts who can give **testimony** in **legal** fights in the art world which center around **copyright*** concerns, contract disputes, fraud, and artists' rights concerns.

Epilogue

While the world of "Art" and "Art History" may seem **inaccessible** to some people because of its many **technical** terms and theories, **access** to Art History in **Liberal** Arts education helps students develop skills of **visual analysis**, research and **communication**. Art History provides you with a basic academic knowledge from which to form your own judgments.

Adapted from a text by Kuniko Abe, PhD
Select Professor
Akita International University, Akita, Japan

Vocabulary

Words From the Second 1,000 General Service High Frequency Word List

aimed	frequently
arrangement	grand
behaviors	handling
bound/boundaries	ideal
cave	information
centuries	inquire/inquiry
century	messages
collections/collective	origin/original
comparative/compare/comparison	path
composition	pattern
connected	perfection
critical	practical
discipline	preservation
during	ruins
engineering	satisfying
especially	scale
essential	skills
examine	taste
explore	universal
formal	weigh

Words From the Academic Word List (AWL)

accurate	aspects
abstract	assessed
academic/academies	assumptions
access	attribution
acknowledged	authorship
acquire	awareness
administrator	capable
affected	categories
analysis/analyze	challenge
appreciate	chemical
approach	circumstances
areas	classical

commission
commodity
communication
complex
components
concept
construct
contemporary
context
contract
contrast
contribution
core
corporate
creation/creative
culture
debate
definition
design
display
distinctive
diverse
dominant
economic/economy
editing
elements
emphasize
empirical
encounter
environment
establish
ethical
evaluative
evidence
evident
evolution
excluded
exhibitions
expertise
finances
focus
found/foundation
framework
frameworks
function
fundamental
gender

hypothesis
identification
identifying
ideology
image
inaccessible
individual
institutions
interpret
investigate
investment
isolated
issues
lecturer
legal
liberal
linked
major
media
method/methodology
mutual
nontraditional
orientation
overall
perceive/perception
period
perspective
philosophy
principle/principally
precise
process
professional
proportion
psychology
publishing
purchase
pursue
qualitative
range
rational
refine
relevance
reorientation
require
research
restoration
role

shifts
significant
sites
specific
stress
style
symbols

technical/technique/technology
themes
theory
tracing
tradition/traditional
vary

Glossary

Aesthetic (adjective): Attractive, beautiful.
Anthropology (noun): The study of man.
Antique (adjective): Old, precious item.
Antiquity (noun): Ancient times—before the Middle Ages.
Architect/architecture (noun/noun): One who designs buildings/the science of designing buildings and structures.
Archivist (noun): A profession that collects and preserves documents for others to see.
Artifacts (noun plural): An object made by humans of historical interest.
Auction/auctioneer (noun/noun): A public sale of merchandise/the person who runs an auction.
Authenticity (noun): Being real, genuine.
Autonomous (adjective): Free from bias.
Baroque (adjective): European art style from 17th to mid-18th century.
Biography (noun): A book about someone's life.
Bon voyage (phrase): French expression meaning "have a good journey"
Canon (noun): A commonly-accepted body of work.
Capitalism (noun): An economic system characterized by private ownership of goods.
Categorize (verb): To put into categories or groups.
Chemist (noun): A profession with expertise in chemistry.
Chronological (adjective): Order in which things happened in time.
Civilization (noun): Culture of a particular place and time.
Clue (noun): Hint or evidence.
Communism (noun): A system of government characterized by collective (state) ownership of all goods.
Connoisseurship (noun): Knowing the principles, techniques, and important details of art.
Conservation (noun): Preservation and protection of something.
Copyright (noun): The legal ownership and right to produce and sell something.
Criticism/critique (noun/noun): Analysis and discussion of the good and bad points about something.
Curation (noun): Selecting the best examples of a body of work to be displayed.
Decorative (adjective): Ornamental.
Depiction (noun): A representation or portrayal of someone or something, typically through art, writing, or images.
Empathy (noun): Understanding others' feelings.
Engraving (verb): Cutting a pattern into something.
Enlightenment (noun): An 18th century philosophy which rejected tradition.
Excavations (noun plural): Digging—especially when trying to find old things from history.
Feminism (noun): A philosophy advancing the rights and interests of women.
Foreshortening (noun): A technique in art to create an illusion visual depth.
Forgery (noun): A fake version of something being presented as the real thing.
Foster (verb): Develop/create.

Galleries (noun plural): Places where art is displayed to the public.
Generalized (adjective): Not highly specific.
Gothic (adjective): A style of architecture in Western Europe from the 12th to 16th centuries.
Grand Tour (noun phrase): A 17th-to early 19th-century custom of a traditional trip through Europe with Italy as a key destination, undertaken by young upper class European men.
Greco-roman (adjective): Of Greek/Roman style.
Hermetic (adjective): Subjects that are difficult to understand.
Historically (adverb): In history.
Homogenizing (verb): Making similar or the same.
Humanistic (adjective): Emphasizing human values and interests.
Iconography (noun): Study of the symbols and representations in artistic work.
Illusion (noun): Something that deceives one's perception.
Impassioned (adjective): Showing great feeling about something.
Inanimate (adjective): Not living/moving.
Interdisciplinary (adjective): Crossing across more than one subject of study.
Intersect/intersection (noun): Passing through or across.
Lascaux (place name): A cave in southwest France containing prehistoric paintings.
Legacy (noun): Something passed down from one generation to the next.
Linear (adjective): In a straight line.
Macroeconomic (adjective): Economic study focused on large populations.
Marxism (noun): The philosophy of class struggle by Karl Marx.
Materiality (noun): Physical substance/matter.
Medieval (adjective): European Middle Ages.
Microeconomic (adjective): Economic study focused on small groups and individual transactions.
Mimetic (adjective): Mimicking/copying.
Motif (noun): Reoccurring themes in artwork.
Multidisciplinary (adjective): Crossing across more than one subject of study.
Mythological (adjective): Related to myths (ancient stories)—especially traditional Greek/Roman stories.
Naturalistic (adjective): Art based on observation of life.
Objective (noun): Goal.
Orthodoxy (noun): Conforming to prevailing views and theories.
Painterly (adjective): A nonlinear art form characterized by lack of sharp outline.
Patron/patronage (noun/noun): A person financially supporting the production of artwork/the system of private financial support for artists.
Peak (noun): The highest point.
Personification (noun): Giving attributes of a person to a nonhuman thing.
Pictorial (adjective): Related to pictures.
Plurality (noun): The most numerous subgroup of a population, while still not constituting a majority.
Portraiture (noun): Art representing a person—particularly the face.
Postgraduate (adjective): Formal studies after graduation from university.
Prehistoric (adjective): The period of human activity before writing and the keeping of records.
Premise (noun): Something assumed.
Provenance (noun): The origin or source of something.
Provoke (verb): Cause to happen.
Psychoanalysis (noun): A form of treatment for mental and emotional disorders.
Renaissance (noun): A period in Europe between the 14th and 17th centuries marked by a revival of classical (Greek and Roman) influences in artwork.
Replicates (verb): To repeat an experiment, process, or action to achieve consistent and reliable results.

Revive (verb): Bring back to life or back into use.
Ritual (noun): Something done according to religious and/or social customs.
Romanesque (adjective): An architectural style around 1000AD.
Sculpture (noun): Art made from metal or stone.
Socialism (noun): An economic system based upon government ownership of the means of production.
Specialize (verb): Have a particular emphasis of study or expertise.
Structuralism (noun): A method of analyzing using techniques from cultural anthropology.
Superstition (noun): Beliefs and practices resulting from fear and ignorance.
Technicians (noun plural): someone who has mastered a particular technique.
Texture (noun): The tactile feel of the surface of something.
Typify (verb): Represent something typical/average.
Undergraduate (adjective): University studies.
Woodcut (noun): Art produced by cutting designs into wood.

SECTION 2

THE SOCIAL SCIENCES: AN INTRODUCTION

As we have **previously defined,** the study of humanities is in essence, the interpretive and subjective study of ourselves as human beings. The social sciences, the next **topic** of **investigation** in this book, is all about our ability to **function** *socially*—that is to say, in groups. Our ability to **cooperate** with one another is a **defining trait*** of our **species*** and is largely responsible for both the **technological** and **civilizational*** progress we have seen in societies across the **millennia***.

Social sciences **research** uses **qualitative** and quantitative methods to study human behavior, societies, and social phenomena. Techniques include surveys, interviews, case studies, **ethnography***, **statistical analysis**, experiments, and **longitudinal*** studies. **Insights** from psychology, sociology, anthropology, economics, and political science are **integrated** to enhance the research **comprehensiveness***.

While few would argue that social behaviour is anything other than a good for humanity it is still notable that social behavior is **complex** and often leads to surprising or unexpected results. We don't always get along—nations go to war, and **individuals** aren't always **cooperative**. The social sciences **seek** to **unravel*** the root causes of such behaviors, as well as to **infer** and to **predict** the results of group tendencies and actions. As such, the social sciences cover a **vast*** field of interests—after all, how many human activities do not **involve** group **dynamics**? In the following chapters, we will cover fields such as **sociology***, **anthropology*** and the geography of public health. Perhaps more surprising to some readers will be the inclusion of business fields such as management, **economics**, and marketing. This **underscores*** just how vast the field of social sciences is. If one carefully considers the matter, business dealings are really just an applied form of social studies, due to the group **dynamics underpinning*** market behaviors, supply and demand, and customer-**vendor*** relationships finally the chapter on **constitutional** law **demonstrates** the **macro***—applications of social sciences, as they bear on entire nations and societies, as a whole. We will see the under-the-surface forces that produce **discernible*** national character and values which **define** the **myriad*** differences we see between human groups across the planet.

Vocabulary

Words From the Second to 1,000 General Service High-Frequency Words List

argue	health
behavior	management
customer	responsible
entire	route
essence	tendency

Words From the Academic Words List (AWL)

analysis
complex
constitution
cooperate
define
demonstrate
dynamics
economics
function
individual
infer
insights
integrated
investigation

involve
methods
phenomena
predict
previously
qualitative
research
seek
statistical
surveys
techniques
technological
topic

Glossary

Anthropology (noun): The scientific study of humanity encompassing its origins, development, societies, cultures and behaviors

Civilisation (noun): A complex and advanced stage of human social and cultural development characterized by urbanisation, technological advancements, organized governance, and various cultural achievements

Comprehensiveness (noun): The quality of including all or nearly all elements or aspects of something, ensuring thoroughness and completeness.

Discernible (adjective): Perceptible; capable of being recognised or distinguished

Ethnography (noun): In-depth study and systematic recording of human cultures through immersive observation and participation.

Longitudinal (adjective): Research that involves repeated observations or measurements of the same subjects over an extended period to track changes and developments.

Macro (adjective): Pertaining to large scale phenomena systems or processes often involving extensive groups or wide-ranging effects

Millennia (noun): Plural of millennium referring to periods of 1,000 years each often used to discuss historical time frames

Myriad (noun and adjective): A countless or extremely vast number; a multitude. Used to describe a diverse range of things

Sociology (noun): The systematic study of society, social interactions, relationships, and institutions, aiming to understand patterns and structures within human communities.

Species (noun): A distinct group of living organisms that share common characteristics and can interbreed to produce fertile offspring

Underpinning (noun): The fundamental basis or support that provides strength and stability to a system concept or structure

Underscore (verb): To emphasize highlight or give importance to a particular point or idea

Unravel (verb): To untangle unwind or solve a complex situation or problem to make something clearer or simpler

Vast (adjective): Extremely large in size extent or scope immense

Vendor (noun): A person business or entity that sells goods or services to others

CHAPTER 11

MACROECONOMICS

Wenti Du
Akita International University, Japan

Introduction

After receiving payment from your part-time **job**, do you save it or spend it? Would you be surprised if I tell you that your action could have an **impact** on your country's **GDP***? Moreover, are you **curious** about the **connection** between your actions and GDP? If you answer yes to this question, studying **macroeconomics** can help you to find the answer.

Macroeconomics deals with the larger **issues** of an **economy** as a whole, instead of the more **specific individual** units in an economy. Have you ever heard of the following terms: national **income**, unemployment rates, and **inflation*** rates? They are examples of what we are usually dealing with in the field of macroeconomics.

Macroeconomists study the various parts, the **aggregate indicators**, which make up an economy as a whole, and ask questions about the way in which our economies work. They **analyze** and **investigate** situations in different economies not only in the short term but also over a long **period** of time. **Research** in macroeconomics helps to **solve** important problems in the world, such as poverty, unemployment, and a lack of **economic** development.

In order to reach economic **targets**, such as economic growth, full employment, and **stable** prices in the economy, there are two main macroeconomic **tools** that are used:

1. **monetary policy** and
2. **fiscal policy**

Monetary policy refers to the actions taken by a country's central bank to manage the supply of money and interest rates. An example of this is the Federal Reserve in the United States lowering interest rates to encourage borrowing and **investment**. Fiscal policy involves **government** spending and tax policies. For instance, **during** an economic recession, a government might increase its spending on infrastructure projects to create jobs and stimulate economic activity.

Macroeconomists also try to understand how effective the **monetary policy*** by the **central bank*** of a country and the **fiscal*** policy by the **government** of a country is at any given time; including how effective it might be in the future. They give central bankers and government officials **information** that helps those people to plan and make better decisions.

History

The **origin** of macroeconomics can be **traced** back to **The Great Depression*** This severe worldwide economic downturn began in 1929 and lasted through the late 1930s. It originated in the United States following the stock market crash of October 1929 and led to widespread unemployment, poverty, and significant **declines** in industrial production and global trade for a **decade** and contributed to the outbreak of World War II. Many economists studied the cause of the Great Depression in an attempt to prevent it from taking place again in the future.

During this period, John Maynard Keynes, a British **economist**, became well-known. Keynes **argued** that during times of unemployment, the government should increase its spending. By borrowing funds and creating job opportunities, the government enables people to earn and spend money, which in turn helps others secure employment. Based on his ideas, a new school of macroeconomics, named **Keynesian Economics,** was developed. On the other hand, Milton Friedman, an American economist, **argued** that the Great Depression could be better explained by looking at money, and thinking about things such as the money supply in an economy. His ideas led to the formation of another school of macroeconomics, called **Monetarism, which** argues that the best way for a government to manage a nation's economy is by regulating the money supply to control inflation. Later, ideas from both **Neo-classical Economics*** and Keynesian Economics, led to the school of **Neo-Keynesianism**, and even later, the school of thought called Post-Keynesianism was developed. People who supported this school of thought argued that Neo-Keynesianism had not fully understood and even **misinterpreted** Keynes' **original** ideas.

Modern-Day Positioning

More recently, a period of **stagflation*** took place in the 1970s.
Stagflation usually includes...

1. **slow** economic growth (also called "**stagnation***")
2. a high rate of inflation* (a period of time when goods and services rise in price).

At the same time as these two things happen, there is often a high rate of unemployment.

Next, the idea of **Rational Expectation*** was introduced into the study of macroeconomics by Robert Lucas. Lucas was also **critical** of the earlier Keynesian ideas and **empirical models**. He argued that the microeconomic **foundations** are very important when we try to understand economic policy **analysis**.

Following the work of Lucas, real business-**cycle** models of macroeconomics were developed. This school of macroeconomics **emphasized** the importance of the supply side of an economy. It was argued that it was the real **shocks** caused by **technology** that led to economic changes. By joining the ideas from earlier schools, new **dynamic** models were developed in the late 1990s, which became known as *New Keynesian Economics.*

Benefits of Studying Macroeconomics

Now, let's consider how macroeconomics helps us in real-life situations. Do you think that people in Japan were happy or **upset** to hear that the sales tax would increase from 5% to 8% in 2014? If you had followed this issue at the time, would you have understood the **arguments** *for* as well as the arguments *against* this change in taxes? With an understanding of macroeconomics, you can **critically analyze** the arguments made by those politicians who want to raise the Japanese sales tax and the arguments made by others against this change in the **fiscal*** policy. By understanding and thinking deeply about these arguments, you can begin to form your own opinions more easily.

Moreover, studying macroeconomics enables you to read and understand articles in newspapers like the Nikkei Shimbun and have deeper **discussions** about present-day economic events. In addition, you can use your knowledge of macroeconomics to offer **insightful** suggestions to such people on questions such as when is the best time to buy a house, and what kind of **mortgage** they should get to pay for it. Moreover, you can also use this knowledge to make such important life decisions for yourself.

Do you, or does someone you know buy **roses** for loved ones on Valentine's Day? Have you noticed that the price of roses is higher than usual around that special day of the year? Such a rise in prices is not surprising and could easily be explained using **The Law of Supply and Demand***. A simple supply-and-demand analysis shows that the price of roses rises because of the increase in demand for roses from **customers**. With a knowledge of macroeconomics, if you expect that the price of roses is going to increase, you could then plan in advance to **avoid** buying overpriced roses at these times when roses are expensive and there is a high demand. For example, you could order and pay for the roses one month earlier, in January. Such economic activity is also known as a **hedge*** in the world of **finance***. Another way, although it might not be as romantic, is to buy the roses *after* Valentine's Day when there is less demand and the desire for flowers **declines**. Flower **shops** often start to have **promotions** in order to get **rid** of the **excess** flower supply in their shops. Of course, if you choose this **option** as a **purchasing strategy**, the people to whom you give the roses might be **disappointed** that they received them a little late.

Employment Opportunities

Do you know any famous Japanese macroeconomists? One of the most well-known Japanese macroeconomists in the school of the *New Keynesian Economics* is Nobuhiro Kiyotaki. Professor Nobuhiro received his degrees from the University of Tokyo in Japan and Harvard University in the United States. Now, he is now teaching at Princeton University in the United States. As a well-known and important New Keynesian economist, Professor Nobuhiro **constructed** various economic models that apply deep microeconomic **foundations** to macroeconomics. Because of the **excellence** of his work, and the **international** recognition he has received, in 1997 he was given the Nakahara **Prize** from the Japan Economics Association.

Besides academic roles, macroeconomics knowledge can lead to various employment opportunities. For example, you can be a **data analyst**, a position that is in high demand in many **sectors** including **consulting**, government, finance and banking, and manufacturing. You could also be a **stockbroker*** and help your customers to make better decisions about where to put their money on the national and international stock markets. Another possibility would be to be an **investment** analyst and to provide information to help your customer's investment **portfolios*** in general. Another job is that of a financial **risk analyst**. A risk analyst studies and considers the **potential** risks or problems customers may face as they use and **invest** their money.

In addition, if you love both macroeconomics and **mathematics**, you could work as an actuarial **analyst** who uses difficult mathematical **formulas** to help businesses such as **insurance** companies and banks, to make good decisions.

Of course, you could always choose to be an **economist** if your field of study falls into macroeconomics. As an economist, you could use your **skills** and knowledge to **predict** future economic **trends** and even help decision-makers to make better decisions that could help a country to be **economically** stronger as well as making life better for its citizens.

Furthermore, macroeconomics knowledge can lead to roles in international organizations such as the International Monetary Fund (IMF) or the World Bank, where professionals work on global economic issues and policies. These roles often involve travel and the opportunity to make a significant impact on international economic development and cooperation. Studying macroeconomics also provides a strong foundation for those interested in pursuing advanced degrees in economics, leading to academic careers where they can contribute to research and teach the next generation of economists. The analytical skills gained through studying macroeconomics are also highly valued in various sectors, making graduates competitive candidates for diverse career paths. By understanding macroeconomics, you gain the tools to navigate complex economic landscapes, make informed decisions, and contribute to the broader economic well-being of society.

Adapted from a text by Wenti Du PhD
Assistant Professor, Economics, Global Business Program
Akita International University
Japan

Vocabulary

Words From the Second 1,000 Words of the General Service High Frequency Word List

argued/arguments
avoid
connection
critical
critically
curious
customer
disappointed
discussions
during
excellence
excess
government
information
insurance
international
lot
models
origin
original
parents
prize
rid
risk
shocks
shops
skills
slow
solve
steady
tools
upset

Words From the Academic Word List

aggregate
analysis/analyst
analyze
benefits
classical
constructed
consulting
cycle
data
decade
declines
depression
dynamic
economic/economically/economics/
   economist/economy
emphasized
empirical
finance/financial
formulas
foundations
impact
income
indicators
individual
insightful
invest/investment
issues
job
misinterpreted
option
period
policy
potential
predict
promotions
purchasing
rational
research
sectors
specific
stable
strategy
targets
technology
traced
trends

Glossary

Central bank: An institution designed to oversee the banking system and regulate the quantity of money in the economy. (*Source:* Mankiw, N. G. (2018). *Principles of macroeconomics. Australia: Cengage Learning*.) The central bank of Japan is the Bank of Japan (BoJ), which was founded on October 10, 1882 (明治15年).

Finance: The field that studies how people make decisions regarding the allocation of resources over time and the handling of risk. (*Source:* Mankiw, N. G. (2018). *Principles of macroeconomics. Australia: Cengage Learning*.)

Fiscal: Something related to government revenue, a good example being taxes.

Fiscal policy: The setting of the level of government spending and taxation by government policymakers. (*Source: Mankiw, N. G. (2018). Principles of macroeconomics. Australia: Cengage Learning*.)

GDP (Gross Domestic Product): The market value of all final goods and services produced within a country in a given period of time. (*Source: Mankiw, N. G. (2018). Principles of macroeconomics. Australia: Cengage Learning*.)

Hedge: A method or strategy to protect against possible loss, usually of a financial nature.

Inflation: An increase in the overall level of prices in the economy. (*Source: Mankiw, N. G. (2018). Principles of macroeconomics. Australia: Cengage Learning*.)

Law of supply and demand: The claim that the price of any good adjusts to bring the quantity supplied and the quantity demanded for that good into balance. (*Source: Mankiw, N. G. (2018). Principles of macroeconomics. Australia: Cengage Learning*.)

Monetary policy: The setting of the money supply by policymakers in the central bank. (*Source: Mankiw, N. G. (2018). Principles of macroeconomics. Australia: Cengage Learning*.)

Neo-classical economics: A school of thought that emphasizes the importance of individual choice and rational decision-making in determining economic outcomes.

Portfolio: A collection of financial assets that may include stocks, bonds and cash.

Rational expectations theory: Argues that individuals base their decisions on their rationality, the information available to them, and their past experiences. The theory suggests that people's current expectations of the economy can influence the future economy. This contrasts with the idea that government policy influences financial and economic decisions.

Stagflation: A combination of stagnation and inflation in an economy.

Stagnation: Very slow (or even zero) economic growth.

Stockbroker: A professional who buys and sells securities on stock exchanges for other people (their clients).

The Great Depression: A period of around ten years from 1929 to 1939, when the world economy was very bad. The Wall Street stock market collapsed, causing banks to fail, and thousands of people to lose their.

CHAPTER 12

SOCIOLOGY

Matthew Ryczek
Akita International University, Japan

Introduction

Are you **unique**? Consider this question for a moment. Your **physical** characteristics are **unique**; you may be **tall**, short, **thin**, or heavy. The kind of person you are, whether you say a **lot** or are **quiet, funny** or serious, makes you different from others. What about your free time activities and interests? How about your **taste** in music or food? Don't all of these qualities make you unique and special?

Well, yes and no. While **physical** characteristics and personal qualities might be different on the surface, our **behavior** is often shaped by social forces outside of our control and **awareness**. **Sociology*** is the study of human behavior in society and **argues** that human behavior is **regular** and that we are more **similar** to each other than we are different. **Sociologists*** are interested in how social relationships influence people's behavior. In addition, it looks at how societies develop and change over time. Sociology is a broad **discipline** (or subject of study) that shares deep **connections** with other social sciences, like **economics**, political science, **anthropology***, and **psychology**. For sociologists, social behavior can be **examined** across two levels: **microsociology*** and **macrosociology***. A microsociologist might examine how divorce **affects communication** between a **parent** and child, while a macrosociologist might examine the **divorce*** rates among married **couples** in different **regions** of a country. Sociologists look at the world from these different **perspectives** in order to understand the relationship between a person and society as a whole.

The ability to see the connection between the **individual** and larger social influences is a **key aspect** of sociology and is known as the sociological **imagination***. Sociologist C. Wright Mills introduced this term in 1959 to help people understand how important social **factors** are in our lives. For example, let's say a young man is unemployed and struggling to pay his bills. Society may judge the man **negatively** and **assume** that he is unemployed because of his own poor choices and individual actions. But if we step back and look at this in another way, we can see a different side to this situation. Perhaps the man worked at a car factory, but is no longer able to work there because a trade disagreement between the leaders of his country and another country **hurt** the market for cars in the country to which he belongs. This may have resulted in many of the workers in the industry no longer being employed. In this example, we used our sociological imagination to see the connection between personal troubles (unemployment) and **structural issues** and poor economic conditions. As you study sociology, your ability to use your sociological imagination will allow you to gain a broader understanding of various social factors and their influences on the individual people's lives.

History

Although examining society and social **interaction** had been done by important **thinkers*** for centuries, it wasn't until the Industrial **Revolution** in the mid-19th **century** that sociology became a recognized social science. The effects of **industrialization*** were more than just the introduction of new technologies, like **steam** power, and **methods** of manufacturing, like the factory system. The Industrial **Revolution** had a great effect on **European*** society in the form of **rapid urbanization*** and the growth of the modern city. Before the industrial revolution, an **agricultural economy** of small-**scale**, often family-owned, farms and businesses were common. At this time social relationships were based on trust, and a shared sense of **community** among people. Since large factories could produce products **cheaply** and **quickly**, many small-scale businesses were forced to close. As these businesses failed, people moved to towns and cities in **search** of work. The rise of the city had serious **consequences** for European society. As people from various **ethnic** and religious backgrounds **suddenly** found themselves living close together, a lack of work opportunities, poverty, **disease**, and **crime**, all increased. **Contemporary** thinkers were concerned about these social issues, as well as for the future of society **during** this time in history. Sociology as a social science grew out of a need to better understand the **rapid** social changes that were taking place at this important time in history.

People of Note in Sociology

Auguste Comte (1798–1857)

As mentioned above, **philosophers** and thinkers had been considering and theorizing about the social behaviors of humans for centuries, but there are a few individuals who have made deep and important **contributions** to the field known as sociology. The French philosopher Auguste Comte (1798–1857) is often considered to be the father of sociology as he made up the term "sociology" himself. Comte argued for an **empirical*** (or scientific) method of studying society rather than one based on personal beliefs.

Emile Durkheim (1858–1917)

The French sociologist Emile Durkheim (1858–1917) built on Comte's ideas in his studies of 19th century European society. Durkheim introduced the **concept** of **social facts*** in his studies of the different rates of **suicide*** found in different regions. Durkheim gathered **data** from **police** on suicides from several districts and discovered that **Catholics*** had a lower suicide rate than Protestants. Using this data, Durkheim believed it was possible that suicide is caused by social factors, not just individual **psychological** ones. He argued that degrees of social **integration*** are different among Catholics and Protestants, and that as social integration **decreases** the likelihood of **committing** suicide increases for the individual. Durkheim's work on the importance of social **solidarity*** was **instrumental** in the development of the macrosociological **theory** known as **functionalism***.

Karl Marx (1818–1883)

Durkheim's belief that social **cohesion*** is **essential** to keeping peace and **balance** in society was very different from that of another important thinker in modern history, the German philosopher Karl Marx (1818–1883). For Marx, the **economic principles** behind our own **self** interest are what make the shape of a society. Marx was particularly interested in the negative effects that **capitalism*** had on society. With the rise of **industrialization*** and the factory system, the individual worker suffered from what Marx called **alienation***. Let's **explore** this concept with an example.

*Let's **imagine** you live in 19th century Europe and run a small business making wooden **barrels**. As the owner of the business, you can control every step of the production **process** of making each and every barrel made in your **shop**: cutting down trees, shaping the wood, building* *the barrels, and even selling them to **customers**. You have a deep connection to your work, to your employees, and to your customers. But recently a large barrel factory in the nearby city has opened and put you out of business. You have no choice but to close your shop and move to the city to work at the barrel factory. The barrel factory is large and there are over a hundred workers. You now work at one station along an **assembly** line and complete just one step in the process of making the barrel. You do this one **task** over and over again all day, every day. You don't talk to the other workers because you don't need to. You never even see a finished barrel. How does this new kind of work **compare** to your old one? Do you think you are **satisfied** with your work?*

This is what Marx means by alienation. The factory worker is **isolated** and **desperate***. He is alienated from the product he makes, from those he works with, and in the end, from himself, as he has lost an important part of his own **identity**. For Marx, the factory worker is a member of the **proletariat***, who lack wealth, power and **status** in society. The factory owners, or **bourgeoisie***, have wealth, power, and status in society and use their position to take advantage of the working class, keeping them in a **weaker** position in society. Karl Marx believed that this situation cannot continue for all time, and that in the end the factory workers will unite and **revolt** against the factory owners, bringing about the end of the capitalist system. For sociology, Marx's theories on class struggle were very important in developing the macro-sociological theory known as **conflict theory***.

Real-World Applications of Sociology

Sociology is not just something we study in a book or in a university class, but can be observed all around us in our daily lives. Let's look at a **typical** morning for a Japanese high school student.

*Before leaving your home in the morning you may **wash** yourself and **style** your **hair**. As you enter the train station you may stand on the left side of the **escalator*** as you go up to the **platform***. While waiting for the train you stand in line **patiently**. Since you didn't have time to eat **breakfast** this morning, you are **hungry**, but you don't eat the **rice** ball you brought from home while on the train. As you walk toward your school you wait at the stop light even though no cars pass by. When you meet your **classmates*** you **greet** them with a friendly smile and say good morning.*

Throughout your typical day you make decisions to do or not do certain things often without thinking about why you are doing them. Why do you spend time styling your hair each morning? Why do you not eat on the train even though you are hungry? Our everyday behavior is controlled by a large number of rules that are not written down anywhere, known as social **norms***. These social norms work to keep order and a sense of unity in society. Where did all of these rules come from? Well you have been learning to follow these rules by **mixing** with and **copying** the people around you, like your parents, teachers, and friends, from the day you were born through the process known as **socialization***. Socialization teaches us how to be good members of a society. We follow many social norms without even thinking, like taking your **shoes** off upon entering your home or stopping at a red light when driving.

What keeps us from breaking some of these rules? Imagine if you stopped styling your hair every morning before school? What would happen? Other members of your class might laugh at you or **tease*** you because you are breaking the social norm connected to taking care of one's physical appearance. Having someone laugh, tease or speaking badly of you are all types of **punishments**, or **negative sanctions***. Members of society use these negative sanctions to make each other follow social norms. Since we usually want to **avoid** these **punishments**, we follow social norms. When we follow social norms we receive **positive sanctions***, like **praise** or smiles, which **encourage** us to continue following those rules. When we go against the norms that society expects us to follow, our behavior may be seen as unacceptable. This is known as social **deviance***. We are all socially deviant at times, but the pressure to **conform** and follow society's rules is always present and influential.

Adapted from a text by Matthew Ryczek
Visiting Foreign Lecturer
Tokyo University of Foreign Studies Center for Global Language and Society in Higher Education
Akita International University

High Frequency Vocabulary—General Service List (GSL) K2

agricultural
argue
avoid
balance
barrel
behavior
breakfast
centuries century
cheaply
compare
connected connection
copying
crime
customers
decreases
discipline
disease
during
encourage
essential
examine
explore
funny
greet
hair
hungry
hurt
imagination/imagine

instrumental
key
mixing
parent
patiently
police
praise
punishments
quickly
quiet
rapid
regular
rice
satisfied
scale
search
self
shoes
shop
steam
suddenly
tall
taste
thin
typical
wash
weaker

Academic Word List (AWL)

affects
aspect
assembly
assume
awareness
committing
communication
community
concept
conflict
conform
consequences
contemporary
contributions
couples
data
economic/economy
empirical

ethnic
factors
identity
individual
integration
interaction
isolated
issues
method
negative
norm
perspectives
philosopher
physical
positive
principles
process
psychological/psychology

regions
revolution
similar
status
structural

style
task
theory
unique

Glossary

Alienation: The somewhat negative feeling a person experiences when they believe they do not belong to or "fit in" with a particular group of people or class.

Anthropology: The study of humans and their cultural development, and how this is passed on to each generation.

Bourgeoisie: The social class that owns the means of production in a capitalist society.

Catholics: People belonging to the Catholic branch of the Christian faith.

Capitalism: An economic system in which ownership of the means of production is in private hands.

Classmates: Members of the same class of students at a school or university.

Cohesion: An act or state of uniting or getting along with other individuals or a larger group of people.

Conflict Theory: The macrosociological theory that examines the ways in which groups disagree, struggle over power, and compete for scarce resources.

Desperate Having an urgent need for something. May become reckless or dangerous due to feelings of despair, hopelessness, or urgency.

Divorce: The legal ending of a marriage.

Escalator: A mechanical moving stairway that takes people up or down.

European: Something relating to Europe or the people of Europe.

Empirical: Information based on scientific observation rather than on ideology.

Functionalism: The macrosociological theory that sees society as a complex system of interdependent parts that work together to ensure its survival.

Industrialization: The shift in production from agriculture to industries, such as mining, transportation, commercial goods, chemicals, and electricity.

Macrosociology: A subfield of sociology that examines large-scale phenomena found in society as a whole.

Microsociology: A subfield of sociology that focuses on the small-scale, face-to-face, patterns of interaction between individuals.

Negative sanctions: Punishments for violating social norms.

Platform: A base point from which other things can happen.

Positive sanctions: Rewards for following social norms.

Proletariat: The working class in a capitalist society.

Protestants: People belonging to the Protestant branch of the Christian faith.

Revolt: To resist and even break away from official authority.

Social deviance: An action or behavior that violates social norms.

Social facts: Aspects of life external to the individual that can be measured.

Social integration: How closely we are connected with other people.

Social norms: Specific rules of right and wrong behavior, usually unwritten.

CHAPTER 13

SOCIOLINGUISTICS

Leigh Bennett
Akita International University, Japan

What Is Sociolinguistics?

"How are you?" When your friends ask you this question, you **probably** have an answer in mind. Maybe you would answer with a common **response** of *"I'm fine."* But what if your school's principal asked this question? What if the question was asked in the early morning or after a difficult **exam*** or what if it was asked **during** a **job interview***? Would your response be the same? In each of these examples, your response would probably be different. The person we are speaking to (a friend or the principal), the situation we are in (job interview), and our **mood*** (early morning) will decide how we answer this question. Our response gives **clues** to the social situation, such as our relationship to the person we are speaking to and the situation we are in. Sociolinguistics shows how language **reveals** the relationships between **individuals,** and it also looks at language across other characteristics. For example, it includes characteristics of **gender,** class, **status,** and race. It also **investigates** different languages in a **community** and people's **attitudes** towards a language. In other words, sociolinguistics is the study of the relationship between language and society.

Background to Sociolinguistics

For many **experts**, sociolinguistics is a young subject. The first official study in 1958 was by John Lyle Fischer (**compare** this to modern **philosophy,** which started in the 17th **Century** over 300 years ago!). John Lyle Fischer was an American-born **professor*** of social **anthropology*** at Tulane University. He was interested in Japanese and American **culture—especially** in Japanese and American family life. Fischer found that school children in **Boston*** did not sound the "g" in words like *"jumping"* or *"singing."* Instead, they would say *"jumpin"* and *"singin."* This was not a **random habit** but, in fact, depended on the child's **gender** and social class. Other **experts** believe the **birth** of sociolinguistics was **thanks** to the work of William Labov in early 1960s New York. Labov worked first as a **chemist*** and only after entering Columbia University did his **career*** in **linguistics*** begin. One of Labov's **landmark*** studies **involved audio tape recordings*** of speech from the people of Harlem. He found that their speech was **connected** to other social characteristics such as age, gender, class, and **education** level. The study **examined** the relationship between how people speak and how they fit into the community. Labov's research resulted in a new branch of sociolinguistics called **variationist*** sociolinguistics. The main teaching of this branch is that **variation** is an **innate*** part of language. In other words, no matter who you are, where you are or what language you speak, the way a language is spoken and written will be different. Even after 50 years, Labov's **research** is still a **model** and an **inspiration*** to other **sociolinguists***.

His research also raised **attention** to the language and status of **minority** groups. Today, sociolinguistics has a much broader **scope**. **Researchers** now **investigate** language and its **connection** to gender, class, region and age. Others are interested in language attitudes, while some look at how sociolinguistics can **benefit** language learners.

Seminal Studies in Sociolinguistics

Published in 1966, the research **titled** "The Social **Stratification*** of English in New York City" by Labov is a **seminal*** study in sociolinguistics that examines the relationship between social class and language variation. Labov's research **focused** on the speech **patterns** of New Yorkers and how these patterns were influenced by social **factors** of **socioeconomic status***, **ethnicity**, and various neighbourhoods in New York City. One of the most famous **aspects** of his research was his study of the **pronunciation*** of the **postvocalic*** /r/ (i.e. the "r" sound in words like "beer," "girl" and "car"). Labov observed that the pronunciation of the /r/ varied **significantly** across different social classes. **Upper**-middle-class speakers were more likely to **pronounce** the /r/, while lower-middle-class and working-class speakers were less likely to pronounce it. This variation in pronunciation served as a marker of social status, with those **aiming** to **project** a higher social status more likely to adopt the **prestigious*** /r/ sound. Labov's study also **explored** how individuals **alter** their speech depending on the **contexts** of **interaction**. This is known as a **phenomenon** known as "**style-shifting**." Labov found that speakers would **adjust** their speech depending on the **formality** of the situation and the social status of the people they were interacting with. For example, in more **formal** situations or when talking to someone of a higher social status, people were more likely to use the "**correct**" way of speaking, like pronouncing the /r/ sound. This showed that how people speak changes based on the situation they are in and is also influenced by social factors. Overall, Labov's work had significant **implications** for understanding the **role** of language in social stratification. It **challenged** the **notion** that language variation is **purely** random or based **solely** on one's **environment** but instead showed that it is **tied** to social **structures**. The study also demonstrated that language is a means to express who we are in society, and that differences in how people speak can both reveal and **perpetuate*** social **inequalities***. Labov's **insights** into the **interplay*** between language and social structure continue to influence research in the field of sociolinguistics, shaping our understanding of how linguistic **practices** are **embedded*** in our communities while at the same time demonstrating how language is not just a means of **communication** but also a social **indicator**.

Attitudes to Language

If you think you need to speak English **perfectly,** then you may be surprised to hear that over 200 years ago, people in the United Kingdom added an **extra** "s." For example, *"birds sings."* People generally believed that this was wrong, so wrong that **categories** of low, very low, **ungentlemanly***, disrespectful and **disgusting** were introduced as a way to **categorize*** nonstandard ways of speaking. Adding the extra "s" **gradually faded** away, and today, we **rarely** hear this form in English, and if it is **uttered***, then it is viewed as a **mistake**. Yet this example shows how language **attitudes underline*** the linguistic choices we make and how we judge other people and their speech. But it is not just with **grammar**. **Dialects*** and **accents** can also have an **impact** on our attitude. Dennis Preston asked university students to rate the speech of northern **regions** and southern regions of America. The students described the north as normal, fast and smart. The southern speech was described as casual, friendly and **polite**. However, not all accents are viewed **positively**. For example, according to the British newspaper, the **Telegraph**, the **Birmingham*** accent in the United Kingdom was rated as the most **unattractive*** and less **intelligent** than those who stayed silent! Of course, having a **positive** attitude to languages and its culture, especially a language one is learning, is an **essential ingredient***. Another **crucial** point to language learning is introduced in the next **section**.

Benefits of Sociolinguistics to the Language Learner

One of the important **aspects** of sociolinguistics for language learners is the idea of sociolinguistic **competence***. This is the idea that a person is able to **adjust** their speech to fit the situation they are in. Without this ability, even the most **perfect grammatical*** **sentences** can give a completely different meaning from what the speaker **intended**. Sociolinguistic competence is often seen in **specific** speech acts. Examples of speech acts include **apologizing***, **requesting** and **inviting**. When apologizing, for example, we usually **apologize** and promise not to do it again. So, we follow a set **sequence** of sentences. But even if we **deliver** the correct sequence in the correct **circumstance**, different cultures use different speech acts in the same situation, so we need to be aware of these differences. For instance, in English, a direct request can appear **rude** to native speakers, so we make it more **polite** by adding *"could I…"* or *"may I…"* but Hebrew does not have any indirect requests and allows for more **directness***. Another example is with **invitations** in American English. Common invitations such as *"Let's get together sometime…"* are often **false** invitations and are instead a **strategy** to show **friendliness*** to the listener. **Overall**, sociolinguistic competence is **demonstrated** in the various speech acts we find ourselves **practicing**. It is also **connected** to culture and our understanding that different cultures will **perform** speech acts using different sequences.

Questions to the Reader

Sociolinguistics covers several aspects of how language and society are connected. As we have seen, these aspects concern individuals such as language learners, communities in New York and Boston and **people's attitudes** towards language. But there are many other **unanswered*** questions in sociolinguistics. For example, how do boys and girls or the old and the young speak differently in your country's language? Do they speak differently when speaking to the **opposite sex** or when speaking to someone of a different age? What is your attitude to learning and using languages? Which dialects and accents are the most **attractive** and least attractive to you? Do you think it is important to develop your sociolinguistic competence? Are there any particular speech acts you find easy or difficult in your native language or in English? After reading this short introduction, you have probably noticed that we are all members of a sociolinguistic community. You know something about your own community and how the people in your community use language with different people in different **settings***. I hope this new **awareness** helps you to understand how language is not only about **correctness** but about the choices we have when answering even the simplest of questions like *"how are you?"*

Adapted from a text by Leigh Bennett, M.A.
Lecturer, English for Academic Purposes
Akita International University, Akita, Japan

Vocabulary

Words From the Second 1,000 General Service High-Frequency Word List

apologize	education
aiming	especially
attention	essential
attractive	examined
birth	explored
century	extra
compare	faded
connect	false
connection	formal
correct	formality
correctness	gradually
deliver	grammar
disgusting	habit
during	intended

invite
invitations
jumping
mistake
model
opposite
patterns
perfect
perform
polite
practice
practices

probably
pronounce
purely
rarely
request
rude
sentence
telegraph
thanks
tied
titled
upper

Words From the Academic Word List (AWL)

adjust
alter
aspects
attitude
awareness
benefit
categories
challenged
circumstance
community
communication
contexts
crucial
culture
demonstrated
environment
ethnicity
experts
factors
finally
focused
gender
impact
implications
indicator
individuals
insights
interaction
intelligent
investigate
involved

job
minority
normal
notion
overall
phenomenon
philosophy
positive
principal
project
published
random
regions
research
response
reveals
role
scope
section
sequence
sex
shifting
solely
significantly
style
specific
status
strategy
tape
variation

Glossary

Anthropology (Noun): The study of humans, their societies, and cultures.

Apologize (Verb): To say "sorry" or express regret for an action.

Audio Tape Recordings (Noun): Sound recordings stored on magnetic tape.

Birmingham (Noun): A city in the UK.

Boston (Noun): A city in the USA.

Career (Noun): A profession or occupation for which someone is trained.

Categorize (Verb): To place into specific groups or classes.

Chemist (Noun): A person with expertise in chemistry.

Competence (Noun): The ability or skill to do something effectively.

Dialects (Noun): Regional or social variations in language.

Embedded (Adjective): Fixed firmly and deeply within something, often referring to ideas, concepts, or systems that are ingrained in a structure or culture.

Exam (Noun): A formal test to assess knowledge or skills.

Formality (Noun): The strict observance of established rules or customs, especially in etiquette.

Friendliness (Noun): Warmth and kindness shown towards others.

Grammatical (Adjective): Correct according to formal rules of grammar.

Inequalities (Noun): The state of being unequal in status, rights, or opportunities, often referring to social or economic disparities.

Ingredient (Noun): A component that is mixed into something larger.

Innate (Adjective): Inborn; naturally occurring rather than learned.

Inspiration (Noun): Something that motivates or influences action.

Interplay (Noun): The interaction or influence between two or more things, such as ideas, forces, or systems.

Interview (Noun): A formal conversation, often before a job is offered.

Landmark (Noun): An event or turning point of significant importance.

Linguistics (Noun): The formal study of the system and structure of human language.

Mood (Noun): A prevailing emotional state or attitude.

Perpetuate (Verb): To cause something to continue indefinitely, often used in reference to ideas or social norms.

Phenomenon (Noun): An observable event or occurrence, often unusual or noteworthy.

Postvocalic (Adjective): Occurring after a vowel, often used in linguistic contexts to describe sounds or letters.

Practices (Noun): Repeated actions or behaviors, often within a particular profession or discipline.

Prestigious (Adjective): Having high status or respect, often associated with recognition or admiration.

Pronunciation (Noun): The way in which a word is spoken, including the sounds and intonation used.

Published (Adjective): Made available to the public, usually referring to printed or online material.

Role (Noun): A specific function or part played in a situation or system.

Seminal (Adjective): Highly influential or original, often used to describe works or ideas that shape a field or topic.

Setting (Noun): The environment or background in which something takes place.

Socioeconomic Status (Noun Phrase): A measure of an individual's or group's economic and social position in relation to others, based on income, education, and occupation.

Sociolinguists (Noun): Experts or scholars who study sociolinguistics.

Stratification (Noun): The hierarchical arrangement of individuals or groups in society based on various factors like wealth, status, and power.

Thorough (Adjective): Complete with great attention to detail.

Tied (Adjective): Fastened or bound together.

Titled (Adjective): Having a title or name, often referring to published works.

Tools (Noun): Instruments or devices used to carry out a function or task.

Unanswered (Adjective): Not responded to or addressed.

Unattractive (Adjective): Not appealing or pleasant to look at.

Underline (Verb): To emphasize or bring attention to something.

Ungentlemanly (Adjective): Rude or not polite, especially in behavior.

Upper (Adjective): Situated higher in position or rank.

Utter (Verb): To speak or say something.

Variationist (Noun): Someone who studies or applies variation theory, especially in linguistics.

CHAPTER 14

CULTURAL ANTHROPOLOGY

Hisako Omori
Akita International University, Japan

Introduction

When you meet someone from a different country for the first time, what are some things you may find surprising? The way she looks may be unfamiliar—she may have a different **skin** color or be much **taller** or shorter than most people from your country. Perhaps she has a broad smile and uses friendly **gestures***? She may speak a completely different language, and you have no idea what she is saying. But, later, you discovered that she grew up watching Pokémon, your favorite childhood TV show. Are you the kind of person who is interested in these kinds of discoveries? If so, you may find **Cultural Anthropology*** interesting. In Cultural Anthropology, we **aim** to understand various kinds of human **behaviors**. We use "**culture**" as a **key** word. But what does culture mean in the **context** of Cultural Anthropology? We use the word "culture" to describe any human behaviors that are not **physically** passed on to us from our **parents**. The way we **interact** with others is a cultural expression, and what we eat is also part of our culture. In Cultural Anthropology, we also use a certain **method** to carry out our studies, or **investigations**.

Cultural Anthropology studies human behaviors in a **holistic*** way. What do we mean by this? When thinking about a certain question, for example, the eating **practices** of a certain group of people, we may also look into their **kinship*** patterns, language, political systems and the natural **environment** in which they live, in addition to the actual food they eat and the ways they eat. How do we do that? Cultural **anthropologists*** use **fieldwork*** as their main **data collection** method. They usually stay at the **research site**, that is, the place where they are going to do their studies, for twelve months or more. They speak the native language of the people there, and eat their food. Cultural anthropologists address research questions while taking part in daily life with the people they study. This method is called "**participant-observation***"—the researchers not only observe, but they also join in the everyday activities of the people they observe.

How is this method of looking at the world, used in Cultural Anthropology, different from the research done in other fields of study? **Economists** would look into **economic** activities, and political scientists would look into the political field when researching their subjects. Cultural anthropologists would look into all of these fields—politics, economics, kinships, languages, **communication**, and so forth—and understand the people's behaviors as being shaped by many different **aspects** of the world in which they live.

History

The **origins** of modern-day Cultural Anthropology go back to the nineteenth **century**. At that time, many Western countries spread their influence over other parts of the world. Many European nations took control of different parts

---

Introducing the Liberal Arts, pages 89–93
Copyright © 2026 by Emerald Publishing Limited
All rights of reproduction in any form reserved.
doi:10.1108/978-1-80592-303-920251014

of Africa, for example, and these Europeans needed to understand the populations of the places they were ruling. Cultural Anthropology has its origins within this colonial history.

We should also note that Cultural Anthropology is the usual term for this field of study in the United States. The same field—with a **slightly** different **focus** and history—is called Social Anthropology in the United Kingdom, while some universities use the term Sociocultural Anthropology.

In the past, Cultural Anthropology was mainly developed by Europeans and Americans to understand people who are seen as social and cultural "others." In its early years, a **typical** way to do Cultural Anthropology was to study a particular people who lived in a place that was far away from developed Western countries and cities.

Colonial relationships between the **researchers** and the people they researched also shaped the field, as those relationships often control who can have easier **contact** with whom. For example, British anthropologists studied **tribes** of people in Sudan (an African country) under British control, and American anthropologists studied native groups in the United States.

Over the centuries, however, Cultural Anthropology has changed greatly. Anthropologists do continue to study tribes of people living in far-off places, but nowadays, larger societies in cities in the Western world are also being studied. As the field develops, the number and kinds of **topics** that Cultural Anthropology covers have also increased.

Why Study Cultural Anthropology?

What are some good reasons to study Cultural Anthropology? One of the most important reasons why Cultural Anthropology should be part of a **Liberal Arts*** **education** is that it would give you a stronger, clearer way of understanding human beings and their cultures based on well-respected ways of thinking that have been developed within this field over a long time.

To explain, in addition to the **information** that you may get through your studies, such as different types of marriage in the world, you would learn how to think like an anthropologist. When looking at the world and its problems, you learn how to look at problems "holistically." This means looking at all the things that shape or cause a problem, not just the problem itself.

Take the case of **toxic breast** milk* in the Arctic, the northern part of Canada, as an example. It was reported that a large number of PCBs, a very dangerous **chemical***, was found in the breast milk of Inuit women living on Broughton **Island**. This is, of course, related to industrial **waste** that arrived from other parts of the world. In the Arctic, the chemical takes longer to break down than in other places due to the low **temperature**. These dangerous chemicals are eaten by fish, and other animals. As the Inuit people need to go fishing and **hunting** for their food, they take PCBs into their bodies from the food they eat, resulting in high levels of dangerous PCBs in the breast milk of the Inuit women.

You can see that this is a very **complex** problem. Many aspects of life, beyond those of the Inuit, shape and cause this problem. We can **approach** this problem in a variety of ways: from a **medical**, environmental or **dietary*** point of view, to name just a few. Those in the **corporate** world can also think about this question from the point of view of the social **responsibility** that businesses have. Cultural anthropologists can also explain the importance of sea animals and fish in Inuit life further. Sea animals and fish mean much more than just food for the Inuit. They are **incorporated** into Inuit art and used in important ways in the Inuit language. As you learn how anthropologists think, you begin to see the special relationships between all the different parts of a culture which you did not see before.

A Well-Known Anthropologist

Do you know the names of any anthropologists? Janice Boddy is a Canadian anthropologist who studies **gender**, the body, **ritual** and **colonialism***. Her **areas** of study may give you a real-life example of a topic that a cultural anthropologist can study—although her field is one of the most difficult. Boddy is best known for her work on **female circumcision*** among the people who live in northern Sudan. This cutting of the private parts of a woman's body causes physical harm, and there are no known **health benefits**. Many people in the West speak and write strongly against it.

Based on her long-term fieldwork, Janice Boddy has provided a careful study of female circumcision as seen from the point of view of the people in northern Sudan themselves. Instead of judging a foreign **custom** using one's own culture, morals and customs to measure what is "good" and "bad," Janice Boddy provided us with very different understandings of this custom by looking at it in its own special cultural context. Her work reminded us of something basic to the proper study of Cultural Anthropology: we should not judge something until we fully understand it from the point of view of the people we are studying. Once we know the meanings behind these practices, only then can we decide how we can understand the practice and those who are subject to it. Though she was just one person, Janice Boddy's work made a big difference to the way Cultural Anthropologists do their studies, and as a result it has helped to change the way we now understand human cultures and customs in our world today.

Real-World Application

It is not so well-known that cultural anthropologists were sent to Africa **during** the **Ebola outbreak*** in different parts of Africa. The World Health Organisation (WHO) called for various **experts** on **disease** control to go and help, including several cultural anthropologists. The Ebola **virus** can spread **quickly**, causing a large number of deaths, and it has to be immediately controlled. With the help of cultural anthropologists, the WHO was able to find out which people had the Ebola virus or had been with people who had the virus, and these people could be kept **apart** from everyone else so the spread of the disease could be more easily controlled.

Why did the WHO need cultural anthropologists for disease control? Because cultural anthropologists are trained to become part of their study groups, they are in a good position to help build strong relationships between local people and experts from outside the **community.** In the case of the Ebola outbreak, cultural anthropologists were able to help build trust between the community members and the health experts, and in doing so they helped to make sure the disease could be controlled.

Cultural Anthropology and the Modern-Day World

You may think Cultural Anthropology is concerned only about faraway people and their lives. People like hunter-**gatherers** who need to **collect nuts** and hunt animals to stay **alive**. You may also think that Cultural Anthropology is no longer important in our lives today, which are filled with iPhones and other modern **tools**. But is this really the case? Where does cultural or social anthropology stand in today's modern world? In recent years, it is common to see cultural anthropologists study modern societies like those in France, the U.S., or Japan. The topics of studies also grow as our life changes. For example, we have an American anthropologist studying modern life in Japan, focusing on the relationships between humans and machines, or a Canadian anthropologist researching the experiences of Muslim women and the views of French people towards **migrants** in Paris. Although the study of Cultural Anthropology began with colonialism and control of others, cultural anthropologists today are concerned about the well-being of the people they study. Some anthropologists work hard to support the groups that they study, and others use their work to try to make powerful people take responsibility for the way they **treat** the people over whom they have power. Wherever you find cultural anthropologists working today, you will find them adding much to our understanding of ourselves as human beings and making a big difference to the world.

Adapted from a text by Hisako Omori PhD
Associate Professor
Akita International University
Japan

Vocabulary

Words From the Second 1,000 General Service Word List

aim
alive
apart
behaviors
century
collect/collection
custom
disease
during
education
female
focus
harm
health
hunt/hunter
immediately
information
island

key
nuts
origin
parents
patterns
practice
quickly
reminded
responsibility
skin
slightly
temperature
taller
tools
tribe
typical
waste

Words From the Academic Word List

approach
areas
aspects
benefits
chemical
communication
community
complex
contact
context
corporate
create
cultural/culture
data
economic/economists

environment/environmental
experts
focus
gender
interact
incorporate
investigations
medical
method
migrants
physical/physically
research/researchers
site
topic

Glossary

Anthropologist/anthropology (Nouns): A person who studies human culture/The study of humans and their culture.

Colonialism (Noun): The practice of controlling another country and using its people and resources for economic gain.

Cultural Anthropology (Noun phrase): The name given to the study of humans and their culture.

Dietary (Adjective): Relating to one's diet or the kind of food that people usually eat.

Ebola outbreak/Ebola virus (Noun phrase): The sudden spread of the disease called Ebola. The Ebola virus is a very small life form that moves from person to person spreading the disease.

Female circumcision (Noun phrase): A cultural practice that removes part of a female's genitalia (private parts). In the West, it is often called "female mutilation"

Fieldwork (Noun phrase): In anthropology, this is the study done in a specific location of a specific group of people.

Gatherers (Noun): People who collect food from the natural environment.

Gestures (Noun): Actions made with the arms, body language.

Holistic (Adjective): Relating to the whole picture. Looking at all aspects of something.

kinship: Family relationship.

Liberal Arts: The areas of study concerned with human beings and the world they live in (not including the hard sciences).

Muslim: A person who follows the religion of Islam.

Ritual: A special ceremony where actions are done in a certain set order.

Toxic breastmilk: Milk from a human mother which is dangerous to the baby because it has dangerous chemicals in it.

CHAPTER 15

THE GEOGRAPHY OF PUBLIC HEALTH

Sig Langegger
Akita International University, Japan

What Is Geography?

Geography* is the study of **locations** on our Earth. It is the study of the **distribution*** of things such as mountains, **oceans**, and rivers, and natural **processes,** for example, how safe drinking water is formed. This branch of geography is called **physical** geography.

However, there is more to geography than physical features such as mountains, oceans and rivers. Geography is also the study of the distribution of people: e.g., rich people, poor people, **sick** people, people who are well, and so on. Geographers are not only interested in where things are but also in how **culture**, **economic** systems, and **social norms*** influence these **patterns** of distribution. For example, when faced with a problem of drinking water that is not **clean**, a geographer would first ask, why is the water safe to drink here but not safe to drink there? Because this branch of geography is also interested in how people live within the physical **environment**, it is called human geography.

What Is Public Health?

We will talk about public **health** and human geography together because people who work in both fields are interested in where sick and healthy people live. Public health also studies how **diseases** move through populations and how the distribution of physical things and social systems adds to, or takes away from, public well-being. Public health is also closely related to **medicine**. While medicine works to help **patients*** one by one, public health works to keep whole populations healthy and free from **injury**. To give an example, while doctors would be concerned with treating an **infection***, or fixing a broken bone, public health workers would be more concerned with limiting the spread of disease-causing **pathogens*** (for example, **bacteria***, **parasites***, and **viruses***), or with ways to make sure that people do not break their **bones** in the first place.

Benefits of Public Health to Humans

We often hear about the discovery of new **medicines** and new kinds of operations that save people's lives, but though we know about the importance of having a physical **check** each year, the importance of public health is not so clear to most of us. In fact, public health does far more to advance the health of a population than medicine does. For example, one study found that the **life expectancy*** (the number of years people can be expected to live) of citizens of the United States of America increased from 45 years to 75 years within the 20th **Century**. The study found that only five of these additional 30 years of life were because of medicine. The other twenty-five additional years of life expectancy came from public health **improvements**, such as better-quality food, better housing, **education** about how to keep clean, better safety in places of work, and better systems to provide clean water and control human **waste**. What is more, it is good for society if the general health of its members is strong because workers produce more, the cost of **insurance** protection goes down, and people spend more money on the things they want and the services they choose to use.

History of Public Health

The history of public health is likely as long as the history of human beings. Any group that protects the health of its members (e.g., by not building a town in a place that **floods** or by taking human waste away from places where humans live) is doing public health. However, the field of study itself began in the 19th Century.

Then, as now, advances in public health often meant that it was necessary to change the wrong ideas that people had about particular diseases. For example, **Typhus***, a disease that can lead to death, was common among poor **Irish immigrants*** who had moved to London in the 19th Century. Many people in the general English public, as well as some doctors, called it the Irish Disease, and because of that, they often **treated** Irish people badly. Once the truth became known that Typhus is spread by small **insects** called body **lice***, which live on human bodies and their clothes, public health workers began to work to stop the disease from spreading in both Irish and non-Irish populations. They did this by **educating** people about the good reasons for keeping themselves clean and by providing places where people could take a **bath** and **wash** their **clothes** in poor neighborhoods. It is interesting to note that Typhus was controlled in this way long before the **antibiotics*** that we use these days to **cure** the disease were **invented**.

19th-century London was also the location of another important advance in public health knowledge. At this time in history, people thought that diseases spread because of bad air or even, as in the case of Typhus, by body **odor***. The **theory** behind this idea was called the Miasmic Theory of Disease. A "**miasma**"* is an unpleasant and/or **unhealthy** kind of gas. In 1854, a particularly bad **outbreak*** of **Cholera*** (a disease that can kill around 80% of untreated people) killed 616 people in the neighborhood of Soho, in London. Public health workers believed that the cause of the disease was the miasma, or the bad air, of Soho.

Today, we know that Cholera is a disease that you can get by drinking water that is not safe to drink because it has **raw** human **sewage*** in it. We now know this because one public health worker named John Snow had a different idea about how Cholera might be spreading. He thought that Cholera was in some way spread by water, not by a miasma.

To test his theory, he used his knowledge of study **methods** from the field of geography. He made a **map** of the addresses of all the people who had died in the 1854 Cholera outbreak. By looking closely at his map, he noticed that there were many deaths on one particular street, Broad Street. He also noticed that there were many deaths in buildings close to the Broad Street water **pump**. After checking to see if the people who had died on Broad Street had indeed been drinking the water from this one water pump, he was able to get the City of London to prevent people from using it. The City put a **lock** on the pump. As soon as they did this, the outbreak of Cholera began to **slow** down. When the city workers checked the pump, they found that the water from the Broad Street pump was full of human waste.

Fields Related to Public Health

As with the so-called Irish Disease, Typhus, many years before scientists found the bacteria that was the real cause of Cholera, and many more years before medicines for Cholera were developed, actions by public health workers were able to prevent many people from coming into **contact** with Cholera bacteria in the first place. These public health actions are what we now call **sanitation***. Sanitation **involves** building systems that **remove** human waste from the city water supply and make it clean before putting it back into the environment. Sanitation also means that water systems bring fresh water to each house so that the people living there have clean, safe water. The water is treated with **chlorine*** to make sure that it is free of diseases and anything else that could be bad for human health.

The field of Public Health will always remain central to organized society. The appearance of new diseases, like **AIDS**, **Ebola**, **Zika** and the **Coronavirus**, each with a different way of entering human populations, will continue to make people in the fields of Public Health and Medicine try to find new ways to stop them from spreading.

Public Health is also closely related to city planning. Planners, both in cities that are growing and also in cities that are losing their populations, will need to continue to work out how to make sure that the health of their citizens is not in any danger. At the same time, they also need to ensure people have a healthy environment and safe places to use, like **parks** and **paths** on which to walk.

Public Health and Public Issues

Public health will always remain important because it is not just about fighting disease. It is also about keeping populations physically safe. For example, public health actions have led to everyday improvements such as **seatbelts*** in cars and safe **crosswalks***.

Public health will always cause people to disagree about what should be done because someone has to pay for the changes to the environment. Better sanitation makes buildings more expensive to build, so some people in the building industry fight against it. Over the last 50 years, seatbelts and **airbags*** have led to fewer deaths in car **accidents**. However, at first, people in the car industry did not want to make these changes to the cars they produced. Safer crosswalks, and the many other changes to city streets, like paths, planting of street trees, and lights at street **crossings*** all make walking in a city a safe and pleasant experience. However, sometimes the people who have to pay for these, that is, the city taxpayers, do not want to pay the taxes needed for these **projects**, even though they know that these things make their city safer and a better place in which to live.

Employment Opportunities in Geography and Public Health

There are many **career paths*** in the space where geography and public health meet. For example, public health officials studying the spread of dangerous viruses like coronavirus in human populations around the whole world must be able to do **advanced mapping*** and know how to use **geospatial tracking technologies***. Another example would be **technicians*** who make sure that a city's drinking water is safe for humans to drink, even after **natural disasters*** like tsunamis or floods. A third example is a career in **urban design**. Urban **designers** make sure that city parks are great places to get exercise or to **relax**, and that city streets are safe for drivers, people riding **bicycles** and people who are walking. They also plan so that city environments do not get too hot **during** summer heat waves or flood during heavy **rains**. In the end, studying the field of Public Health at a **Liberal Arts*** University would be an **exciting** challenge for students who enjoy scientific **research** and who are deeply interested in making it their life work to help us to live healthier, happier lives in an environment that is safe and meets the needs of all.

Adapted from a text by Sig Langegger, PhD
Associate Professor, Geography
Faculty of International Liberal Arts
Akita International University
Japan

Vocabulary

Words From the Second 1,000 General Service High-Frequency Word List

accidents	bicycles
bath	bones

century
check
clean
clothes
cure
disease
during
educating/education
exciting
floods
health/healthy/unhealthy
improvements
insects
insurance
invented

lock
map
medicine
oceans
parks
paths
patterns
pump
rain
raw
sick
slow
treat/treating
wash
waste

Words From the Academic Word List

benefits
challenge
contact
culture
design/designers
distribution
economic
environment
immigrants
injury
involves

issues
location
methods
norms
physical
processes
projects
relax
remove
research
theory

Glossary

Advanced mapping and **Geospatial tracking technologies** (Noun phrases): Modern technology that helps us to map and follow the presence, pathways or movement of something, such as the spread of a disease, or the location of transport systems. The information gathered can be used for policy making and future planning (see http://www.bcc.cuny.edu/academics/geospatial-center-of-the-cuny-crest-institute/what-is-geospatial-technology/)

AIDS (Noun): A disease caused by the HIV virus that weakens the immune system.

Airbags (Noun): Safety devices in vehicles that inflate quickly during a collision to protect passengers.

Antibiotics: medicine to kill or slow the growth of bacteria that cause illness.

Bacteria (Noun): Microscopic organisms, some of which cause disease, while others are harmless or helpful.

Body lice (Noun): Small insects that live on human clothing and skin, feeding on blood and spreading disease.

Career paths (Noun phrase): One's work choices and work experience over a lifetime.

Chlorine: a chemical element. Also called Cl.

Cholera (Noun): An infectious disease causing severe diarrhea and dehydration, usually spread by contaminated water.

Crossings/crosswalks: a safe place for people to cross the street, usually marked by lights or painted lines.

Distribution: the frequency of occurrence or the natural geographic range or place where any item or category of items occur.

Ebola (Noun): A severe viral disease that leads to fever, bleeding, and often death.

Geographer/geography: the study of places and the relationships between people and their environments. Geographers study both the physical parts of the Earth's and the human societies spread across it.

Infection: when a person's body, or a part of a person's body becomes ill because of things that cause disease.

Irish immigrants: People from the country of Ireland who move to other countries. In this case, to London in England.

Liberal Arts (Noun phrase): "Liberal arts is a field of study based on rational thinking, and it includes the areas of humanities, social and physical sciences, and mathematics. A liberal arts education emphasizes the development of critical thinking … the ability to solve complex problems, and an understanding of ethics and morality, as well as a desire to continue to learn." Retrieved from https://www.thoughtco.com/liberal-arts-definition-4585053

Life expectancy: the likely number of years remaining in the life of an individual or class of persons. This number is determined statistically, and is affected by such factors as heredity, physical condition, nutrition, and occupation. The term is used as a common means of measuring the general health of a given population.

Miasma: a dangerous, or deathlike influence or atmosphere.

Natural disasters (Noun phrase): Strong, serious, and dangerous physical events (e.g. tsunami, floods, forest fires, earthquakes, large storms) that cause danger to, or loss of human and animal life.

Novel Coronavirus (Noun): A newly identified virus, such as COVID-19, that can cause respiratory illness in humans.

Odor: a strong smell, usually an unpleasant one.

Outbreak: a sudden event, such as a disease, that spreads quickly

Parasites (Noun): Organisms that live on or inside another living being, gaining nutrients at the host's expense.

Patients: people treated by a medical person (doctor, nurse, dentist etc.) for sickness or injury or special health needs.

Pathogens (Noun): Microorganisms such as viruses or bacteria that cause disease.

Sanitation: services and systems for the safe management of human and other waste for the sake of keeping the public healthy.

Seatbelts (Noun): Straps in vehicles that secure passengers to reduce injury during sudden stops or crashes.

Sewage: dirty water and waste from the human body.

Social norms: "the unwritten rules of behavior that are considered acceptable in a group or society" Retrieved from https://examples.yourdictionary.com/social-norm-examples.html

Technician (Noun): A person who works with and looks after technical equipment.

Typhus (Noun): An infectious disease spread by lice or fleas, causing fever, rash, and body aches.

Urban (Adjective): Of the city.

Viruses (Noun): Tiny infectious agents that reproduce only inside living cells and can cause illness.

Zika (Noun): A viral disease spread by mosquitoes, linked to birth defects in babies.

CHAPTER 16

MANGEMENT STUDIES

Masahiko Agata
Akita International University, Japan

Introduction

When you hear the words "**management**" or "to manage" what **image** do you have of them in your mind? Do they mean to "use your power or **authority**" in order to make your organization run according to your own wishes? Do they mean cold, hard directions by managers with no feeling for their workers? Do they mean that managers use force on the people under them who have no power? Not at all, management is a field within Social Science **seeking** to find better ways for organizations to **perform** so that they can move towards their **goals** using the efforts of humans and **resources** in the most effective way.

The field of management in the social sciences **incorporates** such subjects as **Economics**, Law, **Sociology*** **Psychology** and **Communication** since management deals with a wide **range** of people. These can of course include **customers** and employees with a **focus** on their desires, **behaviors** and activities. If you run a company, you need to think carefully about a variety of situations concerning your markets, society, people, money, and **technology**, etc. Studying management helps you deal with all these things in a more systematic manner. In today's **constantly** changing business **environments**, if you are a **manager**, you need your company to maintain any **competitive*** advantages it may have over other companies. To do that well, knowing how to **manage** your company in an organized and systematic manner is important.

History of Management Studies

The **concept** of Management Studies is thought, by many in the field, to have its early beginnings in ancient **military** life. However, the modern descriptions of Management Studies within the field of Social Science started in the late 19th **century**, growing out of the subject of Economics that followed new **revolutionary technologies*** like the **steam engine** and modern **transportation**.

In the early 20th century, the focus of Management was on driving the workers within each organization towards making a profit. Little notice was paid to the **environment** of organizations or the **motivation** and psychology of the people in places of work. However, soon a new wave of **theories** about management **evolved**. According to these new theories, organizations were viewed more as groups of **individuals** who had a choice as to whether to **participate** in them or not. In this new way of thinking, the most important ideas were (a) finding a **balance** between **inducement*** (what an organization offers) and **contributions** (what individuals provide) and (b) values—not only **economic** value (in other words, making money) but also providing social and **psychological satisfaction** to workers. Thus, a knowledge of management **skills** became necessary. Managers began to realize that they needed to think more about both the goals of their organization and the **motivations** of the individual personalities of the people they employed; they needed to think about the fact that an organization must **satisfy** both of these two things at the same time.

Another important thing that managers needed to think about was their company's **competitive*** situation. This idea lead to the idea of **open system management*** in which a business must remain open and ready to change, depending on the **information** and resources that flow in and out of it. Along with these, the concept of "Leadership in Management" evolved until we now have a more modern idea of leadership. These days, this means that leaders are not just seen as strong persons who control others by using their position and power to **push** or pull their workers, but as persons who **encourage** individuals and build a strong sense of purpose within them. Today's leaders are more interested in motivation and working with their employees to make wise decisions, which in turn drive their organizations **forward**.

One of the biggest changes in the development of ideas within the field of Management was Peter Drucker's study "Concept of the Corporation" (1946), This was the first careful and broad study of applied management that was carried out for the General Motors Company. Since his study became so widely known, Drucker became one of the most widely recognized **theorists** in the field, and is known for his strong support in helping managers build a better understanding of important ideas in the field of Management.

Today Management Studies focuses on several important points of interest; **strategic planning, managing day to day operations, production management, marketing management, financial management, human resource management, information technology management and corporate governance.*** More information about each of these can be found in the glossary below.

Why Study Management?

In the Real World

Concerning business, you may have the chance to study such **specific** subjects as **finance,** marketing and business law. Of course, these subjects will help you **acquire** a deeper understanding of each field. However, these subjects alone do not necessarily help you have a **comprehensive** view of how organizations or companies are run, or how all the different parts of an organization work together to produce a good result. They don't show you how to form a carefully **formulated strategy** for running each part of a company or organization. Studying management will help you know how best you can manage to reach your business or organization's goals. It will help you to have an organization in which all the parts work together in **synergy***, so that in the end, your organization becomes successful. This becomes even more important when you are working within an organization that employs **significant** numbers of people.

In the Academic World

In the **dynamic** and fast-changing business environments of the modern world, the need to **review, analyze** and **innovate** what we are doing is becoming more serious, as is our need to find new ways to do things. The number of fields of study in management is becoming more and more broad. This also means the number of **academic** works in relation to management is also growing. Academics in the field of management studies are always coming up with new ideas and suggestions about how to make our management activities better, which means there is much for students of management to read and learn about. In fact, managers too, need to continue to keep up-to-date with new ideas, and try to include these ideas in their planning and business activities if they want to stay in business and be successful.

It is also interesting to note that these days, an increasing number of academics are being asked to sit on the **Boards of Directors*** of many companies as "**External Directors***." This shows us how concerned companies are to have a Board of Directors that can make better, more **objective** decisions. Companies these days need people who can **"think outside the box"***, people who have broad **corporate** experience, and who are able to be effective leaders in the decision-making that takes place in organizations and in the wider business world.

Application of Management Studies to the Real World

Over time, management has become a popular choice as a subject of study in Western countries. This is particularly the case since universities started to offer **"Master of Business Administration" (MBA)*** courses. In Asian countries, including Japan, courses such as these are increasing in number today. In MBA courses, students study management-related subjects in depth. For example, they can begin to acquire a sense of what real management is all about, through looking at real life **case studies***. In addition, beyond universities, there are many management training opportunities offered to business persons by management **consultants**. However, even though there are so many opportunities to learn about management, cases of management failure have never gone down in number. Rather, they are increasing in real terms year by year. Why is this so?

As Barbara Kellerman of the Kennedy School, in Harvard University, points out in her book, "The End of Leadership" (2012), training opportunities and courses on subjects like management and leadership of organizations have become easy to market. However, many of those management courses have presented the subject only as a limited body of knowledge and **techniques**, or as courses in "how to make your fortune in business." By having such a limited focus, the more important understanding of human values and **ethics** is often left out. These values and ethics, which are part of the true study of **Liberal Arts***, need to be studied together with the more **practical** knowledge and "techniques" of management. Otherwise, business leaders may simply think only of ways of making money for themselves and of their own success, at the expense of the well-being of the people they employ, their organizations, and society generally.

If You Are Thinking of Studying Management

In studying management, you should be thinking carefully ahead to the future. It is desirable that you study management because you believe you will be managing an organization, whether it is a business, a company or any other type of organization, instead of learning the subject merely as a way of building your general knowledge. At universities in many other countries, many business or management students choose the subject because they expect it to help them move towards a future position of real leadership, and for many, this means working in their own businesses and organizations. This is called "**entrepreneurship***."

Entrepreneurship, which is a very basic part of management, comes about when someone has a new business idea and the motivation to start and lead a business of their own. It is important, because successful new businesses help to build a strong economy and can lead to social progress. Instead of working for someone else's company or organization, entrepreneurs start their own, so they are "self-employed." If their business or organization becomes successful, they may in turn provide work opportunities for other people, as well as **exciting** new products and services that did not exist before. This kind of activity is often very helpful for human society in general. Do you have a good business idea? Do you think you have what it takes to become a successful entrepreneur? Then management studies are for you!

In todays' **global** society, Japanese companies also need their **Human Resources Departments*** to think more about growing **diversity** in places of work and in society. They too, need to think about **issues** such as **gender**, the **ethnic** background of their workers, and individual skills, etc. Even if you do not wish to become an entrepreneur, if you do have an interest in business, or if you wish to lead, or be an effective part of a successful organization, you would do well to take management studies at a Liberal Arts university.

Studying management will help to bring about the changes in business and the life of organizations that are needed in today's fast-moving world. Having a background in management can make the difference between being simply a good employee or member of an organization, to being a highly skilled and **competent*** individual who is able to make a real and lasting difference in society. Since businesses and organizations today are looking for individuals with both high motivation and **competency***, those who have studied management, who also have a strong personal motivation to **contribute** their knowledge and skills, will have a big advantage in today's changing world.

Adapted from a text by Masahiko Agata, B.Econ.
Honorary Select Professor
Akita International University
Japan

Vocabulary

Words From the Second 1,000 High Frequency General Service Word List

balance	manage/management/manager(s)
behaviors	perform
century	practical
customers	push
encourage	review
exciting	satisfaction/satisfy
forward	skill(s)
information	

Words From the Academic Word List

academic(s)	individual(s)
acquire	innovate
analyze	issues
authority	military
comprehensive	motivation(s)
concept	objective
constantly	overall
contribution(s)	participate
corporate	psychological
diversity	psychology
dynamic	range
economic	resource(s)
environment(s)	revolutionary
ethics	seeking
ethnic	significant
evolved	specific
focus/focuses	strategic/strategy
formulated	techniques
gender	technology/technologies
global	theories
goals	theorists
image	transportation
incorporates	

Glossary

Board of Directors (Noun phrase): Structured meeting of directors as the highest policy- and decision-making authority at companies. Directors are appointed by the shareholders, commissioned to guide and lead the company's business. Today, the importance of adding directors from outside the company ("**External Directors**") to the board is being emphasized for the strengthening of corporate governance.

Case studies (Noun phrase): A close research study into the development of a particular situation, person, organization or group over time.

Competent/Competency (Adjective/Noun): Relating to an individual person's behavioral patterns that produce good results in tasks. Not staying only at the level of skills, it looks at the combined ability to adapt to varying environments and use various skills to achieve a high level of performance.

Competitive (Adjective): The quality of strongly wanting to be better than others.

Contributions (Noun, plural): Things that are given by one person or group to another (e.g., money, time, labor, or skills given to an employer by workers).

Corporate Governance (Noun phrase): Company's structure in order to ensure compliant process of work while maximizing the success of business on a long-term basis.

Entrepreneurship (Noun): A quality of mind which leads people to design and create a new business despite potential risks, and bring such a business to success.

Human Resources Departments (Noun phrase): "Human resources or HR is the company department charged with finding, screening, recruiting, and training job applicants, and administering employee-benefit programs." Retrieved from https://www.investopedia.com/terms/h/humanresources.asp

Inducement (Noun): Something that leads a person, or persuades a person to do something (e.g., Money given in the form of a regular salary, wages, or a bonus or gift for work well done).

Liberal Arts (Noun phrase): "Liberal arts is a field of study based on rational thinking, and it includes the areas of humanities, social and physical sciences, and mathematics. A liberal arts education emphasizes the development of critical thinking ... the ability to solve complex problems, and an understanding of ethics and morality, as well as a desire to continue to learn." Retrieved from https://www.thoughtco.com/liberal-arts-definition-4585053

Master of Business Administration' (MBA)*: Title of a university graduate degree in the field of Business Management.

Open System Management (Noun phrase): A type of business management in which the organization or business is open to the influence of changing circumstances. This style of management usually means a business or organization becomes increasingly complex over time.

Sociology: A social science concerned with the study of society, human relationships, social behavior, and even how elements of culture are involved.

Steam Engine: A mechanical engine that uses pressure and heat, in the form of water forced into steam, to work. Early trains and ships were powered by this method, before the use of gasoline.

Technologies: Technology is the practical application of knowledge in a specific field. It can be in the form of a process, method or technique or simply actual physical objects developed using the acquired knowledge. However, often it is a combination of the two elements.

Fields of Interest Within Management Studies

Corporate Governance: The process of governing, or managing all parts of a large business by those who own it.

Financial Management: The process of controlling the flow of money within a business.

Human Resource Management: The process of managing the workers within a company or organization.

Information Technology Management: The process of controlling and managing the computers and digital resources and information belonging to a business or organization.

Marketing Management: The process of trying to attract buyers for products.

Operations: The day-to-day activities of a business or company.

Production Management: The process of managing the making of products.

Strategic Planning: The process of making careful plans for the future direction of a business or organization.

References

Drucker, P. (1946). *Concept of the corporation.* The John Day Company.
Kellerman, B. (2012). *The end of leadership.* HarperCollins.

CHAPTER 17

SOCIAL ANTHROPOLOGY

Julian Manning
Nihon University College of Art, Japan

Understanding the Idea of "Culture"

"**Culture**" is a word we hear daily, but what does it mean? The Welsh **academic** who started the field of cultural studies in British universities, Raymond Williams, said "Culture is one of the two or three most difficult words in the English Language." This is because we use it to describe many different things, from the way people live their everyday lives to the beliefs of certain groups of people that we usually think of as being basic to who they are. Here, we will try to explain how the use of the word has developed in the English language and how the idea of "culture" has been understood and used by people for a number of purposes.

In English the word "culture" was related to the idea of "**cultivation**," that is, the raising or growing of things. However, even in this usage, it was not a **neutral** term. The idea also included the belief that there were right and wrong ways to cultivate things, and people. By the late 18th and early 19th **century**, when people spoke of someone as a "cultivated" person, they meant that person had a high social value (Williams, 1985, pp. 87–93).

From the late 18th century, "culture" began to take on political meanings. Broadly speaking, these meanings can be divided into two groups: the meaning given to culture by **universalists*** and the meaning given to culture by **nationalists***.

Both of these views of culture have good points, but they also raise problems. We will move on now to look at the universalist and nationalist arguments in more detail. Then, we will go on to offer another possible way of thinking about culture. This way of thinking is at the centre of the academic field of **Cultural (or Social) Anthropology*** today.

The Universalist Position

In the mid-19th century, an English writer and **critic** called Matthew Arnold (1869) developed a view of culture that remains powerful in terms of its influence on education. In Arnold's view, culture is simply the best form of human thought, writing, music, and production. He saw culture as a set of ideas and products that could help humans reach **perfection**.

In short, the universalist view is that there are **universal** human rights and a set of universal ideas that we call culture, which define "**civilization**" and that humans everywhere will live in "sweetness and light" if only they organize themselves politically to promote these rights and ideas.

Problems With Universalism: High Culture/Low Culture

The idea that **individuals** can escape the limitations of the social positions they were born to by becoming "cultivated" is still powerful in many societies. Education is often believed to be the way to better one's social position. But this raises the question about what particular ideas and products should be included in the set that makes up "culture." For Arnold, this seemed to be very clear. For example, Shakespeare was known to be a great writer, so his works form part of "culture." Mozart and Beethoven were recognized as great musicians, so their works, too, form part of "culture." Plato's ideas, the art of Leonardo da Vinci, Michelangelo and Titian, all would, in Arnold's view, go together to form the necessary parts of "culture." But, even though the ideas and works included on this **list** are important, the list was limited, and this meant that other good ideas and works had to be left out because they were thought less important.

By the 1960s, critics such as Raymond Williams (1958) and the historian E. P. Thompson (1966) were questioning Arnold's view of culture. They claimed that this way of thinking about culture was keeping the divisions between people—the social class system—alive. They claimed that "High Culture," as explained by Arnold's ideas, was a form of knowledge controlled by members of society's **elites*** and used by them to hold onto their power and control. On the other hand, "Low Culture," or popular culture, belonged to the lower social classes and was used to keep them in a lower social position.

Sociologists and cultural critics began to question the systems of power in society that support such ideas of cultural value. Academics began to explain "culture" in what they believed to be a more inclusive, **democratic*** form, in ways that did not **discriminate** between the different 'values' usually given to different cultural products such as music and writing. However, even though universalism claims to support the basic equality of all humans, in practice, this way of viewing culture usually supports existing power systems in society.

The Nationalist Argument: Civilization or "Kultur"?

A **counter-movement*** arose in Europe, known as **Romantic Nationalism***. Romantic Nationalism put more **weight** on the importance of differences between groups of people. It claimed that some people shared certain properties, such as language, that made them basically different from other people. Such groups also shared social behaviors, histories, stories and cultural practices that were **unique**. These unique differences united such people as a group called "nations," and the histories, stories and cultural **practices** that marked them as unique formed their "**kultur**"* (the German word for culture). The nationalists also claimed that such groups should have the right to run their own political affairs in what became known as "nation-states."

"Culture," understood in this way, then becomes the property of national groups. Different nations became known by what people believed were special and basic cultural differences belonging only to those nations. In this way of thinking, culture becomes understood as a fixed set of properties and beliefs that "belong" to a nation.

Early Cultural Anthropology

Nationalists used the idea of culture to mean the particular beliefs and practices of unique national groups of people in order to give reasons for why nation-states should be made to represent those groups and protect what were believed to be the cultures their people were born with. This same idea of culture could also be applied to groups that did not necessarily have a state to represent them but were still, in some way, unique. Such ideas strongly influenced the early practice of what we now know as **Cultural (or Social) Anthropology***.

Early European academics in the field, such as Claude Levi-Strauss or Bronislaw Malinowski, **identified** different cultural groups around the world, making special note of groups that had not been in touch very much before, if at all, with the **industrialized*** nations of Europe and North America. The way of life of people in these "far off" societies was studied by anthropologists who looked at the different ways those people behaved and then looked again at those social **behaviors** that were also found in their own European societies that were considered to be the same in some way.

For example, important life **rituals***, such as marriages and funerals, were seen to be common to both so-called **primitive*** societies and the richer, "developed" societies from which the anthropologists came. These early anthropologists believed that if they could closely watch an event such as a marriage, for example, an event that they thought they understood, then they could uncover the differences in practice between different cultural groups. This would help them to learn about the different belief systems that influenced the way these rituals took place.

Although these early anthropologists believed that they were **treating** different cultures with respect, their ways of working had serious problems. One result of how they worked with different groups was that it strengthened the nationalist position, claiming that cultural differences resulted from differences that people were born with. By working in this way, they also supported the view that real culture was a fixed and unchanging set of ideas and practices. They did not allow for the historical or future development of culture. Cultures were seen as fixed and unchanging objects. These objects were thought to exist separately from human action or historical development.

Problems With the Nationalist Position

Learning from the cultural critics of the 1960s mentioned earlier, later cultural anthropologists such as Fredrick Barth (1969) claimed that culture should not be understood as a fixed set of knowledge, beliefs and practices that never change through time. Rather, a culture should be **defined** by the way the people themselves understand and live their lives.

If a culture changes over time is true, then it must also be true that a culture is not necessarily the property of one particular, unique group of people. Just because we notice differences in cultural behavior between different groups, we cannot say that those differences appeared because of **inherent** differences between people. Moreover, under different conditions, those differences will change or even disappear. From this point of view, culture is not a fixed, basic or necessary property of one group of people; it is a living thing that changes through time. Therefore, culture does not exist as something separate from those who live it. Instead, culture is something that humans make as they build their societies. This is a view of culture that is directly **opposed** to the view that nationalists hold.

Think, for example, of the **gender**, social class, generational or geographical differences that exist among any large group of individuals, even if they believe they share the same "national culture." Is it really possible to claim, for example, that a 16-year-old who was born and raised in modern day Tokyo is culturally the same as an 80-year-old farmer who has lived his or her whole life in Northern Japan? It seems very unlikely that they would be culturally the same in every way. Can we say that they share the very same national culture? Social anthropologists today would say that they would not.

Nationalists, who believe that culture is something we are born with, try to unite people only in the most general or **stereotypical** ways. But we know, from studying people in different parts of the same country, or even people from different age groups within the same country, that they do not share the same beliefs about their social worlds. Nor do they carry out their lives in the very same way.

Therefore, from the point of view of anthropologists, all large groups of people are in some sense **multicultural***. When we think of cultures in this way, our studies in cultural anthropology move away from looking closely at how people do things differently in different places and at different times to why people do things differently. To answer these "why" questions, one cannot simply reply, "They live like this because it is their culture." This way of thinking just goes around and around and, in the end, gets nowhere.

The idea of culture can be used to describe what people do and how they do it, but it cannot explain why people do or believe the things they do. To explain these "why" questions, we must study how historical, political, social, and psychological changes, as well as changes to laws, have developed over time and how these have led to changes in peoples' lives. We also need to try to understand the different forms of power that influence people.

Culturalism* as the New Racism

All people will, if they have the freedom to do so, follow the ways of daily life that they see around them and will learn the cultural practices of society. They will follow these practices according to their own **tastes** and the knowledge they have of the choices they can make.

Take Japan as an example; extreme nationalists might **criticize*** other Japanese people for accepting new "foreign" cultural practices, such as buying **chocolates*** for **Valentine's Day***, or celebrating **Christmas Eve***. In the past, Japanese nationalists criticized people for being un-Japanese if they followed Western styles of dress or hairstyle, but today, except for a very small number of people with extreme nationalist views, such concerns have largely been forgotten. Today, most Japanese people enjoy the new ideas, fashions and tastes that come from outside Japan, just as many people in foreign countries enjoy Japanese culture.

Unfortunately, the kind of cultural nationalism that views cultures as unique, fixed objects that exist separately from time and space, can easily become the source of discrimination. This is particularly true if culture is believed to reflect the "true" **identity** of a nation. In fact, if the **defining** culture of the nation is understood as being fixed in time and space, and if this fixed culture is viewed as the essential "soul" of the nation, then the idea of multiculturalism may be seen as a **threat** to the very existence of that nation and its unique culture. Unfortunately, this view of national culture continues to have a strong influence on social planning within many countries and also plays a part in international politics today, even though cultural anthropologists, who are specialists in this field, can show there are problems with this way of thinking. Cultural anthropologists try to show, through their scientific studies, what the true nature of culture is and what human beings are really like so that people everywhere may live better lives.

Why Study Social Anthropology?

The systematic study of why people believe what they believe is basic to understanding our own lives; however, we should not be happy just to have simple answers to our questions. We need to use knowledge from many academic fields to properly understand the relationships between the ideas of the "individual," "culture" and "society" to make the world a better place for everyone. Studying Social Anthropology, as one of the fields within Liberal Arts will give you a strong, scientific and fact-based way to understand many of the difficult problems that you may face in your personal or working life, or in your larger lives as a member of human society generally.

A background in Social Anthropology provides a strong basis for employment in any field in which you have to think of new ways to solve difficult problems. Whether you become an academic, a teacher, a social worker, an international business person, or work for an NGO*, having an understanding of Social Anthropology will also help you to better understand the people you live and work with, those within your own cultural groups, as well as those who at times seem different from ourselves, with whom we share our wider world.

Adapted from a text by Julian Manning, PhD (Social Anthropology)
Professor of English and Social and Cultural studies
Nihon University College of Art
Japan

Vocabulary

Words From the Second 1,000 General Service Word List

Alive	International
Behavior	List
Century	Opposed
Ceremony	Perfection
Civilization	Practice
Critics	Solve
Cultivation	Tastes
Education	Threat
Extreme	Treating
Fashion	Universal
Funerals	Weight
Hair	

Words From the Academic Word List

Academic
Culture
Define
Discriminate
Gender
Identity

Individual
Inherent
Neutral
Psychological
Style(s)

Glossary

Chocolates (Noun, plural): A sweet type of candy made from the cacao plant.

Christmas Eve: The night before Christmas Day, the festival to remember the birth of Jesus. 24th December.

Counter-movement: A social movement in opposition to an earlier movement.

Criticize (verb): To judge someone in a negative way.

Cultural (or Social) Anthropology: The study of human culture and society.

Culturalism: The belief that culture is the central force that organizes and controls peoples' lives.

Democratic (Adjective): A system of government in which the people freely choose their leaders.

Elites (Noun, plural): Groups of people with power and privilege in society, usually those who are wealthy or who hold high social positions. Upper classes.

Gender (Noun): Either of the sexes. May also refer to one's sexual identity.

Geography: The study of the physical landscape and its relationship with humans.

Imperialism/Imperialists: The idea that a country has the right to expand its territory and take control of other countries.

Industrialized (Adjective): Relates to a type of society that relies on the production of goods, usually with the use of machines rather than agriculture.

Kultur (Noun): The German word for "culture."

Liberal Arts (Noun phrase): A field of academic study grounded in rational thought, including humanities, social and physical sciences, and mathematics.

Multicultural/multiculturalism (Adjective/Noun): the idea of people of many cultures living together in one setting.

Nationalism/Nationalists: The idea that one owes primary loyalty to one's own nation-state, which should be politically independent of other nations. Also, the idea is that the interests of one's nation-state take priority over the interests of other nation-states, even when this goes against the well-being of another nation-state.

NGO (Acronym): Non-Governmental Organization. These organizations are independent of governments and are not run to make a profit. Their goal is usually to try to help people in need.

Primitive (Adjective): Simple or in the early stages of development. Over time, this word has developed a negative connotation and is no longer used by anthropologists to describe people living outside the so-called developed world.

Rituals (Noun, plural): Formal ceremonies or actions that are repeated on given occasions and follow a set pattern. Often related to religion or important life events.

Romantic Nationalism: The idea that the nation-state gets its right to exist from the unity of the common people who belong to it rather than having power exercised from the top down (by a king or queen or emperor, for example).

Stereotypical (Adjective): Relating to a widely held but overly-simplified view of certain types of people. Often, these views are inaccurate.

Universalism/Universalists: The idea that some ideas about human culture apply to all human beings no matter in which social or cultural setting they exist.

Valentine's Day: A day to celebrate love. 14 February.

References

Arnold, M. (1869). *Culture and anarchy*. Oxford University Press.
Barth, F. (Ed.). (1969). *Ethnic groups and boundaries*. Allen and Unwin.
Thompson, E. P. (1966). *The making of the English working class*. Random House.
Williams, R. (1958/1985). *Culture is ordinary*. Chatto and Windus. Keywords: A Vocabulary of Culture and Society. Rev. Ed. New York: Oxford University Press.

Additional Reading

Benedict, R. (1946). *The Chrysanthemum and the sword: Patterns of Japanese culture*. Houghton Mifflin.

CHAPTER 18

LINGUISTICS: HOW DOES LANGUAGE WORK?

Clay Williams
Akita International University, Japan

Introduction

Language is one of the most basic things there is to being human. No matter where humans live, from the forests to the high mountains, from the desert to big cities, all people everywhere use language. Almost every child learns to speak and understand the language(s) of their surrounding **community**, and if the child can't hear, language even flows out from their hands in the form of signs. Language is important to **virtually** everything we do; it is at the center of human **identity**. To study language is to study **humanity***itself, and **linguistics*** is the study of language.

What Does it Mean to Study Language?

Let's **clarify** what is meant when we talk about studying language. Most of us have been in foreign language classes where we try to learn another language. But this is not really what the **focus** of the study of language (or linguistics) is all about. Although the study of linguistics has indeed heavily influenced teaching and learning **methods** in our foreign language classes today, linguistics, as a field of study, is something different. Linguistics, instead, looks at language **abstractly**. It doesn't simply look at the **vocabulary*** and rules of a particular language. Rather, linguistics **seeks** to find the **commonalities*** between all languages, and tries to find the limits of what is a possible human language.

It wasn't always so, however. Languages have been taught and studied since ancient times; there was little thought given to any relationships between languages and any related linguistic **features**. In the past, teachers were more interested in what either helped or **hindered** students to make progress in language learning.

One of the first **major revolutions** in the study of language was the discovery of language families which went far beyond closely related groups (e.g., languages such as Hindi and Farsi are distant **cousins** of English and French). This discovery is believed to have been made by Sir Williams Jones in the late 18th **century**. From the late 19th century there was a strong **push** towards a more scientific study of language which mostly focused on how to **improve classroom*** learning.

For the first half of the 20th century linguistics was heavily influenced by **behaviorism***, a scientific view which held that language was a **collection** of **habits** which could be **reinforced**, either **positively** (+) or **negatively** (−), through a person's experience. These ways of making a habit stronger are called positive **reinforcement*** and negative reinforcement*. In this way of thinking, for example, if a child says something that sounds like "**cookie***," and Mom gives the child a cookie, the child experiences positive reinforcement and will relate the word "cookie" with getting a cookie.

On the other hand, if the child says something bad and is **punished**, this is negative reinforcement which involves something unpleasant happening that the child does not like. Behaviorism says that this kind of negative reinforcement should make the child less likely to say bad words in the future.

The idea that language is formed through experience also led to some related **hypotheses**. For example, in 1929, a Linguist called Edward Sapir said that he believed that language itself actually **defines** how we **perceive** and **categorize*** our experience. To put Sapir's **argument** simply, he thought if an idea doesn't exist in your language, you can't really understand it (e.g., Sapir claimed that Hopi Indians, whose language did not use expressions to mark time, perceived time in a completely different way from other people who speak other languages). **Initially** all of these claims were accepted; however, there would soon come a discovery which would completely change all **previous assumptions** about how humans learn and use language.

In a 1959 book **review**, the famous linguist Noam Chomsky started a major revolution in the field of linguistics that completely changed our way of thinking about language. He pointed out that behaviorism could not explain human language ability. Chomsky's arguments were quite simple. He noted that (1) children often say things that they have never heard **adults** say (e.g., "I goed to school"); (2) the **input** that children receive from adults isn't **uniform** or completely clear; (3) children still learn to speak and understand the language they are surrounded by, and they can do this rather well by the time they are around 5–6 years of age. This happens for children who are learning to speak in all languages. In other words, which language they are learning doesn't matter.

All of these points seemed to **indicate** that language is something we are born with, and that we already have different kinds of "knowledge" about language already **programmed** into our **brains**. This does not mean that we are born knowing a language already, but rather, that when we are born, because we have a human brain, we already "know" some things about language. Chomsky said that it is this inner knowledge that helps young children to figure out the rules that control the language(s) in their own **environment**. For example, Chomsky suggested that **babies** are born knowing what possible speech sounds would be, as well as having an idea of **universal** (common to everyone) **concepts** about **grammar** such as subjects, objects, and **verbs**.

This change to our understanding of language, seeing it as a human ability that we are born with, also **shifted** our understanding about many earlier ideas that were based on behaviorism, such as the hypothesis of Edward Sapir. If language knowledge is something we are born with, then our ability to perceive and organize our experiences is not **tied** to language. Instead, limits to the way we use language would be related to the way we, as human beings, perceive and experience the world. This idea of human **perception** was supported by further study (e.g., the Hopi Indians do indeed perceive time **similarly** to people in the rest of the world but they just don't describe it the way it is described in other languages).

However, a **weak** form of Sapir's ideas still exists. This "weak" view claims that, rather than limiting our perception, languages do still have some influence on our **behavior**, as well as sometimes **restricting** what kind of **information** can be given. For example, in English, when you say "my cousin" people don't know whether your cousin is a man or a woman. The English language, in this expression, does not give you this information. However, if you were speaking in the French language, for example, the words themselves would **reflect** the **sex** of the person. You would have to say "mon cousin" for a man, and "ma cousine" for a woman. Because of the way the French language works you have no **alternative**, when speaking French, but to **reveal** that your cousin is either a man or a woman.

The discovery that language is something we are born with **contributes** greatly to our understanding of ourselves as humans, but we did not stop there. Linguists continue to work hard to learn even more about both how language works and how we use it. People today are re-**examining** and questioning many of Chomsky's ideas, and coming up with new explanations for the way we learn language. As time passes, and the more that linguists learn, the more we have to think again about our past ideas and test them against new information.

More About the Field of Linguistics

As language **affects** almost every **aspect** of human existence, the field of linguistics is therefore **enormous** in **scope**. For this reason, the field is divided into a large number of smaller fields (called **subfields***) which **enable** scientists to focus on the smaller parts of the larger **issue** of language. For example, Historical **Linguists*** look at how languages change over time and **investigate** where languages came from and the relationships between **specific** languages. **Psycholinguists*** and **Neurolinguists*** study how language is stored, **retrieved**, understood, and produced in the mind. On the other hand, **Sociolinguists*** study how language is used in social groups. **Ultimately**, all of these questions come down to the big issues which, **slowly** but surely, linguists are trying to answer: (1) How did language ability develop in the human **species***? (2) How do we learn language? (3) How do we use language?

Why Study Linguistics?

It's easy to see how linguistics would be important to the study of foreign languages (and indeed it is!). However, the types of real-world work applications in the field of Linguistics are **practically** without limit. For example, linguists work as **consultants** for **Hollywood* movies***. Any movie **involving** real, foreign or even made-up languages will often make use of a linguistics consultant. Linguists also work on developing **translation software*** and **artificial intelligence*** (AI) applications. They work as speech **therapists***, **editors***, and speech writers. **Police** departments will sometimes even **contract forensic*** linguists who study speech and writing **samples** to find out who **committed crimes**!

As the world becomes more **connected** in the modern, **digital*** age, the importance of linguistic study will only increase. While products that use **automatic translation software*** may reduce the importance of foreign language study to some extent (at least, for trade and **diplomacy*** purposes), Ultimately, linguistics will still remain an important field. This is because linguistics is not specific to understanding any one language, but rather, the whole system of knowledge by which all humans are connected. In fact, in some very useful ways, linguists will be the people **creating** the **innovations** which will better enable humans to **communicate** even more effectively. While that may negatively affect some **professions** (e.g., language teachers), it may also **create entirely** new **economic sectors** and related fields of work (e.g., **multilingual programming***).

To **conclude**, the "big questions" of linguistics that you read about earlier here, are still not even close to being answered. In the future, it is likely that we will see increasing number of people working together across all fields of learning and **research**; linguists, **historians, economists, sociologists,** and **philosophers*,** for example to try to find answers to these questions. This sharing of research is because of our growing understanding that language is a **key** part of what it means to be human, and that so much of human activity is influenced by the language in which it takes place. By studying linguistics, at a **Liberal Arts** university for example, you too, could become a part of this **exciting** world of learning and sharing.

Adapted from a text by Clay Williams PhD
Professor, Global Communication and Language English Language Teaching Practices
Akita International University
Japan

Vocabulary

Words From the Second 1,000 General Service High Frequency Word List

argument	entirely
babies	examining
behavior	exciting
brains	grammar
century	habits
collection	hindered
connected	improve
cousins	information
crimes	key

police
practically
professions
programmed punished
push
reflect
(book) review
samples

slowly
tied
translation
universal
verbs
weak

Words From the Academic Word List

abstractly
adults
affects
alternative
aspect
assumptions
automatic categorize
clarify
committed communicate
community
concepts
conclude
consultants
contract
contributes
create
creating
defines
economic
enable
enormous
environment
features
focus
hypotheses
identity
indicate
initially
innovations

input
investigate
involving
issue
intelligence
major
methods
negatively
perceive
perception
positive
positively
previous
reinforced
reinforcement
research
restricting
reveal
revolutions
sectors
scope
seeks
sex
shifted
similarly
specific
ultimately
uniform
virtually

Glossary

It is not necessary for learners to memorize these words and expressions.

Artificial Intelligence (AI) (Noun phrase): A term used to describe the ability of computers to perform difficult tasks that normally only humans can do, such as thinking, problem solving and learning. Sometimes called machine intelligence.

Behaviorism (Noun): A branch of Psychology that claims that all human behavior is learned from the environment. Retrieved from https://www.simplypsychology.org/behaviorism.html

Categorize (Verb): to organize and classify into a category or categories.

Classroom (Noun): a room in a school or university in which teaching and learning take place.

Commonalities (Noun): a commonality is a shared feature between two or more things.

Cookie (Noun): a North American English word for a small sweet snack. Often round in shape.

Digital (Adjective): refers to the use of electronic information.

Diplomacy (Noun): the field of international relations.

Editors (Noun): an editor is a specialist who corrects and refines written text, usually for the purpose of publication.

Forensic (Adjective): the application of scientific methods and techniques to the investigation of something. For eg. a forensic linguist.

Hollywood: a famous place in the city of Los Angeles in the USA where movies are produced.

Humanity (Noun): the totality of the human race, all people.

Liberal Arts (Noun phrase): "Liberal arts is a field of study based on rational thinking, and it includes the areas of humanities, social and physical sciences, and mathematics. A liberal arts education emphasizes the development of critical thinking … the ability to solve complex problems, and an understanding of ethics and morality, as well as a desire to continue to learn." Retrieved from https://www.thoughtco.com/liberal-arts-definition-4585053

Linguists/linguistics (Nouns): Linguists scholars who study language. Linguistics = the field of the study of Language.

Movies (Noun): a movie is a moving picture, usually lasting for an extended period of time, that tells a story. Sometimes called a film.

Multilingual programming (Noun phrase): building computer software that can be used in many languages.

Neurolinguists (Noun): a neurolinguist is a specialist trained in neuroscience and linguistics who researches brain function during language use.

Positive/negative reinforcement (Noun phrases): positive reinforcement the act of giving a reward or pleasant outcome, in order to strengthen a desired behavior. Negative reinforcement = the act of punishing, or causing something unpleasant to happen, in order to achieve a desired behavior.

(To) Program (Verb): to have instructions put into something to make it work a certain way.

Psycholinguists (Noun): a psycholinguist is a specialist who researches the psychological functioning of language.

Retrieve (Verb): information recall from one's memory.

Sociolinguists (Noun): a sociolinguist is a specialist who researches how language is affected by social and cultural elements.

Software (Noun): programs that run and operate on a computer or digital device.

Species (Noun): a group of living beings able to produce more of its own kind.

Speech therapists (Noun): a speech therapist is a specialist educated in the study of human communication, its development, and its disorders. They assess speech, language, cognitive-communication, and oral/feeding/swallowing skills. This lets them identify a problem and the best way to treat it. Retrieved from https://kidshealth.org/en/parents/speech-therapy.html

Speech writers (Noun): a speechwriter is a person who is hired to prepare and write speeches that will be delivered by another person. Speechwriters are employed by many senior-level elected officials and executives in the government and private sectors. Retrieved from https://en.wikipedia.org/wiki/Speechwriter

Subfields (Noun): a subfield is a smaller branch within a larger field of study.

Translation software (Noun phrase): computer programs/software that can change one language into another.

Vocabulary (Noun): the body or group of words that belong to a particular language.

Learning activity: Find out what each of these jobs involves....
People who study the different branches of Linguistics
Historical Linguist, Psycholinguist, Neurolinguist, Sociolinguist, Forensic Linguist
People who work in other fields
Historian, Economist, Sociologist, Philosopher, Therapist/Speech therapist, Editor, Speech writer

CHAPTER 19

DEVELOPMENT ECONOMICS

Hideyuki Nakagawa
Akita International University, Japan

Introduction

In 2016, Japanese workers **earned,** on average, **approximately** 4.2 million Yen (figures from The World Bank, 2018). How much do you think people in *sub-Saharan Africa** earn, on average, in a year? The answer is only 160,000 Yen. Of course, we need to consider that there are many reasons for the difference when we **compare** these two numbers, for example, the different price levels in different countries. However, we can safely say that the average population in sub-Saharan African countries is much poorer than those in developed countries, such as Japan for example.

This poverty is caused by many **issues** in daily life: some children have to go to work from the age of ten to help their families instead of going to school; mothers cannot take their **babies** to see a doctor due to **insufficient income**, and sometimes there are no clinics at all within walking distance. At the same time, these problems also **reinforce** poverty because they stop people from having future opportunities to earn more money and get out of poverty.

People who have an interest in these issues often study Development **Economics**. Development Economics is the subject that helps us to better understand the existence of poverty in developing countries. In this subject, students are likely to think about questions such as "Why is poverty so common in Africa?" or "As members of a **global** society, what can developed countries do for these developing countries?" or "What kinds of efforts can reduce poverty most effectively?" These are some of the interesting questions which are studied in the field of Development Economics.

History of Development Economics

The study of Development Economics dates back to the 1950s and 1960s when many former colonies in the third world declared their independence (e.g., 17 countries in Africa became independent in 1960). Before the beginning of Development Economics, many **academic** and political leaders shared the idea that people in developing countries were poor because they were **lazy** and were not ready to become part of the developed *capitalist** world, which values hard work and saving money.

However, early Development Economists such as Theodore Schultz introduced the economic idea of *rationality** into the study of development. This term expresses the idea that people make well-reasoned decisions no matter where they are. Schultz believed that people in poor countries think and make decisions in very much the same way as people in developed countries do, but their surrounding **environments** are simply very different (Schultz, 1964). He suggested that we should help such underdeveloped countries by giving them foreign **aid** and, along with the efforts of their native peoples, this would help to **improve** their quality of life. Shultz's ideas changed people's bad opinions of *underdevelopment** towards a more **positive** view.

Development Economics and the United Nations

In 2000, *the United Nations** set eight big **goals** for development that they hoped to reach by 2015: (1) to do away with **extreme** poverty and **hunger**; (2) to provide *elementary education** for all children; (3) to work for equality between men and women, and give more power to women; (4) to reduce the number of children who die; (5) to improve the **health** of mothers); (6) to fight against *HIV/AIDS**, *malaria**, and other **diseases**; (7) to make sure plans for *environmental sustainability**; and (8) to develop a *global partnership** for development. The *OECD** countries agreed to provide enough money to aid agencies such as the World Bank, the **International** *Monetary Fund**, Asia Development Bank, and African Development Bank in order to reach all eight goals.

It is interesting to note that by 2015 it was almost fifty years after Schultz first suggested his ideas. Has this effort to reduce poverty been successful? This question leads us to an answer with many parts to it. At least the number of people in poverty has been reduced to some degree, and studies show us that the number of people living in extreme poverty has clearly gone down. In 1990, nearly half of the population in the developing world lived on less than $1.25 a day; that dropped to 14% in 2015 (The United Nations, 2015, p. 4). However, poverty still exists in many places. So how can Development Economists help fight against poverty?

Since 2015, much foreign aid has been spent on providing a better environment for the poor. For example, if the farmers in Sub-Saharan Africa suffer from the changing *climatic conditions**, which are bad for farming activities, international aid agencies can plan new **insurance** systems to cover food **crop** failures due to bad **weather**. If there are not enough opportunities for children to be **educated**, **governments** can be given the things they need to help them with large **projects** that are needed, such as building schools.

Recent efforts in development economics have looked more at the effectiveness of aid projects to see if they are working the way they should be working. There are many different ways to spend the money that has been given to fight against poverty. In education, for example, building schools and paying teachers money so that they come to class rather than taking a second **job** to support their families may be effective. (In some cases, it is not students who are not showing up for class, but the teachers!). Other efforts include giving money to poor families in exchange for making sure that their children go to school each day rather than work in *sweatshops**.

Of course, other kinds of aid are also needed. For example, many projects try to improve the health of poor families, or protect the environment, fight against corruption, and so forth. However, we are limited in what we can do. We must spend the limited amount of money that we have for these projects as wisely as possible. To do so, we need to know what kinds of projects are most effective in reducing poverty. For example, one particular project may cost US $1,000 to reach the same result as another project that may cost only US $100.

Checking on the effectiveness of projects is largely done through something called a *randomized controlled trial (RCT)**. RCT is like a science experiment—we divide the *households** or single **individuals** in the study into two groups: a **treatment** group, which receives an aid **program**, and a control group which does not receive any help. Then we measure the effect of the aid program by comparing treatment and control groups. Doing so helps us to know if it is the aid program that is helping us reach the goals we have set or if something else is possibly influencing the groups were are working with. Today, this kind of checking on effectiveness within the aid programs is increasing. Next, you will read about two examples, one in India and the other in Indonesia.

What Is a Better Way to Fight Against Poverty?

In recent years, government officials in the Indian state of Andhra Pradesh have worked hard to check the effectiveness of their aid programs to their elementary schools. They have been looking for the answer to an important question. If a government spends the same amount of money on two different **methods**, which one improves the results of school children the most, providing school supplies such as **pens** and **notebooks**, or paying more money to teachers who do a better job of improving the standard of students' learning? These questions were the basis of a study by two Indian specialists, Muralidharan and Sundararaman (2011).

Answering this question in detail is rather difficult because schools are all different, and you cannot directly compare one school that gets a *subsidy** (or aid) for more school supplies with another school that receives a subsidy for teacher *incentives** (aid money helps to keep its teachers in the *classroom**). To **solve** this problem, Muralidharan and Sundararaman introduced a *randomized experiment**, which is a common way of working in *medical research**. By putting the schools in either a control group or a treatment group (the treatment group being the schools which get the subsidy for more school supplies or one for teacher incentives), they compared the change in the students' results between groups. Muralidharan and Sundararaman found that students' test results improved greatly in both types of schools which received subsidies compared to the schools (in the control group) which did not. They also found that schools with a teacher incentive program had better results than schools that received a subsidy to buy more school supplies. The findings of their study are important to those who give international aid, as it shows that it is not enough just to give money to schools for items such as pens and notebooks if we want students to have better results.

Another example is from Indonesia. In the mid-1990s, Indonesian business owners and people who were starting new businesses wanted better *transportation infrastructures** such as new roads, particularly in places far from the cities. However, there was always a problem with *corruption** in road-building projects because public officials always took some of the aid money for the project for themselves.

The government was looking for a way to solve this problem and reduce the amount of corruption that was taking place. They came up with two possible ideas: *auditing** (that is, checking the use of money by looking at project records) more often by higher-level government officials and having more local people take part in following what was happening as the projects were taking place.

To find which methods reduced corruption more effectively, Olken (2007) put villages into three groups, one control and two treatment groups. The next step was to check how big the problem of corruption was by checking the difference between the official amount spent on the road with a separate **estimate** by **engineers** of what the road would really cost to build. Olken found that when there was more official auditing of the project records, project spending was less. Studies by Development Economists such as these help us to put aid money towards the projects that need it the most and to spend it in more effective ways.

Why Study Development Economics?

I believe that many people, if not all, have **warm** hearts and care about the lives of others who are in need. If the readers of this book want to take action to fight poverty but do not know how then Development Economics is one of the fields to study in the future. Studying Development Economics can help us understand the forces that drive human **behavior**. It is important to understand these behaviors and forces because they are the best ways to help us think about how effective government plans and aid programs are likely to be. Also, using RCTs in order to understand the effects of aid programs has helped us have a better understanding of what governments really need to do to fight against poverty. Today, many well-**qualified** people who hold a PhD in Development Economics join international aid agencies such as the World Bank and other development banks to plan and carry out aid programs. NGOs also want to know about the results of studies done by well-qualified people who work in the field of Development Economics so they can plan their programs.

We are still far from having a full understanding of how to reduce poverty and its effects on the lives of people in need. However, as time goes by, more and more people, who want to change the world in a fair way, will find the directions we need to take to do so. Perhaps, as a student of Development Economics, and then later, as a worker in this field, you might be one of those people.

Adapted from a text by Hideyuki Nakagawa, PhD.
Associate Professor, Development Economics and Applied Microeconomics
Akita International University
Japan

Vocabulary

Words From the Second 1,000 General Service High Frequency Word List

babies	hunger
behaviors	improve
checking	insurance
compare	international
crop	lazy
diseases	pens
earn	program
educated/education	(well-) qualified
engineers	solve
extreme	treatment
government(s)	warm
health	weather

Words From the Academic Word List

academic(s)	goals
aid	individuals
approximately	income
economic	insufficient
economics/economists	issues
environment/environmental	method(s)
estimate	positive
financial	project
global	research

Glossary

It is not necessary for learners to memorize these words and expressions.

Auditing (Verb): Making an official check of financial records.

Capitalist (Noun): Someone who uses their money to make more money through trade and industry.

Classroom (Noun): A room in a school where children work together in a group with a teacher.

Climatic conditions (Noun phrase): Different conditions caused by the climate, eg. wind, rain, temperature, snow etc.

Corruption (Noun): Behavior that is not honest by people in a position of trust. Usually involves money.

Elementary education (Noun phrase): The first level of formal school education.

Environmental sustainability (Noun phrase): The rate of use of environmental resources is not higher than the rate of their use, meaning the environment is not damaged.

Global partnership (Noun phrase): When countries, businesses and organizations from around the world agree to work together.

Household (Noun): A house and the people who live in it; considered as a unit.

Incentive (Noun): Something positive that motivates someone to do something, eg. the promise of higher pay.

Medical research (Noun phrase): Studies in the field of medicine and disease.

Notebooks (Noun, plural): Small books with blank pages in which school children write, draw or calculate.

Randomized controlled trial (RCT)/Randomized experiment (Noun phrase): Studies or experiments in which people are chosen by chance to take part in a research project. Some people are put into a treatment group, while others are put into a control group. The treatment group experiences different conditions, while the control group does not experience any special treatment.

Rationality (Noun): In the field of Economics, this refers to the idea that people make well-reasoned life choices, no matter whether they live in a developed or underdeveloped country.

Sub-Saharan Africa: The name given to the parts of Africa which are south of the Sahara Desert.

Subsidy (Noun): An amount of money given by the government to help support someone in business to keep their prices affordable.

Sweatshops (Noun, plural): Factories or places of work where the workers are forced to work long hours for very low pay, usually in bad conditions.

Transportation infrastructures (Noun phrase): The physical framework that is used to build our system of travel, eg. roads, bridges, railways, air and sea ports.

Underdevelopment (Noun): A condition of being poor and having a low standard of living with bad living conditions and little health care and few opportunities for education.

Diseases

HIV/AIDS: Human Immunodeficiency Virus infection and Acquired Immune Deficiency Syndrome. Serious range of conditions spread by contact with infected body fluids.

Malaria: A serious disease spread by small insects called mosquitoes.

References

Muralidharan, K., & Sundararaman, V. (2011). Teacher performance pay: Experimental evidence from India. *Journal of Political Economy, 119*(1), 39–77. https://doi.org/10.1086/659655

Olken, B. A. (2007). Monitoring corruption: Evidence from a field experiment in Indonesia. *Journal of Political Economy, 115*, 200–249. https://doi.org/10.1086/517935

Schultz, T. W. (1964). *Transforming traditional agriculture.* Yale University Press.

The United Nations. *The millennium development goals report 2015.* United Nations, (2015). http://www.un.org/millenniumgoals/2015_MDG_Report/pdf/MDG%202015%20rev%20(July%201).pdf. Accessed June 10, 2018

The World Bank. (2018). *World development indicators.* The World Bank. https://data.worldbank.org/indicator/NY.GDP.PCAP.CD. Accessed June 10, 2018

CHAPTER 20

MARKETING

Tomas Nilsson
Linnaeus University, Sweden

Marketing—Something We All Know Much About

This **chapter** is about something familiar to you, but perhaps without knowing it. For a start, think of a product you have bought recently. Let us **imagine** it was something you wear. Then ask yourself why you bought it. Was it because you were cold and could buy anything that made you warm? Or was it because you wanted the same outfit as your friends? Or did your parents decide what to buy, and you did not really want it? The answers to these questions are very important when you work with *marketing*. If a company selling clothes knows where, when and why people, or *consumers*, buy what they buy, then they are able to **design**, **distribute** and **promote** the **exact items** the consumers need and want.

Every day, you **encounter** hundreds or even thousands of **commercial messages** when watching TV, listening to the radio or **interacting** on social **media**. All these are examples of marketing activities **aimed** to make you like and buy a particular brand. However, as the examples above **illustrate**, marketing includes much more than "telling and selling." A *marketing manager* must understand what the **potential customers** need and want and then design and **communicate** a marketing offering that delivers superior value to the customers, with the purpose of building profitable and long-term relationships with these customers. In our modern society, where consumers' desire for products changes faster and faster, marketing has become increasingly important for all companies around the world.

History of Marketing

Although the **practice** of designing, manufacturing, distributing and selling goods and services has been around for thousands of years, **theories** about marketing did not **evolve** until the mid-twentieth **century**. One of the earliest and most influential schools of marketing thinking addressed the managerial **aspects** of marketing, asking the **fundamental** question: how should organizations market their product and services? The answer to this question was presented in terms of a "marketing **mix**." The mix **consisted** of **elements** the marketing manager should consider when deciding what **overall** "stimulus" should be used to get the wanted "**response**" from the market. The stimulus was the marketing mix, and the wanted response was an exchange of money for a product or service.

In the book *Basic Marketing: A Managerial **Approach***, (Kotler, 1967; McCarthy, 1960), Jerome McCarthy set the standard for every textbook on marketing management that would come after by **summing** up the marketing mix in a four P's mnemonic: *Product, Price, Promotion* and *Place.* The formation of these 4Ps changed the whole idea of marketing. Rather than just being examples of elements to consider when approaching a particular part of a market (a *segment*), the 4Ps came to **define** what marketing is all about. It is developing a product that **satisfies** customers' needs, **calculating** the optimal price for that product, distributing it efficiently, and **launching*** promotional campaigns to influence the customers' desire to buy.

While McCarthy **focused exclusively** on a business **context**, Philip Kotler later argued that the 4P was a marketing **technique** applicable to all organizations (and even **individuals**) regardless of whether they were for-profit or nonprofit organizations. In a way, Kotler was the better marketer of marketing. Kotler's book *Marketing Management: Analysis, Planning and Control*, became *the* marketing book every marketing student had to read (and is still reading in new **editions**), and Kotler is today often seen, not completely **accurately** though, as *the* **founder** of marketing.

However, the increased focus on services in the 1990s came with **consequences** for "4P marketing." The Ps were difficult to apply to services because services, such as firework **displays**, are activities, not products, which, among other things, led to a widened understanding of what a product is and an **insight** into the importance of *Place* as a space for the **consumption** of experiences. This, in turn, led to a multitude of new definitions of marketing, for example, service marketing, relationship marketing, **interactive** marketing, and experience marketing. Then again, in **contemporary** textbooks on marketing management, most of these aspects are included under some P or another, which leads to the overall **conclusion** that the marketing management **perspective** introduced in the 1960s is still fairly intact.

Contemporary Marketing Challenges

Even if marketing **education** has not changed much in the last **decades,** the very condition for marketing has. The digitalization and **globalization** of society have **dramatically** changed how we communicate, what products and services we consume, and how we live our daily lives. This is something that contemporary marketing managers have to consider when **formulating** and **implementing** marketing **strategies**.

Since more and more interaction between companies and consumers—and consumer-to-consumer—takes place on the internet, it is very easy to **identify** and **track** consumers and learn the details about their buying **behavior** no matter where they are in the world. Besides, suppose the company knows about the consumers and what social media consumers use. In that case, they are able to **invest** in promotion activities in the right media to reach the consumers they find most profitable. On the other hand, today it is very easy for a consumer to **compare** different offerings and choose the **cheapest** with a simple click. If they are **dissatisfied**, they can speak out about it on social media, and **suddenly**, thousands of potential customers are **reluctant** to buy from you. This form of consumer power is an example of the new situation that contemporary marketers have to deal with. This calls for new forms of marketing, and a **reorientation** of old marketing **models**.

Contemporary marketing focuses on value **creation** and customer relationships rather than **satisfying** customer needs a little better than the competitors. Still, marketing is a competitive game. The value a company promises to **deliver** by means of the 4Ps—the so-called *value proposition*—must be different and more **attractive** than the competitors' offerings on common **target** markets and be possible to communicate.

In a more globalized **economy**, where social media dramatically changes how we interact, *branding* is becoming more important. Brands are not just names and **symbols** representing a product, service or organization. They are the **essence** of a consumer's thoughts and feelings about a **specific** value proposition. If brands are managed well, they become *the* **key** asset for a company for years and even centuries. Therefore, brand strategies are now a central part of every company's overall marketing strategy.

A marketing strategy has to cover all aspects and decisions that influence a company's long-term growth in a market. Marketers need to engage in strategic planning to accomplish a fit between the company's objectives and **capabilities** and the **rapidly** changing market, which starts by getting in-depth knowledge about the consumers' behavior, thoughts and feelings.

What Kinds of People Are Attracted to Studying Marketing?

Individuals drawn to the marketing field are creative thinkers who relish the **task** of **generating innovative** ideas for **advertising** campaigns and promotional efforts. Moreover, they **exhibit** a knack for deciphering **data** and discerning consumer **preferences** and **trends, enabling** them to **extract** valuable insights.

Effective communication **skills** are a **hallmark*** of marketing **professionals**, as they must **engage*** with **diverse audiences** and **adeptly*** **convey*** messages. Among this group, some have **entrepreneurial*** **aspirations***, viewing marketing as a vehicle for launching and their own businesses. They are often **fascinated*** by human **psychology** and **excel*** in **roles** related to understanding consumer behavior, managing customer relations, and **driving*** sales.

Adaptability is a valued trait within marketing due to the ever-evolving nature of the industry, particularly in the digital landscape. Tech-savvy individuals adept at navigating digital **tools** and platforms often find themselves well-**suited** to the evolving demands of marketing. Marketers also **frequently** exhibit a deep **appreciation** for brands, **seeking** to shape and **reinforce** brand identities. Others are driven by a strong sense of social **responsibility** and choose to work in nonprofit organizations.

Moreover, marketing professionals are characterized by their **ambition, goal-oriented** nature, and a strong work **ethic**, consistently setting and striving to **achieve** ambitious targets. In essence, they are a **dynamic** people passionate about forging **connections** with others, promoting products or causes, and leveraging their creative and analytical skills to drive success. Whether through captivating advertising campaigns, insightful market **research**, or strategic brand development, they play a pivotal **role** in influencing the popularity of products and ideas.

Careers in Marketing

If you're considering a career in marketing, you're entering a dynamic and ever-evolving field with a wide **range** of employment opportunities. Marketing professionals are in high demand across various industries, and here's a glimpse of the potential career **paths** and job prospects awaiting those who study marketing.

1. Marketing Manager: Marketing managers play a **crucial** role in planning and executing marketing campaigns. They are responsible for developing strategies, managing budgets, and overseeing **teams** to achieve marketing objectives. With experience and **expertise**, you can climb the **corporate ladder*** to become a Chief Marketing Officer (CMO).
2. Market Research Analyst: Market research analysts gather and **analyze** data to help organizations understand consumer behavior, market trends, and competitors. They provide valuable insights that guide marketing decisions, making this role **essential** in any industry.
3. Advertising Executive: Advertising executives work for advertising agencies, where they create and **implement** advertising campaigns for clients. They collaborate with creative teams to design advertisements, **select** media **channels**, and measure campaign effectiveness.
4. Social Media Manager: With the rise of social media, companies are **eager** to **hire** professionals who can manage their online presence. Social media managers create and curate content, engage with followers, and **monitor** social media **performance.**
5. Content Marketing Specialist: Content marketing specialists **focus** on creating valuable and **relevant** content to attract and **retain** customers. They write blog posts, create videos, and develop other content types that align with the brand's messaging and **goals.**
6. Digital Marketing Specialist: Digital marketing specialists are **experts** in online marketing channels such as Search Engine Optimization (SEO), Search Engine Marketing (SEM), email marketing, and online **advertising.** They optimize websites for **search engines**, run paid ad campaigns, and analyze digital marketing metrics.
7. Brand Manager: Brand managers are responsible for developing and **maintaining** a strong brand **identity.** They **ensure** that the brand's values and messaging are consistent across all marketing efforts.
8. Public Relations Specialist: PR specialists manage an organization's public **image** and **reputation.** They create press **releases, respond** to media **inquiries**, and **handle** crisis communication.
9. Sales Representative: Sales representatives use their marketing knowledge to promote and sell products or services to customers. They often work closely with marketing teams to develop sales strategies.
10. **Entrepreneurship***: Many marketing graduates choose to start their own businesses, **leveraging*** their marketing skills to create and promote their products or services. Entrepreneurship allows for creativity and independence in pursuing business **ventures***.

11. Non-Profit Marketing: Nonprofit organizations also **rely** on marketing professionals to raise **awareness**, engage donors, and promote their causes. Working for a nonprofit can be highly fulfilling for those who want to make a **positive impact** on society.

In today's digital age, the marketing landscape continues to evolve, creating new opportunities for **adaptable** and innovative people. With the right education and experience, a marketing career can be **financially rewarding** and personally fulfilling as you **contribute** to the success of businesses and causes.

Future Challenges for Marketing

The world today is not only changing rapidly because of globalization and social media usage. We are also facing large-scale and increasing changes in the whole ecological system. Scientists are united in their **conclusions**: these changes seriously **threaten** all life on Earth. Therefore, marketers can, for example, **inform** consumers about the material used in different clothes and stimulate them to choose clothes with less **harmful** environmental effects. Even more important, marketers need to think beyond short-term customer demand and business performance.

Future marketing strategies must be market-oriented *and* take a **considerably** larger responsibility for how the company **affects** the ecological system as a whole. This makes marketing one of the business world's most stimulating professions and one of the most important if we plan to guide consumer behavior to a more **sustainable** future.

Adapted from a **text** by Tomas Nilsson, PhD.
Senior Lecturer at Linnaeus University, Sweden

Vocabulary

Words From the Second 1,000 General Service High-Frequency Word List

advertising	harmful
aimed	hire
ambition	imagine
audiences	inform
attractive	inquiries
behavior	key
calculate	manager
century	messages
cheapest	mix
commercial	models
compare	paths
connections	performance
customers	practice
deliver	preferences
dissatisfied	rapidly
eager	reputation
education	responsibility
engine	rewarding
exact	satisfies
essence	satisfying
essential	search
frequently	skill
handle	suddenly

suited
threaten

tools
track

Words From the Academic Word List (AWL)

Accurately
Achieve
Adaptable
Adaptability
Affects
Analysis
Analyze
Approach
Appreciation
Aspects
Awareness
Capabilities
Chapter
Challenges
Channels
Communicate
Conclusion
Conclusions
Consumers
Consumption
Contemporary
Context
Considerably
Consisted
Contribute
Corporate
Creation
Crucial
Data
Decades
Define
Design
Displays
Distribute
Diverse
Dramatically
Dynamic
Economy
Editions
Elements
Enabling
Encounter
Ensure
Environment

Ethic
Evolve
Exclusively
Exhibit
Experts
Expertise
Extract
Financially
Formulating
Founder
Focused
Fundamental
Generating
Goal
Goal-orientated
Globalization
Identify
Identity
Image
Impact
Implement
Individuals
Innovative
Insight
Interactive
Interacting
Invest
Items
Maintaining
Media
Monitor
Overall
Perspective
Positive
Potential
Promote
Professionals
Prospects
Psychology
Range
Releases
Relevant
Rely
Retain

Reinforce	Summing
Reorientation	Sustainable
Research	Symbols
Respond	Task
Response	Target
Role	Teams
Seeking	Text
Select	Technique
Strategies	Theories
Specific	Trends

Glossary

accomplish	knack
asset	promoting
campaigns	proposition
corporate ladder	relish
click	superior
competitors	marketers
deciphering	managerial
discerning	mnemonic
digitalization	multitude
driving (verb)	objectives
engage	intact
firework	segment
outfit (noun)	optimal

References

Kotler, P. (1967). *Marketing management: Analysis, planning, and control.* Prentice-Hall.

McCarthy, E. J. (1960). *Basic marketing: A managerial approach.* R. D. Irwin.

CHAPTER 21

CONSTITUTIONAL LAW

Takeshi Akiba
Waseda University, Japan

Introduction

A nation's **Constitution*** sets out the basic **principles** and laws that determine the government's power and responsibilities and its duties to its citizens. **Constitutional Law*** is the study of the **constitution** and how it is applied to actual cases. However, to truly understand constitutional law, you need to learn history, society's current conditions, and political and **legal** culture. For example, does Japan have **gender** equality as described in its Constitution (Articles 14 and 24)? To answer this, you need to learn about Japan's history and society and the historical inequality that led to including these Articles in the Constitution. You must also consider whether inequality has been **overcome** in current Japanese society. Thus, the study of Constitutional Law today also uses the findings of other fields of study, and it looks at the settings in which the law applies, as much as what the written laws and legal decisions actually say.

A History of the Study of Constitutional Law

In Japan, the study of Constitutional Law began with the **practical** desire to bring Japan into the modern age. That is, to bring Japan out of the **feudal-era*** and build a modern nation-state like those in the Western world. At that time, the main **aim** of those who studied Constitutional Law, was to learn about different **models** of Constitutional Law, mainly from European nations, and try to find ways to make these ideas fit to Japan. As a result, the **Meiji Constitution*** was based on the German model, which put most of the political power in the hands of the **Emperor***. This kind of system is called an **Imperial System***.

After **World War II*** Japan's new Constitution was heavily influenced by the United States. For example, it gave the people most of the power in government. This is called **popular sovereignty***. The new Constitution placed importance on protecting basic human rights. It adopted the idea of a separation of powers so that no one person can **govern** the country by his or her will alone.

Since then, the study of the Japanese Constitution has developed along two important **paths**. The first considers the **theory** behind each part of the Constitution. This means thinking carefully about *how the Constitution ought to be*, its basic values and how they should be applied to particular cases. The other path studies and judges the Constitution as the government and the decisions of law courts understand it. In other words *how the Constitution works in* **practice**. There is often a difference between what **scholars*** say about the Constitution (*how it ought to be*), and what the government and law courts say (*how it is in practice*). For example, there is a big difference between scholars' idea of

Introducing the Liberal Arts, pages 131–136
Copyright © 2026 by Emerald Publishing Limited
All rights of reproduction in any form reserved.
doi:10.1108/978-1-80592-303-920251022

Article 9 (which declares **pacifism***) and the actual development in Japanese politics regarding the extent of Japan's **military** power.

Because Japan became a modern nation by learning from other advanced **democracies***, its interest in the practices of other nations is still strong. Some people in Constitutional Law systematically **compare** different systems. This field is called **Comparative Constitutional Law***. Such scholars introduce new developments in foreign law to the Japanese public. For example, they have looked at the US and Europe regarding how to make legal equality between men and women a reality.

Why Study Constitutional Law?

The shared wisdom surrounding a nation's constitution will influence or determine its future and possibly that of other countries. A country's constitution controls how a government works and provides a basis in law for governing **behavior**. For example, if a ruler goes beyond their constitutional limits when going to war, there will be serious effects on the **international community**.

The Constitution, or rather **constitutionalism***, shows us modern ideas of governance. This is the idea that (1) government power should be *limited* by very clear and particular provisions and that (2) people have **individual** rights that the Constitution always protects. People cannot have these rights taken away by those who form a legal **majority** (the government). An effective Constitution provides a necessary basis for a modern society based on respect for individuals.

However, in practice, both of these ideas often face **challenges**. For example, while the whole point of the Constitution is to limit the power of those who rule the country, in practice, those who hold power often try to increase it while being unconcerned about the rights of the people. Also, while the other basic idea of the Constitution is to protect individual rights—meaning that the majority cannot take the rights of individuals away—the rights of **minorities** are still often put in danger by those with political power because those in power represent the majority.

When governments try to find a way around their constitutions, so that they do not have to follow what is written there closely, they often give the reason that it is to protect the nation's safety. Even though it may not be completely legal, they may try to do this, for example, in times of war, or when the **economy** is in serious trouble. There are many examples of this. In the United States, over 110,000 Japanese Americans—many of whom were born in the United States and therefore were US citizens, were sent to **internment camps*** after Japan attacked Pearl Harbor on December 7, 1941, and declared war the following day. In Japan, too, the government has continued to increase the powers of the **Self-Defense Force*** (which is basically a military force in all but name but could not be called this due to Article 9 of the Japanese Constitution). This has occurred despite Article 9, which strongly forbids owning such powers. The growth of this power has also been supported by the public fear that Japan faces threats from its neighbors in Asia.

For the Constitution to be effective, both citizens and those in power need to understand its values and ideas. It is also important for people with social influence, such as scholars, teachers, and **media** reporters, to understand them. Many countries have a Constitution in name only, where the government can actually take no notice at all of the limits of the Constitution, and take away the rights of individuals. The difference between those countries and **constitutional democracies*** rests in whether the Constitution is taken seriously by both citizens and the government. Taking the Constitution seriously means, firstly, that people know their rights under the Constitution well and fully understand the limits of power. Secondly, taking the Constitution seriously also means that those in power fully understand their own limits. Lastly, taking the Constitution seriously also means that there are **institutions** that make it possible to force the people in power to follow the Constitution. Usually, this is done through the law courts (where the courts can stop government actions if they are against the Constitution).

The study and practice of using Constitutional Law is good because it supports the idea of reason in politics, instead of **power grabs***. In the end, studying Constitutional Law and practice, and supporting the idea of limited government protects the rights of the people and makes for a fairer, more peaceful society.

Questions and Issues in the Study of Constitutional Law

Each country has its own particular questions and **issues** regarding its constitutional law. In the case of Japan, several important questions and issues exist.

Our first example concerns Article 9 of the Japanese Constitution, called the **Pacifism Clause***. Article 9 has been the subject of much **discussion** in Japan since World War II. It states (in English),

the Japanese people forever renounce war as a sovereign right of the nation and the threat or use of force as means of settling international disputes. (Clause 1)

and along with this, Japan is to give up possession of

land, sea, and air forces, as well as other war potential

Therefore, according to the Japanese Constitution, Japan should not have a military. However, Japan has a "Self-Defense Force," which is just like other countries' military forces. This has been explained by the Japanese government, which believes that the "**minimum** *forces necessary for self-defense*" mentioned in the Constitution do not count as the kind of armed forces that are forbidden by Article 9. Today in Japan, there are those who wish to increase Japan's "military" power in the world (so that it can even fight wars), and there are others who wish to follow Article 9 more closely (saying that Japan should limit any forces and abilities for going to war). Thus, to what extent such "military" power is allowed within the limits of Article 9 has been one of the hottest issues ever discussed in Japanese constitutional law.

Our second example of an important issue relating to Constitutional Law, is the idea of equality. Recently, the meaning of the word "equality" under the Japanese Constitution has received increased **attention** from both people in the wider Japanese society and the government. Article 14 of the Constitution promises everyone "*equality under the law*" in general, while Article 24 provides for gender equality in particular. However, this does not mean everyone agrees on how Article 14 or 24 should be applied. For example, in 2015, the **Japanese Supreme Court*** was divided, 10–5, over a Japanese law that says married people have to use the same family name. Many women say that in practice, this forces women to give up their family names, which is sometimes bad for their **careers***, and is both expensive and unfair. In another example, more recently, following on from successful legal cases in Western countries, gay and lesbian people in Japan are going to the courts, trying to get real equality under the law, particularly the right to marry. Whether or not they are successful in the courts, such challenges will make the political branches of Japanese society and Japanese people generally think much more deeply about what equality should mean and for whom under the Japanese Constitution.

Another recent issue has been over "**hate speech***," in which people belonging to certain minority groups are publicly attacked with **offensive** language. Whether such ways of speaking about others can be controlled, even though the Japanese Constitution promises "freedom of speech," is a difficult question to answer. It may be said that this is a question of a battle between the values of "freedom" and "equality" under the Constitution. Is it OK for people to march in the streets with big signs and make public speeches that are **racist*** and filled with **hate**—and say that they have a right to do so as part of their freedom of speech? Or should the government pass laws to stop or **punish** such speech and behavior in order to protect the rights of minorities to live peacefully, with as much respect as other members of Japanese society? Some people claim that even though hate speech is bad, stopping people from saying what they choose to say could be dangerous, too, as it could lead to too much government control over people's rights to express their opinions.

When you study Constitutional law, you will encounter many more challenging problems that come to our attention under the Constitution. If you become a scholar of Constitutional Law, you could easily spend years just reading and thinking about *one* of those questions.

Employment Opportunities in the Field of Constitutional Law

There are many fields of employment open to people who specialize in the study of Constitutional Law. Many of these are in the legal system. For example, you could become a judge or a lawyer or a worker in a legal office. You could also become a university teacher who teaches others, writes books and articles, and presents at international **conferences**, helping to build world knowledge in the field.

You could also become an **advisor*** to government officials, or, if you were really interested in becoming a law-maker yourself, you could also enter politics and become a politician.

Conclusion

The study of Constitutional Law relates to many other fields of study. If you become a scholar in this field, you will be studying the law and legal institutions. However, any serious question about the Constitution (such as "what should gender equality under the Constitution mean?") means you would need to have a broader understanding of Japanese history and society. Because the Constitution deals with modern ideas of how to govern a nation, such as democracy, human rights and the rule of law, constitutional scholars and people who work in this field should also know political **theory**.

To have a deeper understanding of the Constitution, your point of view should be based on **Liberal Arts and** not just the study of legal **text**. Understanding the world through the various Liberal Arts fields will give you a far deeper knowledge of the issues facing governments and their people today. Having this broad view will help you to take the Constitution seriously. It will also make it possible for you to support and **promote** its most important values (such as freedom and equality) in the real-life context in which you live. In the end, all citizens need to be well-**informed** and to have the ability to apply all these values for them to save society from the wrong use of power and the loss of human rights.

Adapted from a text by Professor Takeshi Akiba. School of International Liberal Studies at Waseda University

Japan

Vocabulary

Words From the Second 1,000 High Frequency General Service List

aim	international
attention	model(s)
behavior	offensive
comparing	overcome
discussed/discussion	path(s)
forbid/forbidden	practical
govern/government/governance	practice(s)
hate	punish
informed	threat(s)

Words From the Academic Word List

challenge(s)/challenging	constitution
community	culture
conference(s)	economy

gender
individual
institutions
issues
legal
majority
media

military
minimum
minority/minorities
principles
promote
text
theory

Glossary

Advisor (Noun): A specialist or person who gives advice in any particular field.

Career (Noun): One's life work.

Comparative Constitutional Law (Noun phrase): The field of study of differences and similarities between the legal systems of different countries.

Constitution (Noun): The basic principles and laws that determine the power and responsibilities of the government, and the duties it has to its citizens.

Constitutional democracies (Noun phrase): Countries which have a constitution that limits the power of government, protects the rights of all citizens, and in which citizens have the right to elect those in power.

Constitutional Law (Noun Phrase): The laws and rules for institutions that govern a nation, setting out the limits of power and the basic rights of citizens.

Constitutionalism (Noun): The belief in the need to/and the practice of following the Constitution of a country.

Democracy/Democracies (Noun singular/Noun plural): A system/systems of self-government, where those in power are chosen by the majority of citizens in free elections.

Emperor (Noun): One who is the sovereign ruler of a nation.

Feudal-era (Noun): The time when the social system gave power to those who own land. Those who worked the land usually did not own it and had no political power. They had to pay taxes or goods to the landowners in exchange for the right to use the land.

Hate speech (Noun phrase): Threatening and abusive speech or written words directed at minority groups because of their race, religion or sexual orientation.

Imperial System (Noun phrase): The system of government by an Emperor or Empress.

Internment camps (Noun phrase): Places where people are sent (such as prison or other places from which they may not leave) usually during time of war.

Japanese Supreme Court (Noun phrase): 最高裁判所. The highest law court in Japan.

Liberal Arts (Noun phrase): "Liberal arts is a field of study based on rational thinking, and it includes the areas of humanities, social and physical sciences, and mathematics. A liberal arts education emphasizes the development of critical thinking … the ability to solve complex problems, and an understanding of ethics and morality, as well as a desire to continue to learn." Retrieved from https://www.thoughtco.com/liberal-arts-definition-4585053

Meiji Constitution (Noun phrase): Title given to the Constitution of Japan from 1889–1947.

Muslims (Noun, plural): People who follow the religion of Islam.

Navies (Noun, plural): Singular form = Navy. The armed forces of a nation that perform at sea.

Pacifism (Noun): The belief that it is wrong to go to war or to use violence, and that disputes should be settled by peaceful negotiation.

Popular sovereignty (Noun phrase): The system of government that gives political power to the citizens of the nation.

Power grabs (Noun phrase): When a group of people tries to get political power, usually by illegal means.

Racist (Adjective): Someone who feels hostility towards, speaks of, or treats people of other races as inferior.

Scholars (Noun, plural): People whose work involves research and study. E.g. Professors and university academics.

Self-Defense Force (Noun phrase): Title given to the unified military forces of Japan, set up in 1954.

Terrorism (Noun): The illegal use force, violence and threats, usually against regular citizens, by particular groups for political purposes.

The Pacifism Clause (Noun phrase): Another name for Article 9 of the Japanese constitution that describes Japan's legal responsibilities in relation to war and defense.

World War II (Noun phrase): A huge war that began in 1939 and lasted until 1945 between Germany, Japan and Italy, (known as the Axis powers): and the France and Britain, and later the Soviet Union and the United States (known as The Allies).

CHAPTER 22

POLITICAL SCIENCE

James Reid
Akita International University, Japan

Introduction

What makes this subject a science? At first **glance***, it seems unnecessary to study politics scientifically because it looks more like a field of the **humanities*** where politicians use **rhetoric*** to **convince** us about their **motives** or **superiority***. However, some matters within the **sphere** of political science need scientific **analysis** to understand the effects on **policy** and **behaviour**. Political science uses **quantitative* methods** to analyze political **culture** and **inquire** into voting **habits** and public opinion, and **qualitative** methods are used to **interpret** nonnumerical and **textual data** such as political **discourse***, including speeches given by politicians.

Another **aspect** that should be addressed is the **distinction** between political science and history. History is a **chronological*** record of past events and **processes** with an attempt to figure out how they influence the present time, while political science is an analysis of any system of **government** or political behaviour to understand the existing relations of power and even **predict** where such will lead.

Development of Political Science

Political Science has been in existence since ancient times. The earliest recorded political writings are **attributed** to **Aristotle*** (384–322 BCE), who can be regarded as one of the "**founders**" of political science. His famous work "Politics" **discusses** the **role** of the citizen and the **constitution**, providing **insights** that have influenced political thinking for **centuries**.

Over a thousand years later, **Niccolò Machiavelli*** (1469–1527) wrote "The Prince," an **anthropological* treatise*** explaining the behaviours of political leaders and the art of ruling. It was a noticeable **departure*** from standard views on political **theory**, which were centred on politics and **legalism***.

Contributions to the **concept** of the social **contract** were made by **Thomas Hobbes*** (1588–1679) and **John Locke*** (1632–1704) **during** the **The Enlightenment***. In Leviathan (1651), Hobbes **maintained** that without a **unitary*** political power, there would be complete **disorder***. He claimed that if there were no government, people would be free to do whatever they wanted, **anarchy*** would **reign***, and **aggression*** and **strife*** would be **rampant***. To prevent such a state, Hobbes **contended*** that people's rights should be **relinquished*** to a ruler or government whom they are all to **obey** or **risk** the loss of order and security. In **contrast**, John Locke argued in "Oeuvre De Deux Traités Du Gouvernement" (1690) that life, **liberty** and property are rights which belong to **individuals**. It was his view that these rights are what the government is **created** to **maintain** and, **hence**, should be governed with the permission of the people. He argued that if a government did not serve its purpose or became oppressive, the people had the **authority** to **remove** that government. By the 19th century, **Karl Marx's* polemics*** of **class warfare*** and **capitalism***, as **revealed** in his book "The Communist Manifesto," had gained much **traction*** in political circles around the world. Countries that adopted **Marxist-Leninist* governance***—including the Soviet Union, China, Cuba, Vietnam, North Korea, and the **Eastern Bloc***—underwent **profound*** changes in their political systems. The **implementation** of **mandatory* collective** farming in the Soviet Union and China, for **instance**, resulted in **widespread famine*** and millions of deaths.

In contrast to **Communist*** ideology, In his work "**Economy** and Society," **published posthumously** in 1922, **Max Weber*** analyzed **bureaucratic*** and **authoritarian* structures**, along with associated social behaviours. His insights into efficient and **rational organizational* hierarchies** influenced **administrative practices**, contributing to civil service **reforms*** across various nations. These reforms **enhanced professionalism** and **curbed*** political **corruption***. Moreover, Weber's discussion of the **Protestant work ethic* linked** capitalist values to economic development, suggesting that these values led to **significant cultural** costs in many societies.

In the past century, the field of political science **evolved** substantially, driven by **pivotal*** contributions from noted **scholars***. Herbert A. Simon, an influential figure, enhanced the understanding of decision-making within organizations by proposing the theory of **bounded** rationality, which **asserts*** that decision-makers, **constrained** by both the **information** they have and the time **available** to them, often settle for **satisfactory** rather than **optimal* solutions**. Charles E. Lindblom's concept of **incrementalism***, also known as **"muddling through,"* revolutionized** policy-making by suggesting that complex policies **benefit** from small, **sequential adjustments** rather than large, **radical** changes. Robert Dahl's **research** provided deep insights into the nature of **democracy** and **pluralism***, **emphasizing** the variety of political structures and their impact on democratic governance. **Meanwhile**, Gabriel Almond significantly advanced **comparative** politics by developing **frameworks** for analyzing different political systems, helping to classify governments based on their structures and **functions**. These scholars collectively **transformed** political science, making it a more **empirical** and systematic **discipline**.

Contemporary Political Scientists

Current political scientists are significantly enhancing the field by addressing new global challenges. Elinor Ostrom (1933–2012), a **Nobel laureate*** in Economics in 2009, made **groundbreaking*** discoveries regarding communities' ability to manage common-pool resources independently of authorities. In her 1990 book "Governing the Commons," she emphasized the importance of internal community politics as well.

Amartya Sen is another influential figure in contemporary political science. Widely recognized as a leading **proponent*** of welfare economics and social choice theory, his 1999 work "Development as Freedom" **redefined** development economics by **advocating** for the necessity of social and economic provisions for development.

Moreover, Joseph Nye, born in 1937, has made significant contributions to the field, particularly through his concept of "soft power." Unlike **coercive*** "hard power" methods, such as **military** force or economic **incentives**, soft power involves **persuasion** and **attraction**. In his 2004 book "Soft Power: The Means to Success in World Politics," Nye **incorporates** cultural influence and **diplomacy*** into the foreign policies of countries, beyond mere military actions. For instance, Japan's **dissemination*** of anime and manga culture has yielded **impressive*** results, while South Korea has effectively **leveraged*** its K-pop and **film** industries as powerful **tools** of soft power.

Disagreements as Well as Tensions in Political Science

Political science as a field is **fraught*** with significant **contradictions** and **conflicts**. One **major** division lies between two schools of thought: **positivists*** and **interpretivists***. Positivists believe that political **entities** should be studied with scientific rigour, **utilizing** data and **statistics**. In contrast, interpretivists advocate for understanding politics by **exploring** the various meanings individuals **ascribe*** to actions and events.

Another **contentious*** **issue** is the **role** and **relevance** of theory in political science. Some argue that **focusing** on **theoretical** frameworks such as **distributive** justice or **liberalism** merely **highlights** the **internal** conflicts among different political schools of thought. Others question the necessity of such broad theories, suggesting that mid-**range** theories, which address **specific** aspects of politics like electoral behavior or policy processes, are more **practical** and **sufficient**.

Additionally, there is **ongoing debate** about the **impact** of political science on politics and public policy. Political scientists are often **perceived** as **detached***, presenting their findings in **incomprehensible*** ways to **policymakers***. This perception **underscores*** concerns about the practical applicability of political science research in real-world politics and policy-making, highlighting a significant **gap** between academic study and practical implementation.

Potential Perspectives in the Field of Political Science

The field of political science faces a **crucial challenge** as it evolves: **integrating** other disciplines. With the rise of big data and machine learning, political scientists now have **access** to **vast*** **datasets***, allowing for deeper analytical insights. For example, **AI*** **algorithms*** could **monitor** elections or **track** public opinion using large-**scale** data analysis.

International influences and **global** issues, such as **climate*** change, international **migration**, and global security, increasingly require a **worldwide*** perspective in political science studies. Understanding how climate change drives human migration or **contributes** to conflict is crucial for global peace and **involves** analyzing the **intersections*** of race, **gender**, and social class within political **dynamics**.

Moreover, the concept of Human Security is **expanding** in political science. This **approach shifts** the focus from states to individuals as the **primary** subjects of **threats**, **encompassing*** economic, food, **health**, **environmental**, personal, community, and political security. This comprehensive perspective includes addressing nonmilitary threats, such as illnesses caused by environmental **factors**, which can be **mitigated*** through **improved infrastructure**.

These developments represent significant **strides*** in political science, offering a more **holistic*** and **interconnected*** understanding of global and local issues.

Political Science: Associate Fields of Research

Political science encompasses a broad range of studies, integrating perspectives from economics, sociology, and public relations to provide a **thorough** understanding of governance and **societal*** structures.

Integration with History and Economics: Political science **examines** the historical **foundations** of current systems like capitalism and liberalism, exploring how economic factors such as wealth **distribution** and tax policies influence politics and policy-making. This **area**, known as Political Economy, **combines** economic and political analysis to study the impact of government actions on economic activities.

Legal Frameworks and Political Activities: This field studies the **legal** structures that influence political actions, focusing on **constitutional**, administrative, and international laws. It **investigates** how these laws support or **restrict** political **participation**, showing the close relationship between law and politics.

Public Administration and International Relations: Political science studies the theories of **management** and their application in policy implementation aimed at improving societal **welfare**. It also explores international relations, analyzing how countries and organizations **interact** through diplomacy and governance to **tackle*** global issues like climate change, **terrorism***, and human rights.

Political Psychology and Anthropology: These branches of political science examine the interactions between individual characteristics and societal structures, analyzing how these interactions influence political behaviors and **attitudes**. Anthropology within political science looks at cultural and societal **contexts** to understand different political systems, providing a deeper insight into political **phenomena** through social perspectives.

Environmental Studies and Communication: This area studies how state policies **affect** environmental management and how **communication** shapes public opinion and political actions, emphasizing the importance of **media** in political processes and environmental advocacy.

This **comprehensive** approach enhances our understanding of political systems and **equips** scholars to address the **complexities** of modern societies.

Differences in Political Science as a Discipline

Political science **varies** widely across different cultural, historical, and **institutional** contexts and is not **uniform** worldwide. In the USA, the discipline **primarily** focuses on empirical verification and quantitative analysis, exploring public policies, public opinion, and voting behaviors. **Conversely**, in Europe—particularly in countries like Germany, France, and the UK—political science often **leans** towards a theoretical approach, emphasizing the **philosophical** aspects of politics and **diverse** political theories.

In Asia, the approach to political science differs **markedly*** by country. China focuses on state **administration**, Japan **blends*** political sociology with economics, and South Korea **concentrates** on political development and democratic processes. Meanwhile, Latin American political science **frequently** addresses **transitions** to democracy, social justice, and poverty, integrating political analysis with historical and sociological perspectives.

In contrast, African political science is deeply **engaged*** in **domestic** issues such as **decolonization***, governance, and **sustainability**, tackling problems like **corruption***, conflicts, and **regional** integration. In this region, studies often consider the impacts of **political Islam***, **dictatorship***, and **geopolitics***, **reflecting** the **unique realities*** faced by the **continent***.

Employment Opportunities for Political Science Graduates

Those with a degree in political science find employment across various fields. They **excel*** particularly in policy analysis and roles as **legislative aides***. Their **tasks** involve **rigorous*** research and **evaluation** of existing and proposed policies for government agencies, think tanks, and nonprofit organizations. They engage in data analysis, **conduct** thorough research, and prepare **documents** that support policy decisions. Legislative aides **assist** in legislative operations through research, drafting bills, and public interaction, **necessitating*** a deep understanding of legislative processes **alongside*** strong writing and analytical **skills**.

Opportunities in political science and media management are **expansive**. Public relations **practitioners** enhance and protect the **reputations** of organizations or political entities using media, events, and communication **strategies aimed** at shifting public **perceptions**. Social media managers develop and implement communication strategies for political **campaigns***, government entities, and advocacy groups, managing social media platforms and **monitoring** engagement to improve **outreach***.

Political campaigns and advocacy also offer **fertile*** ground for political science graduates. Campaign managers **oversee*** all aspects of voter engagement, **fundraising***, and strategic planning, **requiring robust*** leadership and networking skills. **Lobbyists*** advocate for **organizational***, governmental, or legislative interests, relying heavily on **networking** and **persuasive** skills.

In international relations and public policy, opportunities **abound***. Foreign service officers represent their countries **abroad**, engaging in diplomacy, writing political reports, and protecting nationals **overseas**. Public policy analysts work on implementing and improving **community**-impacting policies, employed by governments, advocacy groups, or research institutions to gather data and **formulate relevant** policies.

For those **inclined** toward **academia**, advancing in political science can lead to **careers*** as researchers or professors who **educate** and **mentor* upcoming*** political scientists. The **versatility*** of a political science degree is **evident** in the broad **array*** of careers it enables, each offering **distinct** ways to engage with and influence politics and governance.

Conclusion

In **conclusion**, political science is a field that blends quantitative and qualitative methods to explore governance and political behaviour. It draws from historical and contemporary perspectives to address modern challenges such as **resource** management and global security. Continuously evolving, political science significantly influences public policy, international relations, and democratic processes, offering solutions to complex issues in our **rapidly** changing world. Studying political science at a liberal arts university **fosters* critical** thinking, interdisciplinary learning, and a broad understanding of diverse cultural and philosophical contexts.

James Reid

Assistant Professor and EAP Coordinator at Akita International University, Japan

Vocabulary

Words From the Second 1,000 General Service Word List

Abroad
Aimed
Argued
Attraction
Behaviour
Bounded
Centuries
Combines
Comparative
Critical
Democracy
Discusses
During
Educate
Examines
Exploring
Film
Frequently
Gap
Government
Habits
Health
Improved

Information
International
Leans
Liberty
Management
Meanwhile
Obey
Persuasion
Persuasive
Practical
Practices
Reflecting
Reputations
Risk
Satisfactory
Scale
Skills
Solutions
Thorough
Threats
Tools
Track

Words From the Academic Word List

Academic
Academia
Access
Affect
Adjustments
Administrative
Administration
Advocating
Analysis
Area
Aspect
Assist

Attributed
Authority
Available
Benefit
Challenge
Civil
Combines
Community
Comprehensive
Concept
Concentrates
Conclusion

Conflicts
Constitution
Constitutional
Constrained
Contributions
Contract
Contradictions
Contrast
Convince
Conversely
Contributes
Cultural
Culture
Data
Debate
Distinct
Distinction
Distributive
Diverse
Documents
Domestic
Dynamics
Economy
Emphasizing
Empirical
Enhanced
Entities
Environmental
Equips
Evident
Evaluation
Evolved
Expansive
Expanding
Factors
Focusing
Foundations
Founders
Frameworks
Functions
Gender
Global
Hierarchies
Highlights
Ideology
Implementation
Inclined
Incorporates
Individuals
Insights

Institutional
Instance
Integrating
Interact
Interactions
Interpret
Internal
Involves
Issue
Legal
Legislative
Liberalism
Linked
Maintain
Maintained
Major
Media
Methods
Migration
Military
Monitor
Monitoring
Motives
Networking
Ongoing
Overseas
Participation
Perceived
Perceptions
Perspectives
Phenomena
Philosophical
Policy
Potential
Practitioners
Predict
Primary
Primarily
Professionalism
Processes
Published
Qualitative
Radical
Range
Rational
Redefined
Regional
Relevance
Relevant
Remove

Requiring
Research
Resource
Restrict
Revealed
Revolutionized
Risk
Role
Scale
Security
Sequential
Shifts
Significant
Solutions
Specific
Sphere
Statistics
Strategies
Structures
Sufficient
Sustainability
Tasks
Textual
Theoretical
Theory
Thorough
Threats
Tools
Transitions
Transformed
Uniform
Unique
Utilizing
Varies
Welfare
Widespread

Glossary

Abound (Verb): Exist in large numbers or amounts.

AI (Noun): An abbreviation for Artificial Intelligence.

Aides (Noun plural): Assistants or helpers, typically to an important person.

Algorithms (Noun plural): Step-by-step procedures or formulas for solving problems.

Alongside (Preposition): Next to or together with.

Array (Noun): An impressive display or range of a particular type of thing.

Ascribe (Verb): Attribute something to a cause.

Asserts (Verb): States a fact or belief confidently and forcefully.

Authoritarian (Adjective): Favoring or enforcing strict obedience to authority at the expense of personal freedom.

Bureaucratic (Adjective): Relating to the business of running an organization, or government with many complicated rules and ways of doing things.

Campaigns (Noun plural): A series of coordinated activities designed to achieve a goal.

Careers (Noun plural): Occupations or professions, especially ones requiring special training, followed as one's lifework.

Climate (Noun): The weather conditions prevailing in an area in general or over a long period.

Communist (Adjective/Noun): Relating to communism, or a person who supports or believes in the principles of communism.

Contentious (Adjective): Causing or likely to cause an argument; controversial.

Corruption (Noun): Dishonest or fraudulent conduct by those in power, typically involving bribery.

Curbed (Verb): Restrained or held back.

Datasets (Noun plural): Collections of data.

Decolonization (Noun): The process by which colonies become independent of the colonizing country.

Democracy (Noun): A system of government by the whole population or all the eligible members of a state, typically through elected representatives.

Detached (Adjective): Disinterested and unbiased.

Dictatorship (Noun): A form of government in which a dictator has absolute power.

Diplomacy (Noun): The profession, activity, or skill of managing international relations, typically by a country's representatives abroad.

Dissemination (Noun): The act of spreading something, especially information, widely; circulation.

Eastern Bloc (Noun phrase): A group of communist states of Central and Eastern Europe during the Cold War.

Encompassing (Verb): Surrounding or holding within.

Engaged (Verb): Involved or busy with something.

Excel (Verb): To be exceptionally good at or proficient in an activity or subject.

Famine (Noun): Extreme scarcity of food.

Fertile (Adjective): Capable of producing abundant vegetation or crops; producing many ideas.

Fosters (Verb): Encourages the development of something (good).

Fraught (Adjective): Filled with or destined to result in (something undesirable).

Fundraising (Noun): The process of seeking financial support for a cause or organization.

Geopolitics (Noun): Politics, especially international relations, as influenced by geographical factors.

Governance (Noun): The action or manner of governing a state, organization.

Groundbreaking (Adjective): Innovative or pioneering.

Holistic (Adjective): Characterized by comprehension of the parts of something as intimately interconnected and explicable only by reference to the whole.

Impressive (Adjective): Evoking admiration through size, quality, or skill.

Incomprehensible (Adjective): Not able to be understood; not intelligible.

Incrementalism (Noun): A method of working by adding to a project using many small incremental changes instead of a few (extensive) changes.

Interconnected (Adjective): With various parts or aspects linked or coordinated.

Interpretivists (Noun plural): Advocates of the interpretivist approach, who seek to understand human behavior from the perspective of those experiencing it.

Intersections (Noun plural): Points where two or more things intersect or cross each other.

Leveraged (Verb): Use (something) to maximum advantage.

Lobbyists (Noun plural): People who engage in lobbying; trying to influence government on behalf of a private interest such as an industry or business.

Mandatory (Adjective): Required by law or rules; compulsory.

Markedly (Adverb): Noticeably or significantly.

Marxist-Leninist (Adjective): Relating to the ideology combining Marxist socioeconomic theory and Leninist political strategy.

Max Weber (Noun): A German sociologist, philosopher, and political economist known for his ideas on bureaucracy and his thesis on the Protestant ethic, among other topics.

Mentor (Verb): To advise or train (someone, especially a younger colleague).

Mitigated (Verb): Made less severe, serious, or painful.

Muddling Through (Verb phrase): Managing to get by despite difficulties.

Nobel Laureate (Noun phrase): Someone who has been awarded a Nobel Prize, especially in the sciences or literature.

Optimal (Adjective): Best or most favorable; optimum.

Organizational (Adjective): Relating to the organization or structure of something.

Outreach (Noun): An effort to bring services or information to people where they live or spend time.

Oversee (Verb): Supervise (a person or work), especially in an official capacity.

Pivotal (Adjective): Of crucial importance in relation to the development or success of something else.

Planners (Noun plural): People who make plans, especially skilled ones.

Pluralism (Noun): A condition or system in which two or more states, groups, principles, sources of authority, etc., coexist.

Policymakers (Noun plural): Members of a government department, legislature, or other organization who create policy (laws or guidelines).

Political Islam (Noun): A movement or ideology that seeks to derive the governmental and legal systems of a state from principles of Islamic law and doctrine, often aiming for the integration of religious and political spheres.

Positivists (Noun plural): Advocates of positivism, a philosophical system recognizing only that which can be scientifically verified or which is capable of logical or mathematical proof, and thereby rejecting metaphysics and theism.

Posthumously (Adverb): After the death of the originator.

Proponent (Noun): A person who advocates a theory, proposal, or project.

Protestant Work Ethic (Noun phrase): A concept in theology, sociology, economics, and history which emphasizes that diligence, discipline, and frugality are a result of a person's subscription to the values espoused by the Protestant faith.

Quantitative (Adjective): Measurable or quantifiable.

Reforms (Noun plural): Changes or improvements that are made to a law, social system, or institution.

Reign (Noun): The period of a monarch's or other ruler's power.

Rigorous (Adjective): Extremely thorough and careful.

Robust (Adjective): Strong and healthy; vigorous.

Scholars (Noun plural): People who are highly educated or have an aptitude for study.

Societal (Adjective): Relating to society or social relations.

Strides (Noun plural): Long, decisive steps in a particular direction or toward a goal.

Tackle (Verb): Make determined efforts to deal with (a problem or difficult task).

Terrorism (Noun): The unlawful use of violence and intimidation, especially against civilians, in the pursuit of political aims.

Upcoming (Adjective): Happening or appearing soon.

Vast (Adjective): Of very great extent or quantity; immense.

Versatility (Noun): Ability to adapt or be adapted to many different functions or activities.

Worldwide (Adjective): Extending or reaching throughout the world.

SECTION 3

THE SCIENCES: AN INTRODUCTION

As we have seen, the Humanities **strive*** to **comprehend*** the **essence** of human existence through the exploration of disciplines such as literature, **philosophy**, history, and religious studies. The social sciences broaden this **exploration** to **encompass*** our **societal* functioning**, with sociology, anthropology, and economics being three representative examples of social science **inquiry**. The Sciences, by contrast, encompass a **spectrum*** of **disciplines** that systematically **probe*** the **physical** and natural **realms***, employing **quantitative*** empirical observations, experimentation, and mathematical **analysis** as their **tools** of **inquiry**.

As we progress, in the **upcoming*** chapters, we will **embark*** on a detailed **exploration** of several **diverse** scientific fields. For example, Biology is **dedicated*** to **unravelling*** the **intricacies*** of life, from the influence of **tiny* organisms*** on **ecosystems*** to **impressive* medical advancements*** and **environmental preservation**. Similarly, Chemistry provides **insights** into the **interactions** of substances, **facilitating** drug development and efforts to **mitigate*** pollution. Next, Physics explores the **foundational* components** of matter and seeks to understand the fundamental principles of nature itself. On a practical level, it leads to **innovations** such as **renewable*** energy. Geology explores Earth's history, **uncovering*** the forces driving the movement of **continents*** and the **creation** of valuable **resources** such as oil. **Environmental** science **examines** the **delicate equilibrium*** of nature, our **impact** on it, and **strategies** for **maintaining sustainability**. **Programming**, crucial in our **digital* era***, **empowers* simulations***, data analysis, and **intricate*** models across fields from **climate forecasting*** to **artificial intelligence**. Zoology, meanwhile, invites us into the fascinating world of animals, studying their behavior, genetics, physiology, and evolution to understand their roles within ecosystems and the broader environmental impacts they have.

Lastly, Mathematics, the common **thread** throughout all scientific **domains, establishes** the basis for inquiry, modelling, and drawing meaningful **conclusions**.

Individually, each scientific **discipline contributes** to our understanding of the natural world. **Collectively**, they offer a **panoramic*** view of the **universe—ranging** from the tiniest particles to **colossal*** geological forces, from life's intricate **patterns** to the laws of **mathematics**, and from **ecosystem* harmony*** to the **frontiers*** of **technological** progress. As we **immerse*** ourselves in these domains, we'll **cultivate** a **profound* appreciation** for the **universe's** intricacies and recognize the **pivotal*** role that scientific **exploration** plays in **expanding** the **horizons** of human knowledge.

Vocabulary

Words From the Second 1,000 General Service High-Frequency Word List

artificial	disciplines
collectively	essence
cultivate	examines
delicate	exploration

148 *The Sciences: An Introduction*

horizons
inquiry
models
patterns
preservation

programming
thread
tools
universe

Words From the Academic Word List (AWL)

analysis
appreciation
chapters
components
conclusion
contributes
contrast
creation
crucial
data
diverse
domains
ecological
economics
empirical
energy
environmental
establishing
expanding

facilitating
functioning
impact
individual
insights
instance
interactions
intelligence
innovations
maintenance
medical
ordered
philosophical
ranging
resources
role
strategies
sustainability

Glossary

Advancements (noun): Developments or improvements, especially in technology or knowledge.

Colossal (adjective): Extremely large or impressive in size.

Comprehend (verb): To understand or grasp the meaning of something.

Continents (noun): Large land masses on Earth, such as Africa, Asia, and Europe.

Dedicated (adjective): Devoted or committed to a particular purpose or task.

Digital (adjective): Relating to or involving computer technology and data in the form of digits.

Ecosystems (noun): A community of living organisms interacting with their environment.

Embark (verb): To start or begin a journey, project, or endeavor.

Empirical (adjective): Based on observation, experience, or experiment rather than theory.

Empowers (verb): To give power, authority, or ability to someone or something.

Encompass (verb): To include or contain a wide range of things.

Equilibrium (noun): A state of balance or stability between opposing forces or factors.

Era (noun): A period of time characterized by particular qualities, events, or developments.

Intricacies (noun): Complex details, nuances, or intricately woven elements.

Intricate (adjective): Complex, detailed, and having many interconnected parts.

Medical (adjective): Relating to the field of medicine or healthcare.

Mitigate (verb): To make less severe, harmful, or intense; to alleviate.

Organisms (noun): Living entities, often referring to plants, animals, or microorganisms.

Panoramic (adjective): Providing a wide and comprehensive view of a scene or subject.

Probe (verb): To investigate or explore deeply and thoroughly.

Quantitative (adjective): Relating to quantities or measurable characteristics.

Realms (noun): Domains or areas of activity, knowledge, or influence.

Renewable (adjective): Capable of being restored or replaced naturally over time.

Simulations (noun): Imitations or representations of real-life situations or processes.

Societal (adjective): Relating to society and its organization or structure.

Spanning (verb): Extending across or covering a certain period or range.

Spectrum (noun): A wide range or variety of something.

Strive (verb): To make great efforts or attempt to achieve something.

Thread (noun): A thin strand or filament; a common theme or element connecting things.

Uncovering (noun): The act of revealing or bringing to light something previously hidden.

Unravelling (verb): The process of uncovering, solving, or understanding something complex or mysterious.

Upcoming (adjective): Approaching or forthcoming in the near future.

CHAPTER 23

MATHEMATICS

Attila Egri-Nagy
Akita International University Japan

Introduction

Clear thinking is needed in everything we do in our working lives. **Mathematics** (**math** or **maths***) is the study of clear thinking. Therefore, you need math regardless of what you choose to study. This **message** does not always get across to students. Even **worse**, sometimes Math looks as if it is the **opposite** of what it really is. Not surprisingly, many people **hate** the subject. If you do too, it is not always your **fault**, but now you have a choice. If you choose not to study math, it may mean that you are choosing to be a less useful professional in your field. On the other hand, taking math courses will often help you to be more successful in your future **area** of work.

Introduction to Mathematics

Let's be **honest**! It is highly likely that you don't like mathematics. It is also likely that you don't feel bad about feeling this way, since many other people do not like math either. Modern **education** has not always done a great **job** in helping people to enjoy this **subject**. Sometimes, it has actually **created** an **image** of math that makes the subject seem more difficult than it really is. As a result, many people actually hate this subject.

In this situation, there is bad news and good news. The bad news is that your dislike of math can get in the way of your studies and may **damage** your future **career***. This is not your **fault**, since the way you have experienced math might have been unpleasant. The good news is that you can fix this problem!

Firstly, let us think about an important question. What is wrong with not taking mathematics courses? To answer this question, we need to think about what mathematics is all about.

Mathematics is about **precise** thinking. No matter what you think about, if you really want to **solve** a problem, then sooner or later you will start writing or drawing something on a piece of paper to help you to build an **abstract model**. As you do this, you leave out unnecessary details. First, you decide what the most important ideas are that relate to the problem itself. You must then think about how they relate to each other. People often do not realize that they are thinking **mathematically*** when they do this.

For example, when you are planning a **holiday** with your friends (you might think that is certainly not a math problem, right?), you might all have different ideas about what to do. Each of your friends may wish to travel at different times, and this can lead to different costs for each person. As you try to make all the **information** clear, you might find it difficult to write down what everyone wants to do in one single **list**, in the order that everyone **prefers**.

For example, visiting a big city is very different from going on a walking **trip** in the mountains; and you might like both, but in different ways. On the other hand, you might clearly prefer one city over the other, while your friends have the opposite point of view. Some possible options are easy to **compare**, while others are not. In the language of mathematics, we would say, "Welcome to the '**theory of partial orders**!'"* Another problem may be that two trips might either be in **conflict** with each other, or they might fit well together in your holiday time, and that can be explained using **graph*** **theory**.

Of course, you can plan your holiday without knowing a **lot** of math. But don't you think that studying the most basic parts of everyday problems, in a less difficult setting, would help us to solve real-world problems? For example, running exercises help us prepare to play **sports**, such as **baseball*** or **soccer***. In the same way that running builds strength for other sports, math is a kind of exercise for building your mental strength and your ability to think in an orderly way. Most of us will **probably** not have to solve difficult math problems every day in our work, but we will certainly need to deal with other difficult problems. Often, if we can think about the problem in a mathematical manner, our mathematical thinking could give us a better **path** to a **solution**. However, in many cases it seems to be true that it is just when the study of math is beginning to become really useful that many students find it becoming more difficult, and so they begin to lose interest.

Maths Is Really About Making Things Easy

Mathematics is an example of an **artificial** language. Over time, it has developed for the purpose of helping us to be very clear in the way we think about problems. Keeping this idea in mind, we begin to see that the whole point of mathematics is to take away uncertainty. How is this so?

In math, the meaning for each expression is clearly **defined**. If we get lost as we try to solve a problem, for example, when we do not know what a mathematical expression means, we can just go back to the **definition** in order to be able to find the solution. It is like learning a foreign language: if we do not understand an unknown word, we just look it up in a **dictionary**. Doing this will help us to understand the meaning. Using this same simple **method** can also help us to solve math problems, and this same method can also help anyone working towards a university degree in mathematics.

On the other hand, in languages like English or Japanese, the meanings of words depend on who is speaking as well as the situation. In other words, meaning depends on **context**, history and **culture**. This means that more background knowledge and **mental** ability is needed to understand meaning. Therefore, it could be said that learning a foreign language **requires** more mental effort than studying math.

Abstraction is a basic operation in mathematics. When we are trying to solve a problem, abstraction is the act of leaving out unnecessary details, with the **aim** being to make thinking easier. All the **symbols** and mathematical **notations*** are used to help reduce the amount of mental work we have to do. Not many people realize that math can be seen as a very helpful form of **shorthand*** notation. Of course, everything can still be said in plain English, but it would be a very long, difficult **sentence** if we tried to write down the meaning of all the information that is contained in a single, **clever** mathematical symbol. Therefore, mathematics was **created** by people with the purpose of making thinking about hard problems much easier.

Why Then Is Mathematics the Most Hated Subject?

In a way, mathematics is a **victim*** of its own success. Because of its precise nature, it is easy to use math to set up and **check** the quality of **standardized tests***. Unfortunately, math is often used as a kind of **weapon** to **punish** students when teachers are **grading** their students. When test **scores*** are not high enough, for example, students are often made to feel they have failed. When mathematics is used like this, it can stop people from taking certain career paths by creating **competition** and **sharp** division between those people who understand math easily and people who don't. This is very **sad**, because at higher levels, mathematical **research** itself is done in **exactly** the opposite way. Research at the university level is usually very social and researchers often do a lot of their work together. In fact, it is important for them to share information and new ideas, as this helps our knowledge of math, and of the world, to grow.

Another failure of math education is **sadly** due to good **intentions**. Take, for example, the **quadratic equation***. The quadratic equation has a special **status** in mathematics, since it is powerful enough to model many things in science, and it is easy to use, so that almost anyone can deal with it.

There is a general **formula** for solving all quadratic equations which is so easy to use that we just need to use three numbers in the equation to get the solution. Thus all we have to do is to give students the formula and tell them how to use it. By using the formula, we save them all a lot of work. How **nice**!

Now look at this from the students' point of view. A student has to remember the formula, which is really just a rather strange grouping of symbols. Remembering a formula is not always easy, because our **brains** are not so good at memorizing these. We are better at remembering stories. Just using a formula takes away the need for thinking about *how* and *why* it is used. Thus, solving quadratic equations becomes a **dull** exercise, with no mental **reward**, since we do not have to think about it very hard. In the end, because it is simply using a formula without much thought, we do not enjoy the success of solving the problem as much as we fear the possible failure if we do not.

On the other hand, we could **derive** the quadratic formula, by finding out how it works for ourselves, instead of just remembering it. This is possible once you know the basic operations of **algebra***. Such exercises, that help us to discover the rules for ourselves, allow us to understand the real power of algebra: by using letters instead of numbers, we can solve an **infinite** number of problems at a time. In this way, mathematics becomes **empowering***. Put simply, it is more helpful for learners to think about *why* we do things a certain way than just *how* we do things.

In mathematics, more advanced ideas build on simpler ones. In other words, if students miss, or do not understand, an early idea, they may not understand the ideas that come later. Unfortunately, it can often be very difficult for teachers to notice problems or **gaps** that learners have in their knowledge, in an everyday **classroom*** setting.

Another **mistake** we make is placing too much importance on the usefulness of math. In reality, mathematics is not useful in a direct sense. For example, you will probably not spend time just solving *quadratic equations* in your daily work. But we still need **focused** thinking and we need to use abstract ideas and different ways of thinking about the same problem. Knowing how to use math is a helpful way to do this.

Opportunities in Computer Programing

Nowadays, there are **exciting** opportunities for moving math education in a more **positive** direction. For example, we could teach **computer programming*** and math together, in a **unified** way because these subjects are **similar** to each other. They are similar because they both use an artificial language to describe and understand our world.

It is becoming more and more difficult to teach mathematics without also teaching programming. Hand-calculated problems are usually too small for modern computer applications. It is also difficult to **motivate** students to use precise notation. When we use a computer, if we are not careful and we make mistakes, what we write has **immediate consequences**. This immediately makes students learn about the importance of mathematical **precision**.

Roughly speaking, mathematics is a programming language. The "programs" are carried out in our heads, without **physical** computers. Moreover, sometimes the notation can do the work by itself. For example, **calculus*** rules can be programmed into a computer, which will then **automatically** solve our math problems for us.

If we unify math and programming, this brings a new usefulness to mathematics. **Functions*** are central in the study of mathematics. The mathematical notion of function is also useful in the **software*** industry. This idea of unifying math and programming is becoming more important as functional programming languages become more and more popular.

Mathematics and Programing in the Liberal Arts

The study of mathematics at Liberal Arts colleges can be more **flexible** than at universities that focus only on science and **technology**. The math courses at a Liberal Arts college can pass over much of the more **technical** material, and focus on helping students understand key ideas in a more general way. We call this "seeing the bigger picture."

Liberal Arts education has a better chance of **improving** the present problems in math education, that we spoke of earlier, by unifying mathematical and **computational** thinking in its courses of study.

In a similar way, mathematical and scientific subjects also need to be studied from a broader point of view. This means the ideas we think about in math and Science need to be related to the ideas found in other subjects, and the ideas we find in other subjects should be related to math and Science, too. As we are learning right now, **technological** developments that do not consider our human nature and needs, which are the focus of the **Humanities*** subjects, can cause huge problems. The present **climate crisis*** is a good example of this.

Now that you know all this, what can you do? Well, perhaps it would be a good idea to make math courses a part of your future study plan. Studying math and other subjects together at a Liberal Arts college would help you to understand the world from a broader point of view for sure.

And, at any time, when you do study math, you should always ask your teachers for explanations that make it clear how formulas are derived. Moreover, it is important for you to know it is right to be **critical** if math is being taught just as a set of rules to follow, without any **connection** to other things you are studying. And it is right to be critical if your study does not require you to think carefully about *how* mathematical ideas are developed and can be used, and *why* they are important in today's world.

Adapted from a text by Attila Egri-Nagy PhD
Professor of Mathematics and Natural Science
Akita International University
Japan

Vocabulary

Words From the Second 1,000 General Service Word List

aim	improve
artificial	information
brain	intention
calculate	list
check	a lot of
clever	message
compare	mistake
competition	model
connection	nice
critical	opposite
damage	path
dictionary	prefer
dull	probably
education	punish
exactly	reward
exciting	sad
fault	sharp
gaps	solution/solve
hate	sports
holiday	trip
honest	weapon
immediate	worse

Words From the Academic Word List

abstract	image
area	interact
automatically	mental
computational	method
computer	motivate
conflict	notion
consequences	physical
context	positive
create	precise/precision
culture	research
define/definition	similar
derive	status
evaluate	symbol
flexible	technical
focused	technique
formula	technology
functions	theory
grading	unified

Glossary

It is not necessary to memorize these words and expressions.

Algebra (Noun): A branch of mathematics that utilizes symbols to represent and manipulate relationships between quantities.

Baseball (Noun): A sport played between two teams using a bat and ball.

Calculus (Noun): A mathematical branch concerned with studying changes in values and rates of change.

Career (Noun): A profession or job typically requiring specialized training, representing one's life work.

Classroom (Noun): A physical location where educational lessons are delivered to students.

Climate Crisis (Noun): A term denoting the issue of global warming and its potential consequences.

Empowering (Verb): Enabling someone to exercise power, control, or authority.

Functions (Noun): An expression, rule, or law that defines a relationship between one variable (the independent variable): and another variable (the dependent variable).

Graph Theory (Noun): The study of graphs, visual representations used to depict relationships between objects or events using lines and connected points or bars.

Humanities (Noun): Various fields of study focusing on human society and culture.

Mathematically (Adverb): Done using mathematical thinking and processes.

Mathematics (Noun): The scientific study of numbers, quantities, and space. (Math in US English, Maths in British English).

Notation (Noun): A system of written symbols employed to represent numbers or quantities.

Programming (Noun): The act of creating a set of instructions (or the instructions themselves): used to control a computer. Programs utilize a specific computer language understood by the machine.

Quadratic Equation (Noun): A mathematical statement expressing a particular mathematical relationship.

Score (Noun): A record of points earned or accumulated in a test or game.

Shorthand (Noun): A system of symbols used to replace whole words, designed to expedite writing.

Soccer (Noun): Also known as 'football,' it is a popular international game played between two teams using a round ball. Players are not allowed to use their hands, except for the goalkeeper.

Software (Noun): A collection of programs and operating information used by a computer.

Standardized Tests (Noun): Tests in which all test takers must respond to questions in the same manner, with results scored uniformly. These tests facilitate comparisons among test takers.

Theory of Partial Orders (Noun): A theory explaining the concept of ordering among different elements or values.

Victim (Noun): Someone who has suffered harm due to an accident, crime, or other negative event or action.

CHAPTER 24

BIOLOGY

Jeanette Dennisson
Tokyo Medical and Dental University, Japan

Introduction

When you were a child, did you ever wonder about where we came from and how living things came to exist? As children, we ask questions like why do some **insects*** fly and some walk? Why do flowers always face the sun? Why do I look more like my sister than my best friend? These simple questions we ask as children are the **foundations** of the **inquiry**-driven field of **biology***. Our first inquiries as children could start an interest in trying to build a bigger understanding of how the living world works. This early interest is how most people who later become **biologists*** first start off. Children interested in insects and animal differences may become **entomologists*** and **zoologists***, children interested in plants and the living world around us may become **botanists*** or **ecologists***, and children interested in human characteristics and **behaviors** may become **geneticists*** and **epidemiologists***.

To be a great biologist, however, we must understand the basics of scientific inquiry. As children, we naturally do this by observing the plants and animals around us. When we are in the **park**, for example, we may count the number of **legs** each insect has and put them into groups of insects that have six legs and those that do not have six legs. We find that if we stop giving water to our plants and do not give them sunlight, they will die. We observe all the characteristics we share and the differences we have with each member of our family. As we observe these things, we start to ask questions of "why" and "how."

Then, when we first go to school, we learn to make questions of inquiry and try to answer them by doing experiments and making further observations. This way of questioning, experimenting and observing is called the **scientific method***. There are four basic steps to this scientific way of working:

1. First, we form a **hypothesis*** based on our earlier observations. We do this by making a statement about what we believe is likely to be true. Our statement is based on what we have seen earlier: **Ants** have six legs, but **spiders** have eight legs. Therefore, other animals with six legs should be like ants, and other animals with eight legs should be like spiders.
2. Second, we make a plan to test our hypothesis: Go to the park and observe all the small **creatures** you find and put them into groups based on the number of legs they have and **identify** their other characteristics.
3. Third, we test the hypothesis with experiments or further observations: At the park, we find many small creatures. We organize them into groups by the number of legs they have. All of them, except the spider and **centipede,** have six legs; the spider had eight legs, and the centipede had so many legs we could not count them easily. Each group had different numbers and kinds of body parts.

4. Last, we **analyze** our observations and relate these to our **previous** knowledge: There are creatures with six legs that we can organise as insects. They have three body **sections**. There are two other groups of creatures with more than six legs, one which we call **arachnids*** with two body sections, and another group, **myriapods** with long bodies, like **worms.**

To begin, this classification of insects (and all animals and plants) were **created** and **utilized** by biologists based on **physical** characteristics. Currently, with the advancement of **techniques** in **genetics***, biologists can now classify **species*** based on their genetic **similarities** to create 'family trees' of all living things. These family trees show how each group of species relates to others. Moreover, genetic studies have proven that humans are very closely related to **chimpanzees** because we share 99% of the same **genes***. Identifying the genetic and behavioral similarities has led biologists to use many species as **models**, for example, **rats** and **mice**, in observation and experimental studies. And studying these model species has helped scientists build a fuller understanding of human **health** and behavior.

Nowadays, young people can **access** a large amount of **information** about the living world through books and the Internet. We know from biologists' observations and genetic studies that there are more than one million insect species. We also know, from biology experiments, that plants move to face the sun and are protected because of **the greenhouse effect***. From studies such as **the Human Genome Project*** and from other studies too, we know that over 20,000 genes play a part in forming physical human characteristics, and changes in certain genes put us in greater danger of getting particular **diseases**. However, there are still so many questions to which we still do not have the answers. It is only through careful inquiry, based on previous knowledge and observation, that the next **generation** of biologists will be able to advance our understanding of the living world.

However, young biologists must be **aware** of the fact that the field of Biology is **dynamic** and always changing. Much of the knowledge we currently accept as fact today, and the information we find in our biology textbooks, was at one time based on **controversial theories**—and in some cases, people are still arguing about these ideas. In fact, Biologists still face many doubts and questions today, not only from people in the **academic community** but also from people in the political world and in **civil** society. Not everyone agrees about everything biologists claim to be true, even when the **evidence** is strong.

In spite of social pressures and political **challenges**, the field of modern biology—through the careful use of the scientific method—has continued to advance greatly, particularly over the last few **decades**. Our understanding of the **ecosystem***, food production and farming, **medicine** and the human **genome***, as well as to the development of new materials for all the products that we buy and sell, has made remarkable progress.

Modern Biology relates to all **aspects** of our world today, from the **environment** and society to health. Let us now look at how the study of Biology has **evolved**, the **issues** biologists face in their research, and think about what the future of Biology may hold.

History of Biology

Biology developed from both medicine and natural history (observation of animals and plants). Since the Ancient Greeks, doctors have been experimenting and carefully observing the human body, while **naturalists*** have been classifying and observing the behavior of animals and plants and making records of **fossils** (the remains of animals and plants that we find in rocks).

Then came **"The Scientific Revolution"*** and **"The Age of Enlightenment"*** from the 15th to the 18th **century**, which led to the common use of the scientific method of inquiry all over the world. From these **initial** experiments and observations and the use of the scientific method, two great figures in modern Biology appeared, Gregor Mendel and Charles Darwin. Their work in the 19th century resulted in two important new **areas** of inquiry: **genetics*** and **evolution**. Biologists who followed these two early scientists led the national movements of scientific progress for modern society as the field of Biology became more popular and well-respected.

This led to a growth in the number of biologists, which in turn led to an increase in specialized fields of study at the beginning of the 20th century. Many new fields **emerged** from this growth, such as modern **biochemistry*** and **microbiology***, to name only two.

All biologists need to have a general understanding of the **formal sciences*** and **physical sciences***. However, Biology is not now and never has been a "stand-alone" field. Biologists often **require** knowledge in other fields too, from the **social sciences*** to **applied sciences***. In the last decade **specifically**, universities have welcomed this growing relationship between different fields of learning and have formed departments in which researchers from these different fields work closely together. A good example of this is the growing relationships between academics working in **STEM*** subjects (science, **technology***, **engineering***, and **mathematics***).

STEM researchers **collaborate** in **research** and development, both in the academic setting and in industry. This continuing shared work amongst STEM researchers has grown into new fields of study, such as **Biotechnology, Bioengineering, Bioinformatics and Biostatistics***. Biotechnology research has provided advances in medicine (e.g., **stem cells***), **agriculture** (e.g., **GMO crops***) and industry (e.g., **cosmetics***). Bioengineering research has helped develop **tools** that support medicine (e.g., **MRI*** and **prosthetics***) and industry (ready-to-eat foods). Bioinformatics research has used **computers** and **software*** to make tools that can identify new medicines and catch criminals, for example, by using their personal biological information. Biostatistics research has helped us to build better public health systems by using population **data** to identify risks and the causes of diseases.

Challenges and Problems in Biology Today

Developments in biology have led to many controversial issues in today's society. First, there are the **ethical** problems. For example, many people in today's society argue about whether animal models and humans should be used in experiments to advance medicine and science. Our ability to **clone*** animals, and possibly humans, and create **designer babies** has led to a great deal of **debate** in the academic and political communities, as well as in civil society.

Moreover, there is a global **consensus** around the world about the ethical problems relating to the development and use of biological **weapons** in times of war. To deal with these current and future ethical problems, specialists in the fields of STEM research have set up ethics committees to put **global** and local standards in place that include rules of behaviour for research and development.

Second, there are concerns about the laws we need regarding human rights and what we consider to be private information. With our present-day **technology** and our ability to gather and store so much information, the question of who has the right to know our personal, genetic, and **medical** information has become more and more important.

Although gathering the genetic information of a large population could progress the development of **cures** for serious diseases and other health problems, we need to ask how we can protect our own private genetic information. When we take a **survey** on the Internet or use our **point card*** to buy something, the company gathers and saves some of our personal information. We can choose not to share our names or say where we are, so our private information may not always be shared. However, in the case of genetic information, it is **unique** only to us, and thus, we cannot keep the information about who we are a secret. Therefore, our medical or health **insurance** company or our new employer could be able to get our personal genetic information and use it for their own purposes.

This problem raises many questions. Could it be possible for these insurance companies and my employer to use my genetic information against me? Could a health insurance company refuse to give me insurance? Could they make me pay more based on my genetic information? Could an employer decide not to employ me due to a genetic marker that shows I am in danger of having **mental** health problems in the future, for example? What if my genetic tests provide **false** results? These false results could lead me to make costly health choices, like having a medical operation I do not really need. While some countries have already begun to make laws to protect people's personal genetic information, many countries still have little clear protection in place for information or no protection at all.

In short, yes, it is true that advances in Biology are helpful for society because they are giving us better health care, protecting the environment, and making our lives safer and more **convenient**. However, these advances raise many ethical questions and present big challenges, both to academics and to those who make our laws.

The Future of Biology

The **focus** of biological research has changed much over the last few centuries, and the rate of change has been very fast. We expect that there will be even more advances in what biologists research and who they will be working together with in the future. Biologists will continue to be important members of **teams** of specialists who will lead the way to new developments and discoveries. Biologists, working together with people in other fields of research and industry, will lead us to new forms of art, new products that are better for the environment, and better kinds of medical care. Future biologists will continue to find much to observe and many new questions we have yet to answer. As well as looking for answers to new questions and problems, they will continue to look again at the questions we have already answered and try to find new and better ways of dealing with existing problems.

Two famous Japanese scientists who have won the **Nobel Prize***, are leading the way for young people today who wish to become biologists in the future. We have much to learn from looking at what they have been able to do.

First, from Osamu Shimomura, who won the Nobel Prize in Chemistry (2008), we can learn about the importance of **persistence** and natural curiosity. Although his research was with **jellyfish**, it has made a big difference around the world in many other fields, including medical science and the fight against serious diseases (Nobel Prize Outreach, 2025a, 2025b).

Secondly, there is Shinya Yamanaka, who won the Nobel Prize in Medicine (2012). From his example, students of Biology can learn about the importance of challenging well-known beliefs and looking again at the hypotheses that many people accept as true. Yamanaka's work has been very important in building our understanding of how human **cells** work and has led to the growth of a whole new field of study, **stem research*** (Nobel Prize Outreach, 2025a, 2025b).

Employment Opportunities for Biologists

Your first inquiries, those questions you had as a child, could one day lead you to study Biology at university. Higher degrees (BS, MS and PhD degrees) and research experience in biology can lead to many employment opportunities in academic research, product development for business companies or employment in which you could even help **governments** to make well-informed decisions that will shape people's lives, and human society for the better.

Moreover, applying your advanced knowledge of Biology to other interests and in other fields, including subjects such as art, **fashion**, and **robotics***, could not only help you to make enough money to have a very good standard of living, they are also good for society. There are artists who make art based on the **patterns** and designs we see in nature; there are fashion designers that make **clothing** from natural materials and **plastic waste***, and there are **biomedical engineers*** who build robots that can do medical operations (**robo-surgeons***). Just think, if you decide to study Biology at a **Liberal Arts*** university, you could be the next person to express the beauty of **bacteria** in a new kind of art or make the next new bioplastic for use in fashion design, or you may even build the next robo-surgeon!

References

Nobel Prize Outreach. (2025a). The Nobel prize in chemistry 2008. *NobelPrize.org*. https://www.nobelprize.org/prizes/chemistry/2008/summary/

Nobel Prize Outreach. (2025b). The Nobel prize in physiology or medicine 2012. *NobelPrize.org*. https://www.nobelprize.org/prizes/medicine/2012/summary/

Adapted from a text by Jeanette Dennisson, M.S. (Molecular Biology)
Associate Professor, Content and Language Integrated Learning (CLIL) and English for Specific Purposes (ESP—Biology)
College of Liberal Arts and Sciences
Tokyo Medical and Dental University
Japan

Vocabulary

Words From the Second 1,000 High-Frequency General Service Word List

agriculture
argued
babies
behavior(s)
century
clothing
creature(s)
convenient
creatures
crops
cures
disease(s)
false
fashion

government(s)
health
information/(well-) informed
insect
inquiry
legs
medicine
models
park
patterns
risk
tools
weapons
worm

Words From the Academic Word List

academic(s)
access
analyse
areas
aspects
aware
challenges
civil
collaborate
community
computers
consensus
controversial
create
data
debate
decades
design
dynamic
emerge
environment
ethics/ethical
evidence
evolve/evolution
focus

foundations
generation
global
identify
initial
insurance
issues
medical
mental
method
persistence
physical
previous
research
require
sections
similarities
specifically
survey
teams
technology
theories
unique
utilize

Glossary

Applied sciences (Noun phrase): Fields that apply science methods of biology and statistics. Examples include medicine, engineering, agriculture.

Biochemistry (Noun): Study of the function of molecules (e.g., proteins, nucleic acids, lipids, vitamins, hormones) in living things.

Biology/biological (Noun/Adjective): The study of life and living things. Biological = relating to the characteristics of life and living things.

Cells (Noun, plural): The smallest unit of life.

Clone (Noun): A living thing that has been produced as a copy of another without using the process of sexual reproduction, which has exactly the same genetic characteristics as the original.

Cosmetics (Noun, plural): A preparation applied to the body to improve its appearance. Eg. lipstick, eye shadow, skin care products, etc.

Ecosystem (Noun): A biological community of living things that exist together within the setting of their environment.

Formal sciences (Noun phrase): Those fields of study based on logic rather than real-world experience. Examples are mathematics and statistics.

Fossils (Noun, plural): The remains of ancient plants and animals that are found and preserved in rocks.

Genes/Genetics (Noun, plural): The biological units of characteristics that are passed from parent to child, which cause the child to be similar to the parent. Genetics = the scientific field of study of genes and the process of how these are passed on from one generation to the next, and changing, recombining or remaining the same.

GMO crops (Noun phrase, plural): GMO (Acronym) = Genetically Modified Organism. Crops = plants grown for food. GMO crops have had their genes changed by scientists with the intention of improving the quality of crops.

Human genome/The human genome project (Noun phrase): Human Genome = The complete set of human DNA sequences. The Human Genome Project = An international scientific project that identified and mapped all of the genes found in the human genome, both physically (what they are) and functionally (what they do).

Hypothesis (Noun): An idea or educated guess based on prior knowledge you test and try to support through observation or experimentation. Plural form = **hypotheses**.

Liberal Arts (Noun phrase): "Liberal arts is a field of study based on rational thinking, and it includes the areas of humanities, social and physical sciences, and mathematics. A liberal arts education emphasizes the development of critical thinking … the ability to solve complex problems, and an understanding of ethics and morality, as well as a desire to continue to learn." Retrieved from https://www.thoughtco.com/liberal-arts-definition-4585053

Microbiology (Noun): field of biology that studies bacteria, viruses, fungi, etc., using microscopes, genetics, and culturing.

MRI (Acronym): **Magnetic Resonance Imaging** is a technique used to take special images of the organs in the body using strong magnetic fields and radio waves.

Nobel Prize (Noun phrase): An international award given to people who do outstanding work in their field, which has significance for the whole world. For more information, visit the Nobel Prize home page. https://www.nobelprize.org/

Physical sciences (Noun phrase): fields of natural science that study nonliving things. These include astronomy, physics, chemistry, and the Earth sciences (meteorology and geology).

Plastic waste (Noun phrase): Plastic objects and material that has not been properly recycled and causes problems in the environment as a result.

Point card (Noun phrase): A special card given to customers by businesses that will give them points each time they buy something. Points can be saved up, then used to get lower prices on other products from the same company in the future.

Prosthetics (Noun, plural): Artificial body parts (e.g. legs, hands, hearts, breast implants).

Robo-surgeon (Noun): A robot that performs medical operations.

Robotics (Noun): The branch of technology relating to robots (machines) that are designed to reduce the amount of work that humans normally do.

Scientific method (Noun phrase): The method in the natural sciences that uses observation, measurement and experimentation to test a hypothesis.

Social sciences (Noun phrase): fields of sciences that study human societies. Examples are anthropology, economics, psychology and sociology (see the Learning Activity below). You can find out more about these subjects in other chapters of this book.

Software (Noun): The programs or operating information that control computer functions.

Species (Noun): A group of animals or plants that can reproduce after their own kind. It is one group below a genus. One example is Homo sapiens (modern humans) from the genus Homo.

Stem cell research *(Noun phrase):* The study of how stem cells develop, repair, and regrow into tissue and organs. The purpose of this study is to better understand diseases so that stem cells can be applied to medical treatments. Example research projects include the study of bone marrow transplantation.

The Age of Enlightenment (Noun phrase): The Enlightenment, also known as the Age of Reason, was an intellectual and cultural movement in the 18th century that emphasized reason over superstition and science over blind faith.

The greenhouse effect (Noun): The trapping of the heat from the sun in the Earth's atmosphere.

The Scientific Revolution (Noun phrase): is the name given to a period of drastic change in scientific thought that took place during the 16th and 17th centuries. It replaced the Greek view of nature that had dominated science for almost 2,000 years.

Some of the People Who Work in the Field of Biology

Biologist (Noun): A scientist who specializes in the study of living things.

Biomedical Engineers (Noun. Plural): Scientists who work across the fields of Biology, medicine and engineering, integrating the knowledge and techniques of each field to solve medical problems.

Botanist (Noun): A scientist who specializes in the growth, structure, evolution, and uses of plants. A famous person who has contributed to botany: Charles Darwin (naturalist).

Ecologist (Noun): A scientist who studies ecosystems and the diversity and behavior of the animals and plants that live there. A famous person who has contributed to ecology: Steve Irwin (wildlife conservationist/television personality).

Entomologist (Noun): A scientist who studies specific kinds of insects. A famous person who has contributed to entomology: Edward Fred Knipling.

Epidemiologist (Noun): A public health professional who investigates patterns and causes of disease and injury in humans and, supports research, community education and aims to improve health policy.

Geneticist (Noun): A scientist who studies variation in genes and their functions and roles in disease and health.

Naturalists (Noun, plural): Scientists that study nature and believe only in what can be observed (and do not believe in supernatural things such as gods, spirits, and souls).

Zoologist (Noun): A scientist in animal biology or ecology who specializes in the behavior of animals. Richard Dawkins is famous scientist who has contributed to evolutionary theory and zoology.

CHAPTER 25

CHEMISTRY

Jeanette Dennisson
Tokyo Medical and Dental University, Japan

Introduction

Have you ever made **slime***, baked a **cake**, or tried to **wash** chocolate out of your **shirt**? For each, we follow a **recipe*** or **instructions created** by **chemists***. The **majority** of these recipes **require** some kind of **chemical reaction**.

Making slime is a chemical reaction and a **fun** way to play around with chemistry. The chemist's recipe explains the **exact ratio** of **reactants*** (glue:borax ratio) and the **correct temperature** and time to **cook** the reactants. If you change the recipe, you will not get the same **product** - the slime may come out hard, **liquidy***, or **grainy***. **Options** to the recipe may include **creating suspensions*** (**mixtures**) which are not **chemical reactions*** but just as fun—just **mix** in **glitter***, **beads***, and coloring to the slime and make all kinds of different **versions** to play with.

Now that you have many types of slime, it is time for a **snack***. To make a cake, you read the **ingredients*** for the cake **batter*** and measure each one **perfectly** (2 **cups** of **flour**, 1 egg, 1 cup of milk…) mix them well, and place in the **oven*** to bake. While waiting, you could not **resist** taking a small **lick*** of the remaining chocolate in the **bowl** and **absentmindedly*** **wiping** your chocolate-covered **fingers** on your new white **shirt**! You then **immediately soak** your shirt in the **sink** with some **laundry detergent*** and **warm** water.

Let's **reflect** on all the **chemistry*** that is going on. First, you mixed the reactants for the cake together. This mixture forms a **suspension** and when heated in the **oven*** goes through a **chemical reaction** to create a **fluffy*** chocolate cake. The chocolate chips change their chemical state from **solid** to **liquid** but do not go through a chemical reaction, and if left on the **counter*** long enough will return to solid chocolate again. The chocolate you ate is now being broken down by **enzymes*** in your mouth, **stomach**, and small **intestine*** for **absorption*** as **energy** in your body. **Finally**, the chocolate on your shirt is **reacting** with the **detergent*** to surround the chocolate stain and **wash** it away into the water. By using warm water, you have sped up the **overall reaction** and with some **scrubbing*** and **rinsing***, you will have the **final** product: a clean white shirt (and **dirty**, chocolate water).

Now, did chemists just use trial-and-**error** to make the slime and cake recipes and create the laundry detergent that works like **magic***? In some cases, the answer is yes. However, modern chemistry uses **empirical** and systematic **methods** that go beyond **guesswork*** to learn about the world around us, allowing us to **efficiently*** create new materials we can use to **improve** our lives. Some **revolutionary creations** by chemists that have changed modern society include **nylon*** for **clothing**, **penicillin*** for **treating bacterial*** **infections***, **plastics*** for many of our common **household*** **items**, and LEDs found in most **electronic*** **devices**. How did the chemists **achieve** such creations? The first step was the discovery of the **atom***.

Let's use Lego building **blocks** for **comparison** to better understand what an atom is. Lego building blocks can be put together to create objects like a house, **spaceship***, or car. Each atom is like a **tiny*** building block that we cannot see with our own eyes. What do the atoms in that orange juice on the table look like? Or why is it that shiny **jewelry*** can be made up of atoms and have no color? Chemists have made machines and developed **techniques** to study atoms up close, and have used that knowledge of atoms to create new materials. Let's find out more about these building blocks of everything on Earth.

Each **unique** atom is known as an **element** each with its own special name and **properties***. Can you name any of the 118 elements **listed** on the **periodic** table? Look around your room and see how many different substances you can find? What elements are they made of? Is the substance a solid? Is it a liquid? Or is it a gas*? Both elements and **molecules*** have unique **physical** states (whether it is solid, liquid, or gas) that can change based on the temperature or pressure. The **dynamics** of elements can be explained through chemistry.

Think about water, as an example. Every molecule looks **identical**, containing **exactly** two hydrogen (H) atoms and one oxygen (O) atom that **connect** together in the same way. Depending on the temperature, water molecules move faster or **slower**; at higher temperatures they move faster and need more space to move. This **extra** space between molecules changes liquid water to a gas **phase** (steam). When the temperature goes down below 0°C the molecules **slow** down and come closer together needing less space, and the liquid water changes to a solid phase (**ice**). Pressure can also change the movement of molecules and force them closer together at higher pressure and **vice versa***. Understanding the **ideal** environment of molecules and how to create those environments for new material creation is the **job** of chemists.

Not all atoms like to connect and may need special environments before they do. When you make the chocolate cake, the mixture will not go through the chemical reaction until heat is applied. Heat increases the **kinetic*** energy of molecules to speed up the chemical reaction that forms the solid cake form (while kinetic energy can also be created with **rapid stirring**, it would not produce enough energy for this chemical reaction). Another way to speed up chemical reactions is to use a **catalyst***. There are many catalysts known as enzymes in our body used to speed the **process** of breaking up food. Chefs and **bakers**, like chemists, experiment with the best **cooking** methods, and even **adapt** the use of catalysts, such as baking **soda***, in their cooking.

Thus, by understanding atoms and how they can **combine** as reactants to make new products efficiently, chemists can better control our environment. So, next time you wonder how a cake is created from the basic ingredients of flour, milk and eggs, remember that chemistry is the **fascinating*** force behind it.

History

Long ago in places like Egypt and China, interest in elements began in the **areas** of metal works, **pottery***, and **medicine**. This was followed by **alchemists*** who desired **longevity*** and wealth and with the **ideal** of changing **copper** into gold and finding the recipe for eternal life. Alchemy's basic **philosophy**, although not so **altruistic***, led to the start of modern chemistry, and alchemists developed experimental **techniques**, devices, and even a special language that **combined** well with empirical observation and systematic experimentation that is still used in modern chemistry today.

It was in the **Scientific Revolution*** between the 16th and 18th **century, during** which **focus shifted** from alchemy to more modern chemistry. In 1662, Robert Boyle experimented on how gasses **behave** and **established Boyle's Law***. Thereafter in the 1770s and 1780s, Antoine Lavoisier, the "Father of Modern Chemistry," found that atoms follow a set of rules he called the **conservation of mass***. He created an easy naming system we use now for elements and **compounds***. The conservation of mass states that atoms can never be lost or created; they just change their **location** or order and form new compounds through chemical reactions. This rule is the basis of all fields of modern chemistry.

The next great discovery in chemistry was by John Dalton who developed the **atomic theory*** in the early 19th century. This theory helps us understand **matter*** and the **components** of matter, namely atoms, which have different masses and properties. These atoms were organized by **mass** by Dmitri Mendeleev in the periodic table in 1869.

Mass is determined by **subatomic particles*** (**electrons***, **protons***, and **neutrons***) which were discovered in turn between the late 19th and early 20th centuries. If atoms are like Lego building blocks, subatomic particles are like the sides of the block, the circular **bumps*** on the top and the circular **holes** on the **bottom**. Each part is **essential** for connecting other blocks to it or allowing them to be placed side-by-side. If one part of the block is changed, the **matching** block could no longer connect. In a **similar** way, an atom (a complete block) connects with another atom (another complete block) in a unique way. We can observe and measure these **connections** between blocks using the technique called **spectroscopy***.

Linus Pauling used spectroscopy to teach us about **chemical bonds*** and **electronegativity***. Chemical bonds are how atoms connect and stay together. Electronegativity is how strongly they stay together. The bond can be **weak** or strong depending on the electronegativity. Let's imagine a building block again. You can **stack*** blocks easily on top of each other in one direction and easily break them **apart** at any point in the stack—a linear **structure** forms a weak bond. On the other hand, if you stack blocks to make a **brick** wall-like structure and **overlap** the blocks a little each time, it becomes more difficult to break the wall at one place than one simple stack of blocks. Atoms work in similar ways. A single bond is like those connections formed in one stack of blocks. There is only one block **attached** on top and one attached at the bottom. A double or **triple*** bond is like the overlapping brick wall with **multiple** blocks attached at the top, bottom, and sides, so they overlap various blocks. The number of connections (bonds) increase the electronegativity and thus the strength of the bonds between blocks. All these dynamics we see with Lego building blocks represent how atoms work at the **microscopic*** level. But how do we know what is really going on between atoms?

Instruments like **nuclear magnetic resonance (NMR)*** and **mass spectrometry*** allow chemists to observe bonds and forces between atoms for any molecule or compound. The NMR **revolutionized** our understanding of the shapes and chemical reactions of molecules, and Bloch and Purcell who discovered NMR were thus recognized with the Nobel **Prize** in Physics in 1952. NMR technology was further developed for current uses in drug discovery, how the body works in a **healthy/unhealthy*** state, and presence of **pollutants*** in environmental **samples**.

Employment Opportunities for Chemists

Chemistry is not just about understanding everyday things; it also helps us **solve** big problems. For example, **environmental chemists*** can **tackle*** the problem of air **pollution*** by trying to figure out what harmful gasses are in the air and how they **affect** our **health**.

Physical chemists* look at the physical properties of substances and how they change when the environment changes, such as how ice **melts** in a warm room. By understanding these phase changes, physical chemists can develop more efficient and **sustainable** energy **sources** like wind and **solar*** energy or create heat **resistant fabric*** for **firefighters***.

Organic chemists* focus on compounds containing **carbon*** (C), the main building block of life. That means they help in the development of **drug*** discovery which includes **antibiotics***, like penicillin, and **pain relievers***, in the creation of new materials such as plastic containers, **packaging***, clothing and even electronics, and in the production of **perfumes***, **beverages*** and foods.

On the other hand, **inorganic chemists*** deal with substances that do not contain **carbon***, like metals and **minerals**. Understanding the properties of metals is important for **medical imaging*** to **detect cancer***, **semiconductors*** for **mobile*** devices, building **construction** materials, and protection of historical **artifacts***. This can allow doctors to **identify** the **severity** of your cancer, help Apple to extend the **battery*** life of your **phone**, and support builders to make buildings resistant to earthquake **damage**.

Lastly, there are **analytical chemists***. They help us stay safe by testing food, drugs, and the air for **harmful** things. They often work **alongside*** the **government** (**police** and environmental agencies) and medical **professionals**.

The job **prospects** for chemists include making medicines, protecting the environment, and creating new **biodegradable*** or **nano-sized*** materials. Many chemists **collaborate*** with other scientists, **academia**, and industry to achieve their **goals**. Moreover, chemists with **computer skills** who like to work with tiny things are **definitely** in demand.

Controversies in Chemistry

Modern chemistry has allowed for many products which make our lives more **convenient**. However, these same products are facing various **controversies, especially** over the last 30 years or more. Let's look at a few examples.

First of all, we use daily household products for **cleaning** and **maintaining** our health. For example, when you wash your **hair** and the **shampoo*** washes away down the **drain***, how will it affect the water environment outside?

If your nylon jacket **repels*** rain, does not **stain** easily and can be washed in the washing machine without **deterioration***, this type of material in your jacket was **chemically** made and was not produced from nature. What will happen to this material once you throw the jacket away? Will the material break down into chemical components or remain **undegradable*** and become **bulk waste**?

Next, let's consider food products such as **mint*** gum, **sour** onion potato chips, and green **tea** chocolate. All these products contain **additives*** which are chemicals created to **artificially** make the **flavors** or coloring of the **original** natural product. Are these additives and **preservatives*** in our foods safe to eat? Will they **harm** us if we continue to eat them? These are the current concerns of many **consumers**.

The Future of Chemistry

The future of chemistry is full of possibilities that can make our world **healthier** and more sustainable. **Imagine nanotechnology***, where scientists create incredibly tiny things. How about the **emerging green chemistry***? We are all **worried** about **climate*** change. Wouldn't it be **cool** if we had drink containers that will break down in a day and leave no waste as a **replacement** for plastic **bottles**? Or if we washed our **clothes** and used the dirty water to **fertilize*** our vegetable gardens?

Powerful computers are also changing the direction of chemistry **research**. **Computational chemistry** will be able to solve **complex** chemical **puzzles** and **design** new materials. Could we **someday*** order a **personalized*** **drug*** to **treat** our cancer? Could we make material that makes a **plane** as light as a car thus reducing the **fuel*** it burns and carbon it produces?

The future of chemistry will be able to help with the **United Nations Sustainable Development Goals*** (SDGs). Chemists will be able to help clean up pollution, create **renewable*** energy sources, and improve **healthcare***. This is a chance for chemists to shape a brighter future for everyone.

Post-reading questions:

1. Explain how temperature and pressure affect the phases of matter.
2. What are catalysts, and how do they impact chemical reactions?
3. Can you name and describe different areas of specialization in chemistry?
4. What are the pros and cons of chemical additives in products?
5. After reading, how does chemistry affect your daily life?

Adapted from a text by Jeanette Dennisson, M.S. (Molecular Biology)
Associate Professor, Content and Language Integrated Learning (CLIL) and English for Specific Purposes (ESP—Biology)
College of Liberal Arts and Sciences
Tokyo Medical and Dental University
Japan

Vocabulary

Words From the Second 1,000 General Service High Frequency Word List

Here is the word list in alphabetical order:

apart	hair
artificially	harm
bake	harmful
bakers	health
band	healthier
behave	healthy
blocks	holes
bottles	ice
bottom	ideal
bowl	ideals
brick	imagine
cake	immediately
century	improve
clean	inside
cleaning	instruments
clothes	liquid
clothing	listed
combine	matching
combined	medicine
comparison	melts
connect	melted
connections	minerals
convenient	mix
cooking	mixture
cool	multiple
copper	orange
correct	original
cream	pain
cup	perfectly
damage	phone
dirty	plane
double	police
during	prize
especially	puzzles
essential	rapid
exact	reflect
exactly	replacement
extra	request
fingers	resist
flavors	resistant
flour	samples
fun	severity
government	shirt

shirt
sink
skills
slow
slower
soiled
solid
solve
sour
stain
steam
stirring
stomach

taste
tea
temperature
treat
treating
warm
wash
washed
waste
weak
wiped
worried

Words From the Academic Word List

Here is the list of words in alphabetical order:

academia
achieve
adapt
affect
areas
attached
bonds
bulk
chemical
chemically
communities
complex
components
compounds
computational
computer
construction
consumers
controversies
created
creating
creations
definitely
design
detect
devices
dynamics
element
emerging
empirical
energy

environment
environmental
error
established
focus
goals
identical
identify
instructions
items
job
location
maintaining
majority
medical
methods
options
overall
overlap
periodic
phase
philosophy
physical
process
professionals
prospects
ratio
reacting
reaction
research
revolutionary

revolutionized
require
shifted
similar
sources
structure
suspension

sustainable
technique
technology
theory
unique
versions

Glossary

It is not necessary for students to memorize these words and phrases

Absentmindedly (adverb): Used to describe the condition of not being fully aware or focused. When you do something **absentmindedly** you do it without paying full attention to the task at hand.

Absorption (noun): Refers to the process where a substance takes in another substance, such as a sponge **absorbs** water.

Additives (noun): Chemicals added to products to achieve specific effects, such as flavor, color, or preservation.

Alchemists (noun): Early scientists of experimental chemistry, often with goals to transform base metals into gold and discover the secret of eternal life.

Alongside (preposition): Next to or parallel to, in cooperation or association with something or someone else.

Altruistic (adjective): Showing selfless concern for the well-being and happiness of others. Unselfish and even benevolent behavior.

Analytical chemists (noun): Scientists who analyze substances to determine their composition and properties and are involved in quality control, research, and problem-solving across industries such as pharmaceuticals, environmental monitoring, food safety, and forensic science.

Antibiotics (noun): Medications that inhibit the growth of bacteria and therefore treat bacterial infections.

Artifacts (noun): Objects made or modified by humans, typically of historical and cultural significance.

Atomic Theory (noun): A theory proposed by John Dalton that explains matter as composed of indivisible atoms with different masses.

Atoms (noun): The smallest building blocks of matter, consisting of protons, neutrons, and electrons.

Bacterial (adjective): Relating to bacteria, which are microscopic single-celled organisms that can be harmful or beneficial.

Batter (noun): A thick, semiliquid mixture used in cooking, primarily baked goods and fried foods. The fish in fish and chips is often cooked in **batter**.

Battery (noun): A device that stores electrical energy and releases it when needed in the form of electrical power.

Beads (noun): Small, often round objects with a hole through the center, made from various materials such as glass, plastic, wood, metal, or stone. Regularly used in jewelry to create bracelets and necklaces.

Beverages (noun): Liquid substances consumed for refreshment, such as water, juice, tea, coffee, or soft drinks.

Biodegradable (adjective): Capable of being decomposed naturally by bacteria or other living organisms and reducing negative effects on the environment.

Boyle's Law (noun): A gas law that describes the relationship between pressure and volume of a gas at a constant temperature.

Bumps (noun): Raised or rounded areas on a surface. Small, protuberant parts or unevenness on an object.

Cancer (noun): A group of diseases characterized by abnormal cell growth and the potential to invade or spread to other parts of the body.

Carbon (noun): A chemical element with atomic number 6 that forms the basis of life on earth. Has many forms, including diamonds and graphite.

Catalyst (noun): A substance that speeds up a chemical reaction without being consumed in the process.

Chemical bonds (noun): Connections between atoms in molecules, determining their stability and properties.

Chemical reaction (noun): A process in which substances (reactants) interact to produce new substances (products) with different properties.

Chemist (noun): A scientist that focuses on the study of chemistry.

Chemistry (noun): The scientific study of matter, its properties, composition, and behavior, and how it changes during chemical reactions.

Climate (noun): The long-term pattern of weather conditions in a particular area of the earth. It includes temperature, humidity and levels of rain.

Collaborate (verb): To work together with others to achieve a common goal or purpose.

Compounds (noun): Substances formed by the chemical combination of two or more elements.

Conservation of mass (noun): A fundamental principle stating that mass is neither created nor destroyed in chemical reactions; it only changes form.

Counter (noun): In terms of furniture this is a flat, horizontal surface, often elevated, that is used for many purposes such as preparing food, assembling items, or displaying objects.

Detergent (noun): A cleansing agent or substance used for washing and cleaning various surfaces, especially clothes and household items.

Deterioration (noun): The process of becoming worse or less valuable over time. The decline in quality or the condition of something or someone.

Drain (noun): A pipe or channel that carries away liquid waste or water from a particular area.

Drug (noun): A substance used to diagnose, treat, or prevent diseases or medical conditions; a medication.

Efficiently (adverb): Describes the manner in which a task or activity is performed with minimum waste of time, effort, or resources.

Electronegativity (noun): A measure of an atom's ability to attract and hold electrons in a chemical bond, showing its tendency to form negative ions.

Electronic (adjective): Refers to machines, systems, or technology that operates using electrical circuits, such as computers, smartphones, and other digital devices.

Electrons (noun): Subatomic particles with a negative charge, orbiting around the nucleus of an atom, involved in chemical reactions and electricity.

Elements (noun): Substances made up of atoms with the same number of protons; they cannot be broken down into simpler substances.

Environmental chemists (noun): Scientists who study the impact of chemicals on the environment and develop methods to reduce pollution.

Enzymes (noun): Biological molecules, usually proteins, that act as catalysts in living things to facilitate and accelerate chemical reactions.

Fabric (noun): Material produced by weaving or knitting fibers together, used for making clothes, upholstery, or other items.

Fascinating (adjective): Extremely interesting, captivating, or enchanting. Holding one's attention due to its intriguing qualities.

Fertilize (verb): To apply natural or artificial substances to soil or plants to promote growth (enriching soil with nutrients).

Firefighter (noun): A person whose profession involves putting out and fighting fires and providing rescue services during emergencies.

Fluffy (adjective): Used to describe something that is light, soft, and airy in texture.

Fuel (noun): A substance burned or used to produce energy, often in the form of heat or electricity.

Gas (noun): One of the three common phases of matter, characterized by molecules with high energy and a lack of definite shape or volume.

Glitter (noun): Small, shiny, and sparkling particles made from various materials, such as plastic, metal, glass, or reflective film.

Grainy (adjective): Something described as grainy often has a coarse or uneven surface and can be made up of tiny, distinct particles that can be felt or seen. For example, sand is **grainy**.

Green chemistry (noun): An approach that focuses on developing environmentally friendly and sustainable chemical processes and products.

Guesswork (noun): Refers to making estimations, predictions, or decisions based on intuition, speculation, or conjecture rather than on concrete evidence, facts, or logical reasoning.

Healthcare (noun): The organized delivery of medical services, including diagnosis, treatment, and prevention of diseases, to maintain and improve health.

Household (noun): Relating to activities, items, or products used within a home or domestic setting.

Imaging (noun): The process of producing visual representations or pictures of the interior of a body or objects, often used in medicine or scientific research.

Infection (noun): The invasion and multiplication of harmful microorganisms, such as bacteria, viruses, or fungi, within an organism's body, leading to signs and symptoms of illness.

Ingredients (noun): Individual elements used in the preparation of food, drinks, or any other products.

Inorganic chemists (noun): Scientists who study compounds that do not contain carbon, often focusing on metals and minerals which are important to fields such as materials science, medicine, electronics, and environmental chemistry.

Intestine (noun): A long, tube-like organ in the digestive system that extends from the stomach to the anus.

Jewelry (noun): Personal ornaments, such as earrings, rings, necklaces, and bracelets. Worn for adornment or as a symbol of status or affection.

Kinetic (adjective): Possessing or having energy due to motion.

Laundry detergent (noun): A cleaning agent used for washing clothes and fabric items.

Liquid (noun): One of the three common phases of matter, characterized by molecules with moderate energy and a definite volume but no definite shape.

Liquidy (adjective): An informal term used to describe a substance that feels and behaves like a liquid.

Longevity (noun): The quality or condition of having a long duration of life, existence, or usefulness. The ability to live or last for a long time.

Magic (noun): Often refers to supernatural or paranormal practices that can influence events, control forces of nature, or achieve mysterious or extraordinary results.

Mass spectrometry (noun): A technique used to measure the mass and charge of atoms and molecules.

Matter (noun): Anything that has mass and occupies space.

Microscopic (adjective): Extremely small and only visible under a microscope.

Mint (noun): A fragrant herb often used in cooking, beverages, or as a flavoring agent.

Mobile (adjective): Capable of being moved or carried. Refers to mobile phones or other devices that can be moved around and even used while in motion.

Molecules (noun): Combinations of atoms bonded together, forming distinct substances.

Nanoparticle (noun): A small group of atoms, molecules, or ions that typically ranges in size from 1 to 100 nanometers.

Nano-sized (adjective): Having dimensions measured in nanometers. Extremely small.

Nanotechnology (noun): The creation and control of materials at the nanoscale level.

Neutrons (noun): Subatomic particles with no electrical charge, found in the nucleus of an atom, adding to its atomic mass.

NMR (nuclear magnetic resonance) (noun): A technique used to study the properties of atomic parts in molecules.

Nylon (noun): A synthetic polymer material, a type of plastic, that is known for its exceptional strength, durability, and versatility.

Onions (noun): Edible bulb vegetables with a strong, pungent taste, widely used in cooking.

Organic chemists (noun): Scientists who specialize in the study of carbon-containing compounds and their applications.

Oven (noun): An insulated chamber or appliance used for heating and cooking food.

Packaging (noun): Materials used to wrap, protect, or contain products for transport, storage, or sale.

Penicillin (noun): A group of antibiotics derived from molds of the penicillium species. It is used to treat bacterial infections and is one of the first and most widely used antibiotics.

Perfumes (noun): Fragrant substances or scents, often in liquid form, applied to the body or objects to enhance smell.

Personalized (adjective): Customized or tailored for a specific individual or purpose, made to suit personal preferences or requirements.

Phase (noun): A state of matter with distinct physical properties, such as solid, liquid, or gas.

Physical chemists (noun): Scientists who study the physical properties of substances and their behavior under different conditions to contribute to advancements in areas like materials science, nanotechnology, and the development of sustainable energy sources.

Plastic (noun): Refers to a synthetic material made from polymers, which can be molded into various shapes when heated and cooled.

Pollutants (noun): Substances or agents, such as chemicals or waste materials, released into the environment, causing pollution and harm to living organisms.

Pollution (noun): The introduction of harmful or toxic substances into the environment, leading to the degradation of air, water, or land quality and posing risks to human health and ecosystems.

Pottery (noun): Objects made from clay that are shaped and fired at high temperatures, including items like dishes, cups, vases, and sculptures.

Preservatives (noun): Chemicals added to products to extend their shelf life and prevent spoilage.

Products (noun): The substances formed as a result of a chemical reaction between reactants.

Properties (noun): Characteristics or qualities that describe a substance or material.

Protons (noun): Positively charged subatomic particles found in the nucleus of an atom, determining its atomic number.

Reactants (noun): Substances that undergo a chemical reaction to produce new substances (products).

Recipe (noun): A set of instructions, usually for preparing and cooking food.

Relievers (noun): Medications used to relieve symptoms or discomfort.

Renewable (adjective): Capable of being replaced or regenerated naturally within a relatively short period of time and sustainable over the long term.

Repels (verb): Forces something away or prevents it from coming near (resists or drives away).

Rinsing (verb): The process of removing residue, dirt, or cleaning agents from a surface or object by washing or flushing it with clean water or another liquid.

Scientific Revolution (noun): A period of advancement in science and the shift from alchemy to modern chemistry.

Scrubbing (verb): The action of cleaning or rubbing a surface with a brush, abrasive material, or a cleaning tool to remove dirt, stains, grime, or other impurities.

Semiconductors (noun): Materials with electrical conductivity between that of conductors and insulators, used in electronic devices like microchips and transistors.

Shampoo (noun): A liquid cleansing product used for washing hair.

Slime (noun): A thin glutinous liquid matter.

Snack (noun): Small amount of food eaten between meals, often eaten quickly.

Soaks (verb): To sink/immerse something in a liquid for a period of time.

Soda (noun): A carbonated beverage, usually sweetened and flavored, often served cold, and contains bubbles produced by carbon dioxide gas.

Solar (adjective): Relating to or derived from the sun and the use of solar energy, such as solar power or solar panels.

Solid (noun): One of the three common phases of matter, characterized by molecules with low energy and a definite shape and volume.

Someday (adverb): At some point/stage in the future.

Spaceship (noun): A vehicle designed for travel or operation in outer space.

Stack (verb): To arrange objects neatly on top of one another in an organized pile.

Sticky (adjective): Used to describe something that has a tendency to cling to or stick to other objects or surfaces.

Subatomic particles (noun): Smaller parts of atoms, including protons, neutrons, and electrons.

Suspension (noun): Refers to a mixture in which solid particles are dispersed in a liquid medium. The particles are temporarily "suspended" in the liquid.

Spectroscopy (noun): A technique used to study interactions between matter and electromagnetic radiation and to study molecular structures.

Tackle (verb): To confront or deal with a problem, challenge, or task directly and effectively. To handle or address a difficult situation.

Tiny (adjective): Extremely small in size, minute or miniature.

Triple (adjective): Three times as much or in three parts. A quantity or size that is three times the amount of another.

Undegradable (adjective): Not capable of being degraded or broken down naturally over time.

Unhealthy (adjective): Adverse to health. Causing harm or having a negative impact on physical well-being.

Sustainable Development Goals (SDGs) (noun): A set of global goals to address challenges such as poverty, inequality, climate change, and environmental degradation.

Vice Versa (adverb): In the opposite way or order from what has been stated.

CHAPTER 26

PHYSICS

Yasushi Nara
Akita International University Japan

Introduction

The development of natural science often **requires** the discovery of a new 'common sense.' In ancient Greece, the **prevalent*** belief was that the Earth was the center of the **universe**. However, Nicolaus Copernicus (1473–1543) **revolutionized** this understanding around 1,500 by proposing that the Earth **orbits*** the sun, which, in turn, is the center of the universe. However, in modern-day **cosmology*** it is believed that there is no center in the universe. Another **illustration** is the discovery of the **expanding** universe. **Initially**, the universe was **perceived** as **static***, but it was later **established** that the universe is expanding, which means that space is a **dynamic entity capable** of expansion. This **phenomenon** can be well described by Albert Einstein's *theory of relativity**.

Physics* is concerned with the most basic **aspects** of nature, such as matter, **energy**, **motion**, and force. Physics is the study of universal phenomena in which general principles are **obeyed** by everything. For **instance**, all objects fall onto the ground, which is a **consequence** of the universal law of **gravity***.

Modern physics is **vast*** in **scale** and not only deals with the history of the universe, **tracing** back 13.8 **billion** years but also has the **capability** to make **predictions** about the future. For example, we can **estimate** that the sun's lifetime is **approximately** 5 billion years. The question arises: how can we understand aspects of nature that are not directly observable? The answer lies in our ability to **investigate** and understand nature by applying the *scientific method**.

To understand nature, scientists first make a **hypothesis** to answer a question or problem. A scientific hypothesis is an **educated guess**. A scientific hypothesis is a reasonable explanation of an observation or experimental result that is not fully accepted as fact until tested **repeatedly** by experiments. With extensive testing, a hypothesis may become a *law* of physics. An **essential** characteristic of a hypothesis is its **testability***—it should be possible to **demonstrate** its **incorrectness***. In science, the ability to **disprove*** an idea is **crucial**. A hypothesis that can only be proved right, without the **potential** for being proved wrong, does not **qualify** as a scientific hypothesis. The **concept** of **falsification*** serves as a widely applicable test to determine the scientific nature of an idea, marking a **significant distinction** between science and **nonscience***.

History

Before **establishing** the scientific method, Aristotle's (384–322 BC) theory had been accepted for nearly 2000 years, and his views were trusted. Aristotle **derived** his theory from direct observations and sense experience. His main **arguments** included (1) force is needed to keep moving, (2) heavier object falls faster than lighter ones, (3) the earth is the center of the universe. These seem reasonable in the sense that they fit "common sense." Later, Galileo (1564–1642) found that Aristotle's theory was wrong: (1) force is not needed to keep an object moving, (2) all objects fall at the same rate, and (3) the earth is not the center of the universe.

How did Galileo arrive at his **conclusions**? Well, he is one of the scientists **credited** with **formulating** the scientific method. Galileo questioned Aristotle's theory about a falling object based on the following reasoning. If a heavier object falls faster than a lighter one, what will happen when a heavier one and a lighter one are **connected**? As a connected object is heavier than its **individual** parts, it should fall faster than the separate object. However, as one part of the connected object falls faster and the other falls **slower**, a connected object must fall at an **intermediate** speed. This difference led Galileo to propose that all objects fall at the same speed regardless of **weight**. To **confirm** his reasoning, he **conducted** experiments. In these experiments, Galileo dropped stones and lead and saw that they reached the ground at the same time. **Additionally***, he noted that when air **resistance** is a **factor**, heavier objects fall faster.

Aristotle considered that the earth is not moving based on the following argument:

When you drop a stone from the top of a **tower**, the tower is carried by the **rotation*** of the Earth from west to east until the stone lands, which means that the stone should not fall at the base of the tower but rather to the west of it. According to Aristotle, the fact that the stone falls along a **vertical*** line **perpendicular*** to the Earth's surface **implies** that the Earth is **stationary***.

Galileo **challenged** this reasoning. He argued that a stone falling from the top of the **mast*** of a ship **hits** the same place regardless of the ship's motion. We can **immediately** agree with Galileo since an **apple** falls in the same place regardless of its motion when it is dropped **inside** a train. This observation has a crucial **implication**: laws of nature are the same in all **uniformly** moving observers, and there is no experiment that **reveals absolute** motion.

In **essence**, Aristotle worked out his theory mainly from sense experience, which leads to a wrong conclusion. Galileo tries to understand nature through **rational** reasoning **incorporating mathematics*** and experimentation, the **primary elements** of the scientific method. It should be **emphasized** that a theory must be changed or **abandoned** when the theory was proven to be **incorrect**.

Aristotle argued that the motion of the **planet*** follows a circular **path**. **Interestingly***, even Galileo accepted this idea without any reason. However, **astronomer*** and **mathematician***, Johannes Kepler (1571–1630) found a very important fact by analyzing the **planetary*** path. He discovered that the **trajectory*** of planets are **elliptical*** and not simply circular in motion. This discovery **disproved*** Aristotle's theory.

Isaac Newton (1642–1727) developed the first systematic physics theory based on the work of Galileo and Kepler and introduced the theory of **gravitation***. Newton's theory successfully explains the motion of objects including planets **governed** by gravitational force. **Subsequently**, James Clerk Maxwell (1831–1879) formulated a theory of **electromagnetism*** that **enables** the description of a wide **range** of electric and **magnetic*** phenomena. Maxwell's theory **predicts** that light is a wave. However, there is a serious problem: Newton's theory is **inconsistent** with Maxwell's theory. Maxwell's theory predicts that the speed of light is absolute: it is always the same for any observer.

However, Newton's theory says that the speed is relative, which means that the speed depends on the observer. For example, while the speed of a train is 100 km/h relative to the ground, it appears as **zero** from the **viewpoint*** of a person inside the train. In this way, the speed of light must be different for different observers in Newton's theory. Which is **correct**: is the speed of light absolute or relative?

Einstein (1879–1955) is the person who **resolved** this **inconsistency**. He developed the theory of relativity, which supports Maxwell's theory and offered a new theory for the motion of an object and gravity. Thus, Newton's theory was proven incorrect. In the 20th **century**, it turned out that Einstein's theory and Maxwell's theory cannot describe the **atomic*** world, and a new theory called *quantum mechanics** was developed, which is conceptually very different from those existing theories.

Outstanding Questions and Future Directions

Scientific theories **evolve** as they go through stages of **refinement**. Einstein's general relativity is a theory of gravity and explains many aspects of the universe. However, it has limitations. For instance, it cannot be applied at the center of a black **hole** and does not address **extreme** conditions such as the earliest moments of the *Big Bang** (a description **coined*** by Sir Fred Hoyle in 1950). **In contrast**, the atomic world can be understood by quantum mechanics. **Nevertheless**, the two theories are very different. A significant challenge in modern physics is how to **unify** these theories, and **exciting** research into this **area** is happening.

As described above, there is currently no theory to explain what happened before the Big Bang. However, it should be emphasized that in the current Big Bang theory, the Big Bang is not an **explosion** of matter within space, but it is an explosion of *space itself*. Some scientists **speculate*** that before the Big Bang, space and time did not exist. In other words, the Big Bang itself **created** time and space and was the beginning of space-time.

Extreme State of Matter

As is well known, matter **undergoes** changes based on **temperature** or **density***, changing between **solid**, **liquid**, and gas states. For example, water **freezes** into **ice** when the temperature drops below 0°C, while it turns into water **vapor*** at temperatures reaching 100°C. What happens when the temperature or density becomes even higher? At such extreme conditions, **molecules*** and **atoms*** **undergo dissociation***, breaking into positive and **negative ions***. Here, a positive ion refers to the atomic **nucleus***, and a negative ion represents **electrons***. This **unique** state of matter is termed **plasma***, recognized as the fourth state of matter. It is **noteworthy*** that 99% of the universe is filled by the plasma state.

Let us consider what happens when the temperature becomes even higher. At such extreme conditions, even the atomic nucleus **undergoes** dissociation, breaking into **protons*** and **neutrons***. Subsequently, protons and neutrons further dissociate into **quarks*** and **gluons***, which are **elementary*** particles. In general, it is **anticipated** that at very high temperatures and/or densities, matter **transforms** into elementary particles. This **distinct** state of matter is called *quark-gluon plasma** (QGP). Questions naturally arise: Does QGP exist in the universe? What are the properties of QGP?

It is well established that our universe began with the explosion called the Big Bang 13.8 billion years ago. The temperature of the early universe just after the Big Bang (up to a few **milliseconds***, 3.3×10^{-5} seconds) is believed to have been very high, and all the matter was broken down into elementary particles. Namely, the QGP state existed just after the Big Bang. A study of the properties of matter under extreme conditions **involving** high temperature and high density is one of the hottest **topics** in physics. The highest-density matter in the present universe is found in the **core** of a **neutron star***. The properties of neutron stars are investigated by theory and observations. **Theoretical** studies **focusing** on the dynamics of high-energy *heavy-ion collisions** are crucial for **exploring** the properties of QGP matter.

What Is the Shape, Fate, and Contents of the Universe?

Cosmology is the scientific study of the large-scale properties of the Universe as a whole. Cosmology particularly tries to give answers to the following **fundamental** questions about the universe:

- The Fate of the Universe:
  - Will the Universe be **expanding forever***?
  - Will the Universe **eventually shrink***?
- The shape of the universe:
  - Is the Universe flat or **curved**?
  - Is the Universe **infinitely** large or **finite**?
- The content of the universe:
  - What is the most common **composition** of the Universe?
  - Is it mostly composed of **atoms***, or is there some unknown matter?

What is the current understanding regarding the above questions?

In 1919, the Hooker Telescope was built at Mount Wilson, which was the world's largest **telescope***. By using the Hooker Telescope, Edwin Powell Hubble (1889–1953) discovered the existence of other **galaxies*** besides the Milky Way in which we live. For example, the **Andromeda Galaxy*** is 2.5 million light-years away. A "light-year" is the distance that light travels in one year, which is 10^{13} kilometers. Hubble also discovered that the galaxies are moving away from the earth and established the fact that the universe is expanding, which is **consistent** with Einstein's general theory of relativity. Nowadays, we have a **vast*** body of **precise data** from new **high-tech*** instruments, such as space **satellites***, **lasers***, and X-ray telescopes.

In 1964, **radio** astronomers Arno Penzias and Robert Wilson first **detected** the **cosmic microwave background*** (CMB), which is the oldest light from the Big Bang that fills the **entire** universe. This **radiation*** is considered the best **evidence** for the Big Bang theory of the universe. Since then, the Big Bang Theory has become the **prevailing*** theory about the **origin** and **evolution** of our universe. If the universe is expanding, we want to know whether it is expanding forever or, at some point, it begins shrinking. This question is closely related to the shape of the universe. The whole universe may have an overall **curvature***. The universe may have a finite size, like the surface of a **sphere**.

Another possibility is that the universe may be infinitely large, and this raises the question of what is the shape of the universe? The density of the universe determines its **geometry***. If the density of the universe **exceeds** some value called the *critical density**, then the geometry of space is closed, i.e., a finite universe. In this case, it is known that the universe will eventually **collapse** back on itself in what is called the *Big Crunch**, due to the strong gravitational **attraction** among all matter in the universe. On the other hand, if the density of the universe is less than the **critical** density, then the geometry of space is open, i.e. infinite. Further experiments in modern times have confirmed the theories that the universe will most likely **expand forever***.

If the universe is **flat**, the density of the universe should be the critical density. However, it turns out that the measured density of the universe is too small and inconsistent with the flat universe, even though the **contributions** of what is termed *dark matter** are included. Dark matter is an unusual matter which is different from ordinary matter. We do not know what it is, but measurement of the very fast **rotation*** speed of the Milky Way requires the existence of dark matter.

Gravity pulls all the matter in the universe; therefore, the universe's expansion must slow down. Surprisingly enough, however, the results of various research studies and observations of distant **supernovas*** have suggested that the growth of the universe is actually **accelerating***. Accelerating the universe **implies** the existence of something that is **pushing** instead of pulling. So, there must be some new form of energy that pushes outward. It is not a matter of either the ordinary or the dark matter because the force of gravity from both can only pull, not push. Something that pushes outward is referred to as *dark energy**. Nobody knows what dark energy is. Dark energy must influence the shape of the universe because energy is **equivalent** to mass and mass **affects** the curvature of space. How much dark energy exists? Observation suggests that dark energy contributes about 70% of the total mass of the universe.

In **summary**, according to the current observations, the universe began with the Big Bang, and the flat universe will keep expanding forever. We do not know much about 95% of the content of the universe, which is called dark matter (26.8%) and dark energy (68.3%). Note that this is the current understanding and is subject to refinement. So far, we have explained some accepted principles that have been supported by research and observation. However, there are many **theoretically** interesting controversies and suggestions, such as the possibility of a **multi-universe***, that will continue to **inspire*** physics research into the future.

Adapted from a text by Yasushi Nara, PhD
Professor, Theoretical and Nuclear Physics
Global Connectivity Program
Akita International University
Japan

Vocabulary

Words From the Second 1,000 General Service High Frequency Word List

absolute
apple
argued
arguments
attraction
billion
century
composition
connected
correct
critical
curved
educated
electric
entire
essence
essential
exciting
expand
exploring
explosion
extreme
fate
flat
freezes
governed
guess
hits

hole
ice
immediately
incorrect
instruments
inside
liquid
motion
obeyed
origin
path
pushing
qualify
radio
repeatedly
resistance
scale
scale
slower
solid
temperature
tower
universal
universe
weight
zero

Words From the Academic Word List

abandoned
affects
analyzing
anticipated approximately
area
aspects
capability
capable
challenged
collapse
concept
confirm
conducted

conclusions consequence
consistent
contributions
contrast
core
created
credited
crucial
data
detected
derived
developed
distinct

distinction
dynamic
elements
emphasized
enables
energy
entity
equivalent
established
establishing
estimate
evidence
evolution
eventually
exceeds
expanding
expansion
factors
finite
focused
formulating
fundamental
implies
individual
initially
innovation
inconsistent inconsistency
inspire
instance
intermediate
investigate
involving
illustration

ions
molecule
nevertheless
nucleus
orbit
oversee
phenomenon
plasma
predictions
precise
principles
range
rational
requires
resolved
revolutionized
shrink
significant
sphere
speculate
static
stationary
study
suggest
summary
theory
trajectory
undergo
unique
unify
uniformly
vary

Glossary

It is not necessary for students to memorize these words and phrases.

Additionally (adverb): In addition to what has already been mentioned; furthermore.

Andromeda Galaxy (noun): A spiral galaxy approximately 2.5 million light-years away from Earth, the nearest major galaxy to the Milky Way.

Atomic (adjective): Relating to atoms, the smallest unit of matter.

Astronomer (noun): A scientist who studies celestial bodies such as stars, planets, and galaxies.

Atoms (noun): The basic units of matter and the defining structure of elements.

The Big Bang (noun): The theory that the universe originated from an extremely dense and hot state and has been expanding ever since.

The Big Crunch (noun): A hypothetical scenario where the universe's expansion eventually reverses, causing it to collapse.

Coined (verb): To invent or create a new term or phrase.
Cosmic Microwave Background (CMB) (noun): Radiation that is the remnant of the Big Bang, filling the universe and providing evidence of its origin.
Cosmology (noun): The scientific study of the origin, structure, and development of the universe.
Critical Density (noun): The exact density required for the universe to stop expanding and eventually collapse.
Dark Energy (noun): A mysterious form of energy that is believed to be responsible for the accelerated expansion of the universe.
Dark Matter (noun): A form of matter that does not emit light or energy, making it invisible, but its presence is inferred from its gravitational effects on visible matter.
Density (noun): The degree of compactness of a substance, typically measured as mass per unit volume.
Disprove (verb): To demonstrate that something is false.
Dissociation (noun): The process by which molecules or atoms split into smaller particles such as ions or radicals.
Disproved (verb): To show that a theory or hypothesis is incorrect.
Elliptical (adjective): Having the shape of an ellipse, an elongated circle; used to describe the path of planets.
Electrons (noun): Subatomic particles with a negative charge that orbit the nucleus of an atom.
Elementary (adjective): Related to the most basic or fundamental aspects of a subject.
Forever (adverb): For all future time; endlessly.
Galaxies (noun): Massive systems of stars, gas, dust, and dark matter bound together by gravity.
Geometry (noun): The branch of mathematics that deals with the properties and relationships of points, lines, surfaces, and shapes.
Gravity (noun): The force that attracts a body toward the center of the Earth or any other physical body having mass.
Gluons (noun): Elementary particles responsible for holding quarks together in protons and neutrons.
High-tech (adjective): Involving advanced technological developments, particularly in computing and electronics.
Incorrectness (noun): The state of being wrong or inaccurate.
Ions (noun): Atoms or molecules that have lost or gained one or more electrons, giving them a positive or negative charge.
Interesting (adverb): In a manner that arouses curiosity or interest.
Mathematician (noun): A person who specializes in the field of mathematics.
Mathematics (noun): The abstract science of number, quantity, and space.
Milliseconds (noun): One thousandth of a second.
Multiverse (noun): A hypothetical collection of multiple universes that exist parallel to each other.
Neutrons (noun): Subatomic particles with no electric charge, found in the nucleus of an atom.
Neutron Star (noun): A type of extremely dense star composed mostly of neutrons, typically formed after a supernova explosion.
Nonscience (noun): Ideas or activities that are not based on scientific principles or methods.
Noteworthy (adjective): Worth paying attention to or noticing; remarkable.
Orbits (verb): The curved path that an object follows as it moves around another object due to gravitational forces.
Perpendicular (adjective): At an angle of 90 degrees to a given line or surface.
Planet (noun): A celestial body that orbits a star, is spherical, and has cleared its orbit of other debris.
Plasma (noun): A state of matter consisting of free electrons and ions, often considered the fourth state of matter.
Prevalent (adjective): Commonly occurring or widely accepted.
Protons (noun): Subatomic particles with a positive charge found in the nucleus of an atom.

Quantum Mechanics (noun): The branch of physics that deals with the behavior of very small particles on the atomic and subatomic scale.

Quark Gluon Plasma (QGP) (noun): A state of matter consisting of quarks and gluons, believed to have come into existence just after the Big Bang.

Quarks (noun): Elementary particles that combine to form protons and neutrons.

Radiation (noun): The emission of energy as electromagnetic waves or as moving subatomic particles.

Rotation (noun): The act of spinning around an axis.

Satellites (noun): Man-made objects placed in orbit around Earth or another planet to collect information or for communication.

Scientific Method (noun): A systematic process for gathering knowledge and testing hypotheses through observation and experimentation.

Shrink (verb): To become smaller in size, typically due to external forces like gravity.

Speculate (verb): To form a theory or conjecture without firm evidence.

Stationary (adjective): Not moving; fixed in place.

Static (adjective): Lacking movement or change.

Supernovas (noun): The explosion of a star that has reached the end of its life cycle, resulting in an extremely bright and powerful burst of energy.

Telescopes (noun): Optical instruments designed to make distant objects appear closer and more detailed.

Testability (noun): The capacity for a theory or hypothesis to be proven wrong through experimentation or observation.

Theory of Relativity (noun): A theory by Albert Einstein that explains the relationships between space, time, and gravity.

Trajectory (noun): The path followed by an object moving under the influence of forces like gravity.

Vapor (noun): A substance in the gas phase, particularly one that has evaporated from a liquid or solid.

Vertical (adjective): Oriented in an up-and-down direction, perpendicular to a horizontal surface.

Viewpoint (noun): A particular perspective or way of considering something.

Vast (adjective): Of very great size or extent; immense.

CHAPTER 27

GEOLOGY

James Reid
Akita International University, Japan

Introduction

Geology is a science that combines **disciplines** such as chemistry, biology, physics, and geography. It explores the composition of the Earth, its ability to support life and the **management** of its valuable **resources**. Geologists, with their extensive understanding of the Earth, take a forefront **role** in tackling societal and **environmental issues**. Their **expertise aids** in **locating** resources, such as oil and gas, for financial gain, and **anticipating** natural calamities, **preserving soil**, enhancing **agricultural** yield, and decoding global climate variations. By acting as Earth's guardians, geoscientists develop **solutions** and **formulate policies** for resource conservation, environmental safeguarding, and public well-being.

Catastrophism

As a **formal** science, Geology dates back to the 18th **century**. But it only **emerged** a century after the **Scientific Revolution***. So, why this delay? The answer was that early geologists **sought** to **match** the Biblical understanding of **creation** with the geological **evidence** being found. This led to the **theory** of Catastrophism, which proposed that Earth's history has largely been influenced by **sudden**, catastrophic events rather than **consistent, gradual processes** over extended durations. For **instance**, those subscribing to this idea might believe that the Rocky Mountains formed due to a massive earthquake rather than through gradual uplift and **erosion** over millions of years.

One of the originators of Catastrophism was the influential British theologian Bishop James Ussher (1581–1656). He deduced from the ages of people in the Bible that the Earth was **established** in 4004 BC, which led him to **assume** that all Earth's surface **features** must be under 6,000 years old, originating from violent disruptions or catastrophes.

Similarly, Baron Georges Cuvier (1769–1832), a French anatomist, **aimed** to align the fossil records with the Biblical chronicles. He theorized that various sets of fossil **creatures** were born and later went extinct due to geological catastrophes, the most recent being the **Biblical Great Flood***. In Cuvier's view, each of these cataclysmic events was **responsible** for the demise of the creatures in the fossils and the **sedimentary deposits*** that became the rocks **enclosing** them.

Uniformitarianism

However, present-day studies suggest the Earth is around 4.5 **billion** years old. The first scientist who **argued** that the world must be much older than the Catastrophists supposed was James Hutton (1726–1797), dubbed the "first modern geologist." Hailing from Scotland, Hutton's keen observations of the geological features of his farmland led him to **challenge traditional** beliefs about Earth's age, **advocating** for a much older planet. He introduced the **concept** of "Deep Time" as he realized that most geological processes were so slow the Earth must be unimaginably old. Thus, his **principle** of Uniformitarianism portrays Earth's evolution as a blend of **slow**, continuous changes punctuated by sporadic catastrophic events. Although not recognized at the time, James Hutton's wife, Mary Horner Lyell (1808–1873), was also a geologist who greatly **assisted** him in his work.

In the year that James Hutton died, another Scottish geologist named Charles Lyell (1797–1875) was born. His three-volume book "Principles of Geology" (1830–33) **empirically** established Uniformitarianism, allowing it to gain mainstream recognition in the Scientific community.

Lyell's work greatly influenced Charles Darwin (1809–1882), who proposed the Theory of Evolution by Natural Selection*. He carried a **copy** of the "Principles of Geology" on his famous **voyage** aboard the ship HMS Beagle. He realized that, like the very slow process of geological change, the evolution of species must also take an unimaginably long time, giving more credence to the incredible age of our planet.

Continental Drift and Plate Tectonics

The next **paradigm shift*** came with Alfred Wegener's (1880–1930) theory of continental drift, which reshaped geology. Using a **diverse range** of evidence—from fossils to geological formations—Wegener proposed that continents were once **unified** but had drifted **apart** over eons. This precursor laid the **foundation** for **plate** tectonics, an idea fully expressed in the mid-20th century.

Plate tectonics revolutionized geology. It explains how Earth's crust—divided into lithospheric plates—moves, **interacts**, and reshapes our world. These plates glide atop the semifluid **asthenosphere***, meeting at convergent, divergent, or **transform boundaries**.

There are two types of convergent boundaries, also known as destructive boundaries. In convergent collision boundaries continental plates come together, forming mountain ranges like the Himalayas*, as India crashes slowly but irrevocably into Asia. In such cases, powerful earthquakes can occur, but there is no magma so volcanoes cannot exist. However, in convergent subduction boundaries, the denser oceanic plate **slides** beneath the continental plate and drags water, carbon dioxide and plankton downwards whereupon the gases bubble up through the crust causing volcanoes. When the plates get stuck and then suddenly release themselves powerful earthquakes occur. We see this in the **Pacific Ring of Fire*** that encompasses western South America, Indonesia and Japan, amongst others.

At divergent boundaries, also known as constructive boundaries, two tectonic plates drift apart. Earthquakes **frequently** happen in these **regions**, and **magma*** from the Earth's **mantle*** ascends to the surface, **cooling** and forming new **oceanic crust***. The **Mid-Atlantic Ridge*** exemplifies such divergent plate boundaries. The island of Tristan da Cunha in the South Atlantic Ocean, about midway between southern Africa and South America, experienced a mid-Atlantic volcanic eruption in 1961, leading to the entire population being relocated to England.

At transform boundaries, plates slide **alongside** each other. When built-up **stress** is **released**, it leads to earthquakes. An example of this is the San Andreas **Fault**, where a **section** of western California, associated with the Pacific Plate, moves north-northwestward in relation to the rest of North America.

Though Wegener first introduced the idea of continents moving, the discoveries in the mid-20th century truly **validated** and **expanded** upon his thoughts. Plate tectonics unravels the Earth's geological mysteries and helps us understand events of **enormous** magnitude. Take, for instance, the Grey's Landing **supereruption*** in **Yellowstone***. This volcanic event was the most massive in Yellowstone's history, discharging a staggering 2,800 km³ of volcanic materials. The **immediate** aftermath saw vast regions of America covered in volcanic glass. On a global **scale**, **ash** particles would have circulated the atmosphere, **impacting** regions far and wide.

Exploring Earth's Rock Types

Geology offers a fascinating glimpse into the fabric of our planet's inner **constitution**, showcasing the rich variety of rocks that form it. These can be classified into three main **categories**: igneous, sedimentary, and metamorphic.

Igneous Rocks are the product of **molten*** material or magma. Depending on where they cool and **solidify**, they can either form on the Earth's surface as lava or deeper within, **emerging** as **intrusive rocks***. Familiar examples include **granite***, **basalt***, **and obsidian***. Recognizable by their **crystalline* structures**, these rocks are commonly found in volcanic regions and **constitute significant** sections of the Earth's **crust***.

Sedimentary rocks form from the **accumulation** and compression of sediments, including **eroded** rock fragments, organic materials, and **minerals**. Over time, these sediments solidify into rocks like **sandstone*** and **limestone***. Processes like erosion, **weathering**, and **dissolution*** reshape large rocks into smaller sediments. Additionally, chemicals in water **precipitate*** to form rocks, as observed in locations like California's Death Valley, where lakes dry up. The **weight** of overlying materials results in **lithification***, compacting these sediments into rocks. Notably, sedimentary rocks often contain fossils, providing insights into Earth's past and the immense periods of time required for evolution.

Metamorphic rocks have a history of transformation. Originating from preexisting rocks, they undergo significant changes when subjected to extreme temperatures, pressure, or the intrusion of fluids. Such changes are primarily seen deep within the Earth's crust, often associated with tectonic activities. Examples like **marble***, **quartzite***, **slate***, and **gneiss*** stand out with their distinct textures and mineral compositions. Their often **foliated*** or **banded** appearance, as can be seen in places like Death Valley, US, speaks volumes about the intense conditions they have been through.

Collectively, these rock types are **instrumental** in deciphering Earth's geological narrative, providing valuable insights into its historical events and the conditions that led to their creation.

Geology Is a Time Machine

You may remember that we now consider the Earth to be approximately 4,500,000,000 million years old, about one-third the universe's age. Therefore, the study of Geology can be likened to a time machine, offering a profound **dive** into Earth's vast past and illuminating the varied geological phenomena, climatic conditions, and landscapes that have sculpted our planet through the ages. Powering this time machine requires the rigor of scientific enquiry and the techniques it has generated. Five of these techniques and theories will now be **fleshed out***.

Through meticulous **examination** of rock structures and the fossils they contain, geologists unravel ancient mysteries. The different layers of rocks signify different timeframes, with the embedded fossils revealing tales of ancient life. Such findings pave the way for tracing the evolutionary **path** of life on Earth and the movement of continents. For instance, fossils of the reptile Mesosaurus are only found in southern Africa and South America, suggesting that these continents were once **connected.**

Stratigraphy is the discipline that focuses on studying strata, or rock layers, providing insights into the timeline of rock formation. By discerning these layers' relative positions and arrangements, geologists gain a window into past environments and associated geological events. Wegener's study of stratigraphy revealed that rock layers from the east coast of South America and the west coast of Africa fit together, **lending** yet more evidence they had once been a single landmass.

Another significant technique is Radiometric Dating, which allows geologists to assign precise ages to rocks and pivotal historical events. The method hinges on analyzing the **decay patterns** of radioactive isotopes within minerals. Through radiometric dating of the oldest rocks on Earth, as well as moon rocks and meteorites, scientists have **calculated** that the Earth is approximately 4.54 billion years old, with an error margin of about 1%.

Paleoclimatology brings past climatic patterns **to the fore***. By delving into geological records such as sediment deposits, **ice** cores, and age-old tree rings, scientists sketch out historic climatic variations. Paleoclimatology adds evidence to the fact that some continents used to be closer to the polar regions, and some were close to the equator. For instance, plant fossils from the Arctic Svalbard island of Norway were of tropical plants, suggesting that the region was once located in the tropics.

Finally, we have already discussed the revolutionary field of Plate Tectonics, which **sheds light on*** the movement of Earth's tectonic plates over millennia. Such insights enable geologists to reconstruct historical continental patterns such as Pangea. This **supercontinent*** thrived during the late **Paleozoic*** to early **Mesozoic*** eras, forming around 335 million years ago and fragmenting roughly 200 million years later. Situated on the equator and bordered by the expansive Panthalassa Ocean, Pangaea is both the most recent supercontinent and the first to be charted by geologists. However, it will not be the last. Geologists estimate the world might develop a new supercontinent within 200 million to 300 million years as the Pacific Ocean shrinks and closes.

Careers for Students of Geology

A degree in geology paves the way for a wide range of job opportunities. Industries like oil, gas, mining, construction, water, and **engineering** frequently seek geologists. Positions they might occupy include sustainability advisors, geological **mappers**, **waste** management experts, and **hydrogeologists***, among others. One **exciting** opportunity is that of a Planetary Geologist. These geologists map off-world landscapes, gather information from asteroid remnants, or **guide** robotic space missions. The endeavors of **NASA's Mars Rovers*** epitomize planetary geology, examining **Martian terrain*** for crucial geophysical evidence, including potential life signs, which we have yet to find. Though most Planetary Geologists are immersed in computational studies or lab experiments, a select few experience their subjects firsthand. Harrison Schmitt stands out as the first Planetary Geologist to collect **samples** right from the moon's surface. In the future, planetary geologists will no doubt travel to other planets in our solar system and perhaps beyond.

Whether you go into space or not, an **education** in Geology will equip you with versatile **skills** such as effective communication, analytical thinking, technological expertise, mathematical ability, research acumen, and project oversight. These competencies are sought after in many **professions**, not just those **tied** to geology.

James Reid
Assistant Professor and EAP Coordinator at Akita International University, Japan

Vocabulary

Words From the Second 1,000 General Service High-Frequency Word List

agricultural	disciplines
aimed	dive
apart	education
argued	enclosing
arrangements	engineering
ash	examination
billion	exciting
banded	fault
boundaries	flood
calculated	formal
century	frequently
collectively	gradual
combining	guide
connected	ice
cooling/cool	immediate
copy	instrumental
creatures	lending
decay	management

mappers/map
match
minerals
mysteries
oceanic/ocean
originated
path
patterns
plate
preserving
professions
responsible
samples
scale

skills
slides
slow
solidify
soil
solutions
sudden
tied
universe
violent
voyage
weathering
weight
waste

Words From the Academic Word List (AWL)

accumulation
advocating
aids
anticipating
assume
assisted
categories
challenge
concept
consistent
constitution/constitute
creation
deduced
diverse
emerged/emerging
empirically
enormous
environmental
eroded/erosion
established
evidence
expanded
expertise
features
foundation
formulate

global
impacting
interacts
instance
issues
locating
policies
processes
range
regions
released
resources
revolution
role
section
sought
stress
structures
significant
theory
traditional
transform
unified
validated
variations

Glossary

Asthenosphere (noun): The upper layer of the Earth's mantle beneath the lithosphere, characterized by a partially molten or plastic-like state.

Basalt (noun): A common extrusive igneous rock formed from solidified lava, typically dark in colour and fine-grained.

Biblical Great Flood (noun phrase): The catastrophic flood described in the Bible's Book of Genesis, which, according to the narrative, covered the Earth and destroyed most of humanity.

Compression (noun): The action of pressing or squeezing together, often associated with tectonic forces that lead to the shortening and thickening of rocks.

Crust (noun): The outermost layer of the Earth, composed of solid rock and divided into tectonic plates.

Crystalline (adjective): Composed of crystals or having a regular atomic structure.

Dissolution (noun): The process of breaking down or dissolving rock or minerals, often due to chemical weathering.

Fleshed out (verb phrase): Developed or expanded upon, adding more details or substance to an idea or concept.

Foliated (adjective): Having a layered or banded appearance due to the alignment of mineral grains, commonly found in certain metamorphic rocks.

Gneiss (noun): A coarse-grained metamorphic rock with a banded appearance formed from preexisting rocks undergoing intense heat and pressure.

Granite (noun): A common intrusive igneous rock composed of quartz, feldspar, and mica.

Himalayas (noun): A vast mountain range in Asia extending through several countries, including India, Nepal, Bhutan, and China.

Hydrogeologist (noun): A scientist who specializes in the study of groundwater and its interactions with geologic formations.

Intrusive rocks (noun): Igneous rocks that formed from magma cooling and solidifying within the Earth's crust, typically exhibiting coarse-grained textures. Examples include granite.

Limestone (noun): A sedimentary rock composed primarily of calcium carbonate, often formed from the accumulation of marine shells and coral.

Lithification (noun): The process of compacting and hardening of loose sediments to form solid rock.

Magma (noun): Molten rock material beneath the Earth's surface, which may erupt as lava during a volcanic eruption.

Mantle (noun): The layer of the Earth's interior between the crust and the core, composed of solid rock.

Marble (noun): A metamorphic rock formed from limestone that has undergone recrystallization, often used for sculpture and architecture.

Martian terrain (noun phrase): The physical characteristics and landscape features of the surface of Mars.

Mesozioc (noun/adjective): A geological era lasting from about 252 million to 66 million years ago, known for the dominance of dinosaurs and the rise of mammals.

Mid-Atlantic Ridge (noun): An underwater mountain range located along the floor of the Atlantic Ocean, formed by divergent tectonic plate boundaries.

Molten (adjective): In a liquefied or melted state, usually referring to hot, liquid rock or metal.

NASA's Mars Rovers (noun phrase): Robotic spacecraft designed by NASA to explore the surface of Mars.

Obsidian (noun): A natural volcanic glass formed by the rapid cooling of lava, often black or dark in color.

Oceanic crust (noun): The outermost layer of the Earth's lithosphere beneath the oceans, composed mostly of basalt.

Pacific Ring of Fire (noun phrase): An area surrounding the Pacific Ocean known for its high seismic and volcanic activity.

Paleozoic (noun/adjective): A geological era lasting from about 541 million to 252 million years ago, known for the diversification of life forms.

Paradigm shift (noun phrase): Refers to a profound and transformative change in the fundamental concepts, assumptions, and approaches that shape a particular field of knowledge or understanding.

Precipitate (verb or noun): To cause a solid substance to be separated from a solution or the solid material that forms in this process.

Quartzite (noun): A metamorphic rock formed from sandstone that has undergone recrystallization, composed mainly of quartz.

Sedimentary deposits (noun phrase): Layers of sediment that accumulate over time, forming rocks such as sandstone, limestone, and shale.

Sheds light on (idiom): To provide insight or understanding into a topic or situation.

Slate (noun): A fine-grained metamorphic rock derived from shale, typically used for roofing and flooring.

Supercontinent (noun): A large landmass consisting of multiple continents merged together into a single landmass.

Supereruption (noun): An extremely large and powerful volcanic eruption capable of ejecting massive amounts of volcanic material.

The Scientific Revolution (noun): A period in history, roughly from the 16th to the 18th century, marked by significant advances in science, mathematics, and philosophy.

The Theory of Evolution by Natural Selection (noun phrase): Charles Darwin's scientific explanation for how species gradually change and diversify over generations through the process of natural selection favouring advantageous traits.

To the fore (idiom): Prominently in view or at the forefront of attention or importance.

Yellowstone (noun): A national park located primarily in the US states of Wyoming,

CHAPTER 28

PROGRAMMING

Florent Domenach
Akita International University, Japan

A Short Introduction to Programming

Almost everyone agrees that the biggest cause of societal and industrial change over the last 50 years is computers and, more recently, the ability computers have to **connect** different systems and applications. However, how many of us can understand what a computer is or even master what it can do?

Even though computers are **ubiquitous*** in our lives, most of us still don't understand what happens within one. We **treat** them as black boxes, enjoying their **convenience** and fearing anything that would go wrong, **relinquishing*** our agency to these **tools**. My main **argument** here is that, as **Liberal Arts*** students or even as active citizens, everyone should learn **programming**. As Steve Jobs, the famous **inventor** and co-**founder** of the technology company Apple, said in an interview in 1995: "But much more importantly, it had nothing to do with using them [programs] for anything **practical**. It had to do with using them to be a mirror of your thought **process.** To actually learn how to think." Though learning **coding** might be useful, learning programming is more important if we wish to become actors in control of our own lives, not just computer users. Learning programming is all about problem-solving, logical thinking, and creativity, all of which are **fundamental** components of an **enlightened*** spirit.

Before discussing programming and why you should learn it, it is important to look at what computers are and why they are so important in our society. Computers come in many shapes and sizes, from big, heavy **desktop PC's***, to shiny **tablets*** and **smartphones***. Computers are in our **fridges***, cars, and even **clothes**. They are present in every part of our lives. However, computers are really just tools, like a **hammer** or **scissors**. But unlike hammers and scissors, computers are not made to do only one particular thing. Rather, they are *tools that can make other tools*! This is to say, a computer can do almost anything you want it to do, or whatever you can think of, within the limits of its **hardware***. This **incredible*** **flexibility** is the main reason why computers were at the heart of the industrial revolution 3.0, which **transformed mechanized*** and human **labor** into **digital*** and **automated** operations. Your computer can be used to operate a factory, fly a spaceship to the moon, play games, watch **movies***, and listen to music, and you can write, draw, and so on…. The possibilities are, in fact, endless. And if you want to do something that is not currently possible, well, you just have to make a plan and write a program for it! A **core concept** of computer science involves **algorithms*** that are used to **program** computers, which control so much of our lives, from our **credit scores*** to our possible love interest on dating **sites**.

Introducing the Liberal Arts, pages 193–198
Copyright © 2026 by Emerald Publishing Limited
All rights of reproduction in any form reserved.
doi:10.1108/978-1-80592-303-920251029

What Is Programming?

Well, to answer the question above, programming is just the user giving **instructions**, step by step, for what the computer should be doing. Think about a recipe for your favorite dish, explaining one step at a time what you need to do to make beautiful pies (my favorite dish to cook!). These sets of instructions are called algorithms, and these algorithms lie behind everything that your computer does, from keeping a record of all your friends on social **media**, your Instagram feed, the suggestions that Amazon sends you about what you should buy, your **Google* searches**… in fact, almost every single piece of software that we use every day is based on algorithms.

History of Programming

So, where does all this come from? Your understanding of where computing came from depends on what you think computers (and computing) are. Most **researchers** would agree that the work of Alan Turing, with his written **model** of **computational** machines that was **published** in 1936, is a **key** work. Turing was a British **mathematician***, who worked at Bletchley Park (a **military** center in England) during World War II. He was part of the large group of men and women working there, which broke the famous **Enigma** machine **code***. The work of Alan Turing and the **subsequent** breaking of the Enigma code was estimated to have ended the war about two years earlier than it would have ended.

In this 1936 article, Alan Turing wrote about computers, calling them "**universal** machines." Turing showed that any other computing model can be reduced to his model, which is why he called it "universal"; in other words, it was a tool to make other tools (Alan Turing, 1936). Often referred to as Turing machines, they are **theoretically equivalen**t to modern computers **despite** differing in many practical **aspects**. The **genius*** of Alan Turing wasn't limited to this theoretical model: he introduced the concept of uncomputable numbers in the same article. These are numbers that cannot be computed by any Turing machine. It had deep **implications**—the universal machine that Alan Turing **envisioned*** was, in fact, limited in its ability! This **apparently insurmountable* contradiction** became the **focus** of most of Turing's life.

To **solve** this problem, Turing wanted to make computers able to "think." In other words, he wanted to make **intelligent** computers, just as humans are, to be able to tackle these limitations. Because of this, he is also considered the father of **Artificial Intelligence (AI)*** and developed the famous Turing test, a **method** to determine whether a computer is intelligent. Because AI and programming are closely connected, you need to understand programming to understand the importance of AI fully. Fortunately, most Liberal Arts universities offer classes where you can learn more about these subjects.

Despite his multiple **accomplishments***, Alan Turing had a **tragic*** end of life. As **homosexuality*** was considered a **crime** at the time, he was **convicted*** in 1952 and sentenced to **chemical castration***, a process **intended** to reduce **libido***. He **committed suicide*** on June 7, 1954, by eating an apple containing cyanide poison. It was only in 2009 that the British government issued a formal apology and a **royal pardon*** in 2013.

Kinds of People Attracted to Programming

So, should everyone learn how to program? Isn't it reserved for **math geeks***? After all, it is hard enough to learn how to operate a computer and to find your way around the thousands of existing **software*** applications, let alone understand these cryptic programming languages full of zeros and ones…

This view of programming is unfair, as people who think this way often think programming is the same as coding. It is not. Programming, or writing algorithms, is as simple (or as difficult) as writing down the steps of how to **cook** something or explaining to your little **cousin** how to **tie** their **shoelaces***. Conversely, coding is the set of instructions written in a particular machine language (with strange names such as C#, Python, Ruby, Perl, Java, etc.). This is usually what we see in movies and elsewhere, with all its hidden jargon (or special words that only **coders** understand):. However, coding is the last and least important programming step, not its starting point.

Benefits of Learning Programming

Human existence can be characterized by using tools, from hammers to computers. As a tool, programming is a basic part of how we pass on knowledge. It does this not by providing the **solution** to a problem but by giving us a way to solve or to reach that solution. Computers are tools to make tools (to solve a problem), algorithms are the way to think about these solutions, and coding is the method to implement them.

Why is this important? Well, understanding *how* a problem can be solved develops our **logical skills** and **creativity**. It trains us to **think critically** and deeply about the issue at hand, to understand all the requirements that are needed, not only technically (logically) but more **broadly**, about who will use our software solution and in which situation. It forces us to work **collaboratively**, pull different personal experiences and expertise together, and appreciate **multiple viewpoints**, as the algorithms we create are never unique. After all, finding a better way to solve any problem is always possible.

This is why it is important for all students to learn programming and to have a basic understanding of what a computer can do. Today, students usually learn useful software tools like Word or Excel, but learning programming is far less popular. However, learning the software program, "**Office***," without knowing anything about programming limits a student's general **education**. It is like learning how to read *but not how to write*. Not learning about programming means that you subject your digital life and experiences to other people's choices and decisions!

The good news is that this divide between active **creators** and basic users is decreasing as time goes by. This has been helped by popular teaching programs like "**Hour of Code***," programmable robots like "Lego Mindstorms," or the growing use of very cheap computers like the "**Raspberry Pi***." These things will possibly begin to change the place of computers in our lives. They will help people lose their fear of computers and the belief that programming is too difficult for ordinary people to master.

This change in the way we think is important if we are to take back control of our living **environment**, and **governments** all around the world are taking the change seriously. For example, the **Japanese Ministry of Education (MEXT)*** has recognized the importance of programming education in its latest curriculum reform. From 2020, all students must learn programming from the earliest school level, starting with **unplugged activities*** and **Robotics***.

Employment Opportunities

So why is it important to learn about programming while planning for the future? One important reason, as mentioned before, is that programming is the door leading to the understanding of machine learning and Artificial Intelligence (AI).

AI is leading the current fourth **industrial revolution***, and, like the other industrial revolutions, it is making us think again about who the real leaders of our age are. This new revolution of our digital age is also shaping the way in which we live our lives and taking us in new directions. For example, it is believed that half of the types of jobs that exist today will disappear or be heavily changed in the future because of the spread of robotics and AI. Having the ability to do programming could, therefore, make a big difference to your future.

Whatever happens in the future, computers will continue to be very important in our lives. Truly understanding how they work, how we can use them, and how to program the software that runs on them will become even more important as time goes by. As stated earlier, understanding programming will give us the tools that we need to become actors who have control in our lives, not mere users of programs and systems that other people have made and that other people control. It is the people who understand programming, people with jobs as **Software Engineers, AI Architects* and Computer Systems Analysts** who will shape the way we live well into the 21st **Century**.

Adapted from a text by Florent Domenach, PhD
Professor, Computer Science
Akita International University

Vocabulary

Words From the Second 1,000 General Service High-Frequency Word List

argument	inventor
aspects	key
attracted	model
century	practical
clothes	programming
connect	scissors
convenience	searches
cook	shoe
cousin	skills
crime	solution/solve
education	tie
governments	tool
hammer	treat
intended	universal

Words From the Academic Word List

apparently	implications
automated	instructions
benefits	intelligent
code/coding	jobs
contradiction	labor
core	logical
computer	method
committed	military
concept	process
creativity/creators	published
despite	researchers
environment	sites
equivalent	technology
flexibility	theoretically
focus	topics
founder	transformed
fundamental	

Glossary

It is not necessary for students to memorize these words and phrases.

Accomplishments (Noun): are things that have been achieved successfully, typically through effort, skill, or perseverance.

Artificial Intelligence (AI) (Noun phrase): A term used to describe the ability of computers to perform difficult tasks without being explicitly programmed to perform these tasks. Tasks such as thinking, problem-solving and learning. This is sometimes called machine intelligence.

Algorithm (Noun): A series of clear instructions necessary to perform particular tasks.

Chemical castration (Noun): Refers to the use of medication to reduce libido and sexual activity, typically by lowering testosterone levels in males.

Coders (Noun): People who construct and write computer programs (aka computer code).

Convicted (Adjective): Means having been declared guilty of a criminal offense by the verdict of a jury or the decision of a judge in a court of law.

Credit score (Noun phrase): A way of ranking a person's financial status and trustworthiness. Used by banks and companies when making decisions about who to lend money to or who to allow to buy expensive items such as cars and refrigerators.

Desktop PC (Noun phrase): A large computer that sits on top of a desk, usually with a separate screen and keyboard.

Digital (Adjective): Refers to technology that uses discrete (often binary): data, typically involving computers or other electronic devices.

Enigma machine code (Noun phrase): A top secret machine to code secret messages, used by the Germans in World War II to communicate.

Envisioned (Verb): Means imagined or visualized something in the mind, especially as a future possibility or plan

Enlightened (adjective): means having or showing a rational, modern, and well-informed outlook. For example, "she had an enlightened spirit, always open to new ideas and perspectives."

Geeks (Noun): People with a very strong interest in one thing (e.g. computers, anime, chess): and who may not have developed strong social skills because they spend a lot of time following their interests.

Genius (Noun): Refers to exceptional intellectual or creative power or other natural ability (Adjective): describes someone or something that shows exceptional intellectual or creative ability.

Google (Noun & Verb): A brand name for a famous search engine owned by the huge American multinational technology company Alphabet Inc. "To Google something" is used as a synonym for searching the web.

Hardware (Noun): The physical parts of a computer.

Homosexuality (Noun): Refers to the romantic or sexual attraction to people of one's own sex.

Hour of Code: The name of an online course that teaches people about computer programming. See https://hourofcode.com/jp/en (English version): and/or https://hourofcode.com/jp (Japanese version).

Incredible (Adjective): Means something that is hard to believe because it is extraordinary or amazing.

Industrial revolution (Noun phrase): An expression used to describe a time in history, starting in the UK, when steam engines were invented and machines began to produce goods for people on a large scale. Many people moved away from the countryside to work in factories in the cities.

Insurmountable (Adjective): Means too great to be overcome or dealt with successfully

Japanese Ministry of Education (MEXT): The part of the Japanese government that controls the formal education system in Japan.

Liberal Arts (Noun phrase): "Liberal arts is a field of study based on rational thinking, including the humanities, social and physical sciences, and mathematics. A liberal arts education emphasises the development of critical thinking ... the ability to solve complex problems, and an understanding of ethics and morality, as well as a desire to continue to learn." Retrieved from https://www.thoughtco.com/liberal-arts-definition-4585053

Libido (Noun): refers to sexual desire or the drive for sexual activity.

Math (Noun): American English short form of "mathematics," the study of numbers, quantity, and space. The short form in British English is "maths."

Mathematician (Noun): A person who is a specialist in mathematics.

Mechanized (Adjective): Means operated or performed by machinery rather than by human labor.

Movies (Noun): Short form of "moving pictures" or cinema film.

Network Architects (Noun): People who plan, design and build computer networks.

Raspberry Pi (Noun): Name of a basic computer system made of several single boards, that is often used to teach computer science to children. See https://www.raspberrypi.org

Relinquishing (Verb): Means giving up or letting go of something.

Robotics (Noun): The study of robots. Robots are machines that are made to do particular jobs. Many robots can work by themselves, without human help.

Shoelaces (Noun): The strings used to tie shoes closed, so that they do not come off your feet.

Smartphone (Noun): An electronic device that has the functions of a cell phone and small handheld computer that includes access to the internet.

Software (Noun): The programs, and other information used to operate a computer or run on a computer. E.g. "Office" or "Excel."

Suicide (Noun): Refers to the act of intentionally causing one's own death.

Tablet (Noun): A small, hand-held computer, smaller than a desktop PC and larger than a phone, operated by touching the screen rather than with a separate keyboard.

Tragic (Adjective): Means causing or characterized by extreme distress or sorrow, often related to serious and sorrowful events.

Ubiquitous (Adjective): Describes something present or found everywhere. For example, computers are ubiquitous in modern society.

Unplugged activities (Noun phrase): Learning activities that do not require a computer, but are used to teach children about computing, often in the form of puzzles or games.

Reference

Turing, A. (1936). On computable numbers, with an application to the Entscheidungsproblem. *Proceedings of the London Mathematical Society, 42*(1), 230–265.

CHAPTER 29

ENVIRONMENTAL SCIENCE

James Reid
Akita International University, Japan

Introduction

How do we **tackle* urgent* global challenges** like **climate change***, **biodiversity loss***, **ecosystem* degradation*** and pollution? **Environmental** science addresses these **critical issues** by developing strategies for **conservation*** and **sustainability**. This **complex discipline** covers various **areas**, allowing for the **investigation** of **diverse phenomena**. Examples include how **rainforest*** loss **affects precipitation* patterns** and **contributes** to atmospheric and water pollution. For instance, **deforestation*** in the **Amazon rainforest** leads to reduced **rainfall*** both locally and globally, leading to **drought***. Another area of **research** is that by **examining** small groups of trees, environmental scientists can **infer** the health of **expansive** forests. **Monitoring** growth rings in these trees allows them to work out past **climatic*** conditions and **predict** future **outcomes**, including the likelihood of forest fires and **disease**. Environmental science also looks at the **impact** of human actions on nature. For example, Central Park in New York City not only **improves** air quality by **removing** 1,821 tons of **carbon dioxide*** (CO_2) a year but also **enhances leisure*** activities and **urban*** biodiversity. The field **continually* evolves** to address **practical** challenges by **framing** them within broader **contexts, posing** targeted questions, and developing **theories** for **evaluation**.

Past and Present

Environmental science **emerged** as a **distinct academic** discipline in the 1960s and 1970s, driven by growing concerns over pollution, **resource depletion***, and environmental **damage**. In 1958, American scientist Charles David Keeling was the first to measure **atmospheric*** CO_2 concentrations at the **Mauna Loa*** Observatory in Hawaii. His work provided some of the earliest **data** on the impact of human activities on Earth's climate.

Twelve years later, Rachel Carson's book "Silent Spring" **highlighted** the dangers of **pesticides***, **sparking*** the modern environmental movement. Her **compelling* narrative* illustrated** the **severe consequences** of in**discriminate*** pesticide use, leading to **widespread** public concern and a **ban*** on the use of **DDT*** (Dichlorodiphenyltrichloroethane) a pesticide that was very **harmful** to **birdlife***. **During** the same **period**, the **publication** of the "Earthrise" **photograph** by **Apollo 8* astronauts***, showing Earth from space, provided a powerful **visual** that **emphasized** Earth's **fragility*** and **interconnectedness***. This **image** became a **symbol** for the emerging environmental movement, helping to **catalyze*** the **establishment** of Earth Day in 1970 and **fostering*** a global **push** for environmental **activism***.

In the latter part of the 20th **century, technological advancements*** like **satellite*** imagery and computer **modelling revolutionized** environmental science. These **tools enabled precise** monitoring of **ecological*** changes such as deforestation and climate **shifts, facilitating** targeted **interventions. Innovations** such as the **restoration** of **wetlands*** in the **Mississippi river delta*** have **combated* coastal* erosion**, improved water quality, and supported **wildlife* habitats*, showcasing*** the practical applications of environmental science.

Environmental Research and Management Process

The environmental research and **management process consists** of **creating** and **evaluating policies** that **minimize** the **impacts** of human activities or human systems on nature. It usually begins with a description of the problem in general, for example, how polluted the air in the city is or what the condition of the particular **coral reef*** is. For example, in **New Delhi***, studies showed **excess** amounts of **PM2.5*** and **PM10*** pollutants in the air pollution levels, leading to measures **aimed** at **decreasing** the **usage*** of private cars and enhancing mass **transit** systems. Other examples include the prevention of **desertification*** and **cleaning** the **oceans** of plastic. The Great Green Wall **initiative** in the **Sahel region** has seen millions of trees **stretching** 8,000 km. planted to combat the spread of the **Sahara*** desert, restore **landscapes*** and create **jobs. Meanwhile,** advanced **technologies*** have been **deployed*** to prevent **The Great Pacific Garbage Patch***, a **massive*** amount of plastic **debris*** in the ocean, from getting **worse** than it already is. Another example is **The Great Barrier Reef Marine Park Authority***, which **imposed** a ban on tourism and fishing in the **regions** affected by **coral bleaching*** to help the reef **recover**.

Key Areas of Environmental Science Application

Environmental science has many **aspects** that are important in the **resolution** of world problems. For instance, increased deforestation of the Amazon rainforests increases the concentration of CO_2 in the **atmosphere,** leading to climate change. That is why special **projects** have been developed, such as the United Nations' REDD+ (Reducing **Emissions*** from Deforestation and Forest Degradation), which is a process that helps countries prevent forest loss and improve their carbon content. For instance, in Brazil, REDD+ projects have helped local people protect the forest by giving them **financial incentives** and training on how to farm sustainably.

Environmental science has **engendered*** a number of recent policies aimed at **encouraging** sustainability and reducing environmental impact **worldwide***. For instance, in Europe, the **purchase** of plastic bags has been **curtailed***, and single-use plastics like **straws, cutlery*** and **plates** have been banned. At the same time, there has been **tremendous*** growth in the **funding** of **renewable*** sources such as wind energy, **solar*** energy, and **hydroelectric*** energy. Moreover, in India, **agricultural** policies **advocating** the planting of drought-resistant rice, such as Sahbhagi Dhan, help **secure** food, reduce pesticide use, and ensure future-proof rice production as droughts increase.

Careers and Applications in the Real World

Careers **involving** environmental science are numerous; for example, ecologists are **engaged*** in studying particular ecosystems and the **role** of human beings in these ecosystems. For example, ecologists in the Amazon study how the loss of habitat affects **pollinators*** like **bees***, which are **crucial** for **maintaining** biodiversity and local farming. Environmental **engineers** are **responsible** for developing **methods** for pollution control and **waste** management. An example of this is the engineering of **filtration*** systems that **capture* stormwater runoff*** in Los Angeles. This measure reduces water pollution and **replenishes*** the **groundwater*** supply. **Marine biologists*** or **oceanographers*** work on issues like water pollution and the degradation of coral reefs. They can even restore coral reefs by **cultivating** coral **larvae*** to **mitigate*** the effects of coral bleaching caused by rising sea **temperatures**. Wildlife biology **focuses** on conservation issues by providing an understanding of species, their ecology, and **interactions** with human populations. Environmental policy **analysts** engage in research and other activities that create policies that will strengthen the **legal**

regime that **governs** the conservation of the environment and its use in a sustainable manner at the regional, national, and **international** levels. An international example includes the European Green Deal, which plans to make the EU climate-**neutral** by 2050. It will also include a carbon **border** tax on imports from countries with lower environmental standards in order to financially **disincentivize*** companies from moving production to such regions.

With regards to sustainable agriculture, some **experts** work on improving farming **techniques**, such as **intercropping***, **cover cropping*** and **crop rotation***, that do not lead to the depletion of **soil** and water resources. Hydrologists analyze the **hydrological*** cycle and **distribution** of water for its efficient management. Examples include the use of **GPS***-guided **tractors***, **drones***, and **sensors*** in Spain to **optimize*** **irrigation*** and **fertilizer*** **usage*** in **arid*** regions and advanced computer modelling in California to maintain efficient water **reservoir*** levels.

The management of pollution, **disposal** of trade effluent, soil erosion, and so on need the involvement of environmental experts working for private or public organizations preparing plans and **arrangements** to minimise such consequences as far as **practicable***. Environmental **consultants** **advise** companies and **governments** on green **practices**, legal **compliance***, and sustainability measures. Climate change analysts look at the climate and find ways and means of dealing with the **potentially** destructive impacts climate change may bring. **Finally**, environmental lawyers, act on **behalf** of organizations on legal policies and **regulations** affecting the environment.

Disputes* and Issues in the Field of Environmental Science

Like most fields of study, environmental science is subject to controversies. **Global warming*** remains the most **debatable** **concept** concerning its modelling, impact, and the measures that should be put in place to **alleviate*** the situation. While most governments accept **anthropomorphic global warming*** as true, the debate over the economic **burdens*** imposed on societies trying to become sustainable is a **paramount*** concern.

Seeking to reduce **greenhouse gas emissions*** and address climate change, some **argue** for a **radical** shift to renewable energy, while others propose a **transitional** process. Some argue that a strategy that involves **fossil fuels***, **especially** natural gas, **mixed** with renewable energy can mitigate economic and security **shocks** during the transition period, **whereas** others argue that continuing fossil fuel usage is **counterproductive*** in terms of **overcoming** climate change and will result in a **delay** in the **uptake*** of cleaner energy sources.

Another **contentious*** issue is **Hydraulic fracturing***, or fracking, which has its share of supporters and detractors. The former argue that it increases the **domestic output** of oil and prevents dependence on foreign crude oil, as can be seen by the fact that the USA has become energy independent due to fracking, whilst the latter raises **alarm*** over the **risks** of pollution of groundwater and increased **seismic*** activity.

Conclusion

The study of the environment is critical in addressing global issues like climate change, biodiversity loss, and pollution. If you study environmental science, the knowledge you gain will be invaluable for understanding the complex ways in which people impact the environment. This field of study equips you to identify potential environmental **threats**, enhances your understanding of sustainable development, and prepares you to engage actively in debates on energy **diversification**, the **controversies** surrounding fracking, and the extent to which pollution can be controlled.

As the field of environmental science continues to evolve, it will need to address challenges that **span*** **demographics***, economics, and technological changes, necessitating an **integrated approach**. By studying environmental science, you will learn to consider both current and future **implications**, which is essential for developing solutions that support **planetary*** health and human well-being. This education provides you with the necessary knowledge, skills, and abilities to contribute to solving pressing global problems and advancing sustainable development both locally and globally.

James Reid
Assistant Professor and EAP Coordinator at Akita International University, Japan

Vocabulary

Words From the Second 1,000 General Service High-Frequency Word List

aimed	meanwhile
advise	mixed
agricultural	modelling
argue	oceans
arrangements	overcoming
border	patterns
century	period
cleaning	photograph
consequences	plates
critical	practical
cultivating	practices
damage	publication
decreasing	push
delay	resistant
disease	responsible
discipline	rice
during	risks
encouraging	severe
engineers	shocks
especially	soil
examining	straws
excess	stretching
framing	symbol
governs	temperatures
governments	threats
harmful	tools
illustrated	visual
image	waste
improves	widespread
International	worse
management	

Words From the Academic Word List

academic	consists
advocating	consultants
affects	contexts
analysts	contributes
approach	controversies
areas	creating
aspects	crucial
behalf	cycle
challenges	data
complex	debatable
concept	distinct

disposal
distribution
diverse
diversification
domestic
emerged
enabled
energy
enhances
environmental
erosion
establishment
evaluation/evaluating
evolves
expansive
experts
facilitating
financial
finally
focuses
funding
global
highlighted
imagery
impact
implications
imposed
incentives
integrated
infer
initiative
innovations
involving
interactions
interventions
investigation
issues
jobs
legal
maintaining
methods

minimize
monitoring
neutral
outcomes
output
phenomena
policies
posing
potentially
precise
predict
process
projects
purchase
radical
recover
regions
regime
regulations
revolutionized
removing
research
resolution
resource
restoration
role
secure
seeking
shifts
sources
strategies
sustainability
symbol
targeted
technological
techniques
theories
transit
transitional
whereas

Glossary

It is not necessary for learners to memorize these words and expressions.

Alarm (Noun): A sudden fear or anxiety, often due to a sense of danger.

Alleviate (Verb): To make something, such as pain or hardship, less severe.

Amazon rainforest (Noun Phrase): The world's largest tropical rainforest, located in South America.

Anthropomorphic global warming (Noun Phrase): The concept of attributing human-caused activities to climate change and the resultant global temperature rise.

Apollo 8 (Noun Phrase): The NASA space mission that first sent humans around the moon in 1968.

Arid (Adjective): Extremely dry, typically referring to land or climate.

Astronauts (Noun): People trained to travel and work in space.

Atmospheric (Adjective): Related to the atmosphere, the layer of gases surrounding a planet.

Ban (Verb): To officially or legally prohibit something.

Bees (Noun): Insects known for pollination and producing honey.

Biodiversity (Noun): The variety of life in the world or a particular habitat.

Birdlife (Noun): Birds collectively, especially the species of a particular region.

Burdens (Noun): A heavy load, especially one causing hardship or stress.

Capture (Verb): To take possession or control of something, often by force.

Careers (Noun): Occupations or professions undertaken for a significant period of a person's life.

Carbon dioxide (Noun Phrase): A colorless, odorless gas produced by burning carbon and respiration.

Catalyze (Verb): To cause or accelerate a reaction or process.

Climatic (Adjective): Pertains to the climate, describing anything related to weather patterns and conditions over time.

Climate change (Noun Phrase): Long-term changes in temperature, precipitation, and weather patterns.

Coastal (Adjective): Located on or near a coast.

Combated (Verb): Fought against or opposed something.

Compliance (Noun): The act of adhering to or following regulations or guidelines.

Compelling (Adjective): Evoking interest, attention, or admiration in an irresistible way.

Concentrations (Noun): The abundance of a constituent within a mixture, often in terms of chemical substances.

Conservation (Noun): The protection and preservation of the environment and wildlife.

Continually (Adverb): Occurring without interruption or repeatedly.

Contentious (Adjective): Causing or likely to cause disagreement or controversy.

Counterproductive (Adjective): Having the opposite effect to what was intended.

Coral bleaching (Noun Phrase): The whitening of corals due to stress from temperature changes, often leading to coral death.

Coral reef (Noun Phrase): A diverse underwater ecosystem made from the calcium carbonate skeletons of coral polyps.

Cover cropping (Noun Phrase): The practice of growing specific crops to protect and enrich the soil.

Cutlery (Noun): Eating utensils like knives, forks, and spoons.

Curtailed (Verb): Reduced or limited something in extent or quantity.

Debris (Noun): Scattered fragments, typically of something wrecked or destroyed.

DDT (Noun): A synthetic insecticide, once widely used but now banned in many countries due to environmental harm.

Degradation (Noun): The process by which something deteriorates or declines.

Deployed (Verb): To move into position or make use of resources.

Depletion (Noun): The reduction in the number or quantity of something.

Demographics (Noun): Statistical data related to the population and particular groups within it.

Desertification (Noun): The process by which fertile land becomes desert, typically as a result of drought, deforestation, or inappropriate agriculture.

Disincentivize (Verb): To discourage someone from doing something by providing a disincentive.

Disputes (Noun): Disagreements or arguments.

Drones (Noun): Unmanned aerial vehicles used for various purposes, including surveillance and agriculture.

Drought (Noun): A prolonged period of abnormally low rainfall, leading to a shortage of water.

Earthrise (Noun): The view of Earth rising above the moon's horizon, famously photographed during the Apollo 8 mission.

Ecological (Adjective): Related to the relationships between living organisms and their environment.

Ecosystem (Noun): A biological community of interacting organisms and their physical environment.

Emissions (Noun): Gases or pollutants released into the atmosphere, typically from human activities.

Engage (Verb): To involve oneself in an activity or become occupied.

Engendered (Verb): To cause or give rise to a situation or feeling.

Fertilizer usage (Noun Phrase): The application of chemical or natural substances to soil to increase its fertility.

Filtration (Noun): The process of removing unwanted substances from a liquid or gas by passing it through a filter.

Fossil fuels (Noun Phrase): Nonrenewable energy sources like coal, oil, and natural gas formed from the remains of ancient plants and animals.

Fragility (Noun): The quality of being easily broken or damaged.

Fostering (Verb): Encouraging the development or growth of something.

GPS (Noun): Global Positioning System, a satellite-based navigation system.

Global warming (Noun): The long-term increase in Earth's average surface temperature due to human activities, primarily the emission of greenhouse gases.

Greenhouse gas emissions (Noun Phrase): Gases, like carbon dioxide and methane, that trap heat in the atmosphere, contributing to global warming.

Groundwater (Noun): Water stored beneath Earth's surface in soil and rock formations.

Habitats (Noun): The natural environments where organisms live and thrive.

Hydraulic fracturing (Noun Phrase): A technique used to extract oil and gas by fracturing rock with pressurized liquid.

Hydroelectric (Adjective): Related to electricity generated by water power.

Hydrological (Adjective): Concerning the study of the movement, distribution, and management of water on Earth.

Indiscriminate (Adjective): Done at random or without careful judgment.

Interconnectedness (Noun): The state of being connected with each other.

Intercropping (Noun): The agricultural practice of growing two or more crops in proximity.

Irrigation (Noun): The artificial application of water to land to assist in crop growth.

Larvae (Noun): The immature form of an insect or other animal that undergoes metamorphosis.

Landscapes (Noun): Natural environments and terrains, often described in terms of beauty or aesthetics.

Leisure (Noun): Free time spent away from work or obligations.

Marine (Adjective): Related to the sea or ocean.

Marine biologists (Noun Phrase): Scientists who study ocean life and ecosystems.

Mauna Loa (Noun Phrase): A massive shield volcano in Hawaii, known for its role in climate science as a CO_2 monitoring site.

Massive (Adjective): Extremely large or heavy.

Mitigate (Verb): To make something less severe or harmful.

Mississippi river delta (Noun Phrase): The region where the Mississippi River empties into the Gulf of Mexico, characterized by wetlands.

Necessitating (Verb): Making something necessary or required.

New Delhi (Noun Phrase): The capital city of India.

Narrative (Noun): A spoken or written account of events; a story.

Oceanographers (Noun): Scientists who study the physical and biological aspects of the ocean.

Optimize (Verb): To make something as effective or functional as possible.

Paramount (Adjective): Of utmost importance.

Pesticides (Noun): Chemicals used to kill pests, especially insects that damage crops.

Planetary (Adjective): Relating to planets or the entire Earth.

PM 2.5 (Noun Phrase): Fine particulate matter in the air, measuring less than 2.5 micrometers, harmful to health.

PM 10 (Noun Phrase): Particulate matter in the air measuring 10 micrometers or less, also harmful to health.

Plastic (Noun): A synthetic material made from polymers.

CHAPTER 30

STATISTICS

Eric Yanchenko
Akita International University, Japan

What does it mean when the **weatherman*** says there is a 75% *chance* that it will **rain tomorrow**? How can a **poll*** of 1,000 **registered** voters tell us anything about the *likely* voting **patterns** of millions of citizens? How does Netflix know what movies to **recommend** to me?

Introduction

Statistical thinking is an **indispensable*** tool for every **aspect** of modern-day life. **Sadly**, however, it is all too often **relegated*** to a list of **formulas** and **procedures** to memorize in introductory classes. Yet from **weather predictions** to political polls to social **media** recommendation systems, no **domain** is free from statistics' reach.

First, the word *statistics* **requires clarification** as it has two related but **distinct definitions**. The first meaning of the word is a set of facts or figures. For example, the **GDP*** of the United States, the total population of India, and Shohei Ohtani's batting average are all statistics. The *field* of statistics, however, is not only concerned with such **summary** measures but rather decision-making under uncertainty. Since we are **constantly** making decisions without complete **information**, it's clear that statistics **impact** our daily lives. By **converting** scientific questions into **mathematical** ones, **collecting data**, fitting **models** and **analyzing** the results, statistics provides a principled decision making **framework**, useful for answering everything from local to **global** questions.

History

Compared to its scientific **cousins**, the field of statistics is still relatively young. While several Christian **philosophers engaged*** with the **concept** of **probability** in the middle of the second millennium, including Thomas Acquinas (1225–1274) and Thomas Bayes (1702–1761), statistics did not become a proper scientific **domain** until the early 20th **century**. The one man most **deserving** of **credit** for this **statistical revolution** is Sir R. A. Fisher (1890–1962). A fiercely opinionated and unapologetic pipe-smoker, Fisher was a true **Renaissance*** man who developed many of the most popular statistical **techniques during** his **career**. Throughout his time as a **researcher** in England, he developed countless statistical tools, from **ANOVA*** to **t-tests***. Fisher was also **foundational*** in the field of **Design** of Experiments, which is concerned with setting up experiments for **optimal*** statistical properties. His work was **originally motivated** by **agricultural** applications, such as understanding the effect of growing conditions on **harvest** yield, but he

Introducing the Liberal Arts, pages 207–214
Copyright © 2026 by Emerald Publishing Limited
All rights of reproduction in any form reserved.
doi:10.1108/978-1-80592-303-920251031

also applied his **methods** to the fields of **biology*** and **genetics***. Fisher's methods continue to be **ubiquitous*** today, partly because he could make deep mathematical concepts accessible to nonmathematical researchers. Indeed, his textbook *Statistical Methods for Research Workers* (1925) was a **staple*** on **lab benches*** across the world for years, and introductory statistics courses today are still filled with methods he developed.

Statistics continued to grow in popularity during the 20th century, marked by **giants** such as George Box, Gertrude Cox and C. R. Rao. One **deserving** of special mention is the Japanese statistician Hirotsugu Akaike (1927–2009). A **graduate** of the University of Tokyo, Akaike began working at the **Institute** of Statistical Mathematics in Tachikawa during the 1950s. There, he developed the Akaike **Information Criterion** (AIC), one of the most widely-used **model selection tools** today. Model selection is a **classical** statistical **task** where the **goal** is to **discriminate** between two **competing** models. In other words, given two or more potential explanations of the data, which fits the best? AIC gives a principled way to **compare** models, and led to Akaike receiving **international** recognition for his **contributions** to statistics.

Finally, a huge **leap*** forward in **computing** power led to the latest statistical revolution that began in the later part of the 20th century, and continues to this day. **Whereas** Fisher may have worked with tens of data points, and Akaike with hundreds, present-day statisticians can easily access and **analyze** data sets with thousands, millions, or even **billions** of lines of data. One method which **leveraged*** the **improved computational** power was the **bootstrap***, developed by Stanford statistician Bradley Efron (1938-). There's an old **adage*** in the English language to "pull yourself up by your bootstraps." Well, if you know anything about **physics***, or have ever worn shoes, you know that it's impossible to lift yourself off the ground by pulling on the **straps** on your **boots**! Even though it is an impossible **feat***, the saying is used to mean you succeeded at something without external help. English aside, the bootstrap method developed by Efron allows for the (**seemingly***) impossible task of **generating** uncertainty **estimates** without needing to **collect** more data. The **key** is using computers to re-**sample** from the original data set and **recompute*** the statistic of interest many times, something **infeasible*** by hand. From bootstrapping your data to **artificial** intelligence and every method in between, the modern field of statistics is completely shaped by the rise in computational power.

Statistical Processes

With some historical context in hand, we can begin to see what statistics is and how it can be used. At its **core**, statistical thinking is about decision-making under uncertainty. There are four main **components** of the statistical process: Question, Data, **Analysis** and Decision.

First, we have our question of interest. This could be: a **regulatory** agency asking if a new **drug** is safe to take; a small business owner wondering if social **media** users like their new product; or a group of friends trying to decide on where to eat **dinner** tonight. There is something in the "real world" that we want to know about, and we will use statistical **procedures** to learn about it. Once we have settled on our question, the next step is data. As Sherlock Holmes said himself, "Data! Data! Data! I can't make **bricks** without **clay**!" In other words, we can't begin to make a **principled** decision without having information on the subject. For testing new drugs we **conduct clinical*** trials; to **gauge*** social media user's sentiments, we may look at their posts, likes and follows; and for our dinner decision, we may **consult** our friends or Google **reviews**.

Once we have collected our data, it's time to analyze. Depending on our application and question of interest, there are many models to choose from. As statistical methods become easier to **implement thanks** to **online programs** and **web apps***, it's **paramount*** that the user understands the methods to **ensure** proper **usage***. A **major hallmark*** of statistical methods is their **emphasis** on uncertainty **quantification***. Understanding the **variability** in the **data-generating process**, observations, and model, are **key** to making **informed** decisions, which is the **final component**. Once we have fit a model and **analyzed** the **output**, we have to make a decision. We can't simply say that a drug has a 90% chance of being effective, we must decide whether to **approve** it or not. **Similarly**, it's not enough to say that we **probably** will like the new restaurant, we have to make up our mind and eat! In countless applications, the **final** decision comes down to a **binary*** decision, but thanks to the statistical process, we can make our decision with **confidence** by understanding the associated **risks**.

What Does Probability *Mean*?

One **major appeal*** of statistics is the number of different **disciplines** that it **intersects***. From **philosophy** to mathematics to social science and everything in between, statistics is **inherently** an **interdisciplinary*** field. As an example, let's consider the philosophy of **probability**. Probability serves as the mathematical foundation of statistics. The **topic** has interested **polymaths*** since as early as the 18th **century**, but the **debate** over its **precise definition intensified** in the early 1900s.

There are two **major camps** when it comes to the **interpretation** of probability. The first is the *frequentist** view which depends on the long-run *frequency* of observations. **Imagine** a drug company says there is a 90% chance their new drug will protect you from a certain **disease**. Under the frequentist interpretation, this means that if 100 people take the drug, we would expect 90 of them to be protected while the other 10 would still get sick. This is a natural way to think about probability, and can be **validated empirically**, i.e., we can count the proportion of people who get sick. This **definition**, however, depends on observing the process in the long-run. In other words, it requires the data-generating **process** to be *repeatable** and tells us nothing about a *single event*, in this case, a single person. This can lead many people to **mistakenly criticize*** the **probabilities** as incorrect. If there's a 90% protection **guarantee**, and you still get sick, some may say that the prediction was wrong. However, the probability makes no guarantees for a single **individual**, but rather the average over many people. So while mathematically a **valid** statement, knowing that 90% of other people will be protected likely brings you little **solace*** if you get sick!

The other popular interpretation is the *Bayesian** view. Here, the interpretation of probability is based on *subjective** belief*. For example, a 25% chance of rain tomorrow means my belief that it will not rain is three times greater than my belief it will rain. This definition now allows us to **assign** a probability to a single event, i.e., the probability it rains *tomorrow* or the probability that *I* get sick. Indeed, this is the only sensible definition for assigning probabilities to, e.g., historical events like the bodily **resurrection*** of Jesus of Nazareth, as historical situations cannot be repeated. One **con*** of this definition is that it's not completely objective. Indeed, two people could look at the same weather report, and give a different probability of rain.

The **appropriate** definition usually depends on the situation. If an experiment can be **replicated***, then the frequentist definition may make more sense. On the other hand, if a single event is of interest, then a Bayesian belief is required. Regardless, an understanding of the interpretation of probability is necessary to **evaluate** claims **encountered** in daily life. Moreover, if you are interested in philosophy, **hopefully** this **discussion whets*** your **appetite*** to study statistics!

Real-World Relevance

There are many benefits to studying statistics, but I will briefly touch on three. First, as almost every **discipline collects** data, every discipline needs statistical analysis. This means that if you are interested in the social sciences, statistics is for you. If you are interested in **medical** sciences, statistics is for you. Business, **economics**, **chemistry***, **ecology***, **agriculture**, political science, **engineering**, law, **epidemiology***, no matter the field, statistics plays a **vital*** role. One example of this is in the field of **psychology**. Many **psychological theories** are tested and validated using experiments. Statisticians are used not only to analyze the data once it has been **collected**, but also to set up the experiment to **ensure** the scientific **conclusions** are statistically valid. While a particularly **complicated** experiment may call for a trained statistician to **consult**, many **projects** are run by psychologists alone who need to understand the statistical **procedures** themselves.

The second reason to study statistics is its **relevance** to machine learning (ML) and artificial intelligence (AI). Both AI and ML have **generated considerable buzz*** over the past **decade** and have already become a part of everyday life. Using Face ID to **unlock** your iPhone, **instantly translating entire documents** into another language with *DeepL*, movie **recommendations** on *Netflix*, and *ChatGPT* are all examples of AI we **encounter**. Beyond their **ubiquity*** today, ML and AI also promise many future **advancements***: self-driving cars in cities where **traffic jams*** are distant history; **personalized*** medicine giving each **patient** a tailored medical plan; **removal** of **menial* labor tasks** in offices; and more. Understanding many of these methods, however, requires a knowledge of statistics.

Finally, beyond the walls of **academia** and **self**-driving cars, sound statistical thinking can have **enormous** benefits in your daily life. First, humans have an **incredible*** ability to **detect patterns**. While this is a wonderful God-given ability, it can also lead us to find "patterns" that do not truly exist. For example, imagine you own a **bakery*** and you start to notice that whenever you leave the main door open, you get more **customers**. You **deduce** that opening the door *leads* to more customers, so you decide to leave the door open all the time, even on the coldest days. In reality, leaving the door open had little to do with the amount of customers, rather, you opened the door on days with **nice weather**, when there is more **foot traffic** in general. Now all that opening the door is doing is increasing your heating bill! This is a **quintessential*** example of "**correlation*** not **implying causation***." In other words, just because two **phenomena** are related, e.g., open door and increased sales, does not mean that one causes the other. Truly **demonstrating** causation is a **laborious*** process and any such claims should be met with **appropriate skepticism***. Statistical thinking allows you to analyze claims of causation, as well as test for them in your own **circumstances**.

Beyond **mistakenly attributing causal*** effects when there are none, statistical thinking **combats*** other common **biases**, e.g., **selection, confirmation, survival**, etc. A common example of **survival bias** is something almost every college student will **encounter** at least once. Imagine you are finishing your third-year and trying to decide whether to go to graduate school or start working after graduation. To find out what **graduate** school is like, you speak with your **professors** and find that *every one* of them had a great experience in graduate school, and they all highly **encourage** you to go. You might think that grad school is for you! While that might be the case, you must beware of survival bias. The very fact that someone is a professor almost certainly means they had a positive experience in **grad*** school, because, well, that's why they are in **academia**. There are **scores*** of people who have very poor grad school experiences, but almost none of them stayed in academia. Thus, only consulting professors, means only consulting those who "survived" grad school, and will give you a very **warped*** perception of it. Sound statistical thinking can give you more **principled** ways of addressing this question. For what it's worth, if you want my **unbiased** opinion, you should **definitely** go to grad school; I had a great experience :)

Conclusion

Sadly, statistics is far too often taught as a **list** of rules and **procedures untethered*** to any real-world application. **Unsurprisingly***, many students **dread*** taking a statistics course, and are **relieved** to receive a passing grade to finally forget about the subject! From the philosophical **underpinnings*** to its wide-**array*** of applications, statistics is a rich and **exciting** field worthy of careful study. Moreover, with the **ascension*** of the "**big data" era***, **statistical literacy*** has become a **requisite*** skill for the modern citizen. Beyond the in-demand skills of many employers and **relevance** to **virtually** every field, sound statistical thinking can **reap*** many benefits in your daily life. Here's to being certain about studying uncertainty!

Adapted from a text by Dr. Eric Yanchenko
Assistant Professor of AI & Data Science
Akita International University
Japan

Vocabulary

Words From the Second 1,000 General Service High Frequency Word List

agricultural	billions
agriculture	bricks
approve	camps
artificial	century
aside	clay

collect
compare
competing
complicated
confidence
cousins
customers
deserving
dinner
discipline
discussion
disease
during
encourage
engineering
entire
exciting
fiercely
foot
forward
frequency
harvest
imagine
improved
incorrect
information
informed
instantly
international
key
list
medicine
mistakenly

model
nice
original
patient
patterns
pipe
probability
probably
programs
rain
recommend
recommendation
relieved
repeated
restaurant
reviews
risks
sadly
sample
self
shoes
sick
skill
straps
tailored
thanks
tomorrow
tonight
tool
translating
unlock
weather

Words From the Academic Word List

academia
access
accessible
analysis
analyze
appropriate
aspect
assign
attributing
benefits
bias
briefly
circumstances

clarification
classical
component
computational
computers
computing
concept
conclusion
conduct
confirmation
considerable
constantly
consult

context
contributions
converting
core
credit
criterion
data
debate
decade
deduce
definitely
definition
demonstrating
design
detect
discriminate
distinct
documents
domain
economics
emphasis
empirically
encounter
enormous
ensure
estimates
evaluate
external
finally
formulas
foundation
framework
generated
global
goal
grade
guarantee
impacts
implement
implying
individual
inherently
institute
intelligence
intensified
interpretation
labor
liberal
major
media

medical
method
motivated
objective
perception
phenomena
philosophers
philosophical
philosophy
positive
potential
precise
prediction
principled
procedures
process
projects
proportion
psychological
psychologists
psychology
registered
regulatory
relevance
removal
required
research
researcher
revolution
role
selection
similarly
statistic
statistical
statistically
statistician
statistics
summary
survival
survived
task
techniques
theories
topic
unbiased
valid
validated
variability
virtually
whereas

Glossary

It is not necessary for learners to memorize these words and expressions.

Adage: Old saying; proverb
Advancements: Improvement
ANOVA: Analysis of Variance—a statistical test to compare means
Appeal: Request
Appetite: Strong urge or desire
Apps: Computer or mobile application
Array: Orderly arrangement
Ascension: Rising; moving upwards
Bakery: Place where bread and pastries are produced
Bayesian: Relating to an interpretation of the concept of probability
Binary: In two parts
Biology: The study of living organisms
Bootstrap: A leather strap on the rear of a boot which is pulled on to put the boots on
Buzz: Excited discssion
Causal: Expressing a cause/reason for something
Causation: The act of causing/initiating something
Chemistry: The science of the composition and properties of physical matter
Clinical: Involving direct observation of patients
Combats: Fights; battles
Con: A negative point
Correlation: The tendency for two variables to change in a related manner
Criticize: Find fault with
Dread: Fear
Ecology: The science of the relationship between organisms and their enviornment
Engaged: Involved with
Epidemiology: The study of diseases in populations
Era: Time period
Feat: Accomplishment
Foundational: At the base; what everything else relies upon
Frequentist: An advocate of frequency probability (that probability is defined by limits of relative probability)
Gauge: Measure
GDP: Gross Domestic Product (measure of all market value of all goods and services produced in a country)
Genetics: Branch of biology dealing with heredity and transmission of characteristics
Grad: Postgraduate
Hallmark: A distinguishing characteristic
Incredible: Unbelievable
Indispensable: Necessary; essential
Infeasible: Not capable of being accomplished
Interdisciplinary: Drawing from two or more separate professional disciplines

Intersects: To cut across; cross
Lab benches: Workbench in a laboratory
Laborious: Requiring hard work
Leap: Jump
Leveraged: To use effectively
Menial: Work appropriate for a servant
Paramount: Of highest importance
Personalized: According to individual needs
Physics: The science of matter and energy
Poll: Survey or election
Polymaths: A person whose knowledge spans multiple subjects
Quantification: Counting; measuring
Quintessential: Most typical
Reap: Yield
Recompute: To calculate again
Relegated: To assign to an inferior position
Renaissance: A revival of classical art, architecture, and learning in 14–16th century Europe
Repeatable: Able to be repeated
Replicated: Done again in the exact same manner
Requisite: Required; essential
Resurrection: To come to life again after dying
Scores: A count of 20
Seemingly: Appearing to be
Skepticism: Doubt
Solace: Comfort
Staple: Something used by many people
Subjective: Depends on someone's point of view
T-tests: A statistical test comparing group means
Traffic jams: When road traffic is blocked and not moving
Ubiquitous/Ubiquity: Being everywhere at the same time
Underpinnings: Foundation; the support which strengthens something
Unsurprisingly: Does not cause surprise or alarm
Untethered: Not connected
Usage: Use
Vital: Necessary
Warped: Bent
Weatherman: Someone who forecasts and reports on weather
Whets: Sharpen; make more acute

CHAPTER 31

ZOOLOGY

James Reid
Akita International University, Japan

Introduction

Have you ever wondered about the **incredible*** ways animals have **evolved** and **adapted** to their **environments** over millions of years? What **mysteries** can we uncover within the **behaviors, structures,** and **ecosystems*** of the animal kingdom, and how do they **connect** to our understanding of life on Earth? Zoology, the scientific study of animals, **beckons*** us to **explore** these **enigmas*** and more. It takes us on a **journey** through the **astonishing diversity** of life on our **planet***, from the **tiniest* microorganisms*** to the largest **mammals***. For example, consider the **unique** adaptations of the **octopus***, which can change color and **texture*** to **blend*** into its **surroundings***, **showcasing*** the incredible ways animals have evolved. By scrutinizing animal behaviors, **physiology*, genetics***, and **ecological*** roles, zoologists **reveal** the secrets of the natural world, shedding light* on our place within it.

History of Zoology

Zoology has ancient **roots**. Various civilizations, such as the Egyptians, Greeks, and Romans, observed and **documented** aspects of the animal kingdom, often **intertwining*** their understanding with **mythology*** and **superstition***. The true beginnings of zoological study are often **attributed** to the ancient Greek **philosopher** Aristotle (fourth **Century** BCE). His work "Historia Animalium" laid the **foundation** for zoological classification and observation, setting a **precedent** for future **investigations**. For instance, Aristotle's detailed observations of **marine*** life, including the octopus and its behaviors, were **groundbreaking*** for his time.

During the Middle Ages, zoological knowledge was largely **preserved** by **Islamic* scholars***. In **The Renaissance***, European **naturalists*** like Conrad Gessner and John Ray began to systematically **catalogue*** and describe animals. **The Age of Exploration*** in the 17th and 18th centuries brought back many new animal specimens*, leading to the development of **taxonomy***. Carl Linnaeus, an 18th-century Swedish biologist, is known for his **binomial nomenclature system***, still used today to name and classify **species***. Linnaeus's classification of whales, which were **previously** thought to be fish, **revolutionized** marine biology.

The 19th century was a **pivotal*** period for zoology. Charles Darwin's **Theory of Evolution by Natural Selection***, presented in "On the **Origin** of Species" (1859), revolutionized the field, providing a **unifying framework** to understand the diversity of life and how species change over time. Darwin's observations of **finches*** in the Galápagos **Islands**, which led to his theory of natural selection, remain one of the most famous examples of evolutionary biology.

Introducing the Liberal Arts, pages 215–224
Copyright © 2026 by Emerald Publishing Limited
All rights of reproduction in any form reserved.
doi:10.1108/978-1-80592-303-920251032

In the 20th century, zoology **expanded rapidly** with **technological** advancements, genetics, and ecology, leading to investigations into animal behavior, genetics, physiology, and **conservation biology***.

Today, zoology **encompasses*** various sub-**disciplines**, including ethology (the study of animal behavior), marine biology, entomology (the study of insects), ornithology (the study of birds), herpetology (the study of reptiles and amphibians), and more. Zoologists play a critical role in **wildlife*** conservation and **habitat*** preservation in **response** to the threats faced by many animal species. For example, conservation efforts for the critically **endangered*** Sumatran rhinoceros have been informed by zoological research on their habitat and behavior.

Notable Zoologists

Several notable figures have made **significant contributions** that have **profoundly*** shaped our understanding of the natural world. Carl Linnaeus (1707–1778) developed a structured **approach** to naming and classifying species. Charles Darwin (1809–1882) produced the theory of evolution by natural selection, **reshaping*** our **comprehension*** of evolution and species diversity. Although Darwin published first and conducted more extensive research, Alfred Russel Wallace (1823–1913) independently **formulated** the same theory based on his research. Wallace's studies in the **Malay archipelago*** provided critical **insights** into species **distribution** and the concept of the **"Wallace Line."***

Konrad Lorenz (1903–1989) made influential contributions to animal behavior studies, notably through his work on **imprinting*** in birds. Rachel Carson (1907–1964), a marine biologist and **author,** raised **awareness** about the **environmental impact** of **pesticides*** with her **seminal*** work "Silent Spring." Barbara McClintock (1902–1992) made groundbreaking discoveries in genetic **regulation**, earning her a Nobel Prize in Physiology and reshaping our understanding of genes and their **functions**. E.O. Wilson (1929–2021), an **expert** in ants and **biodiversity***, **championed*** the preservation of Earth's diverse life forms and introduced the **concept** of "**biophilia***." David Attenborough (1926-present), a naturalist and **broadcaster***, has **inspired*** millions through his **captivating*** wildlife **documentaries*** like "The Blue Planet" and "Planet Earth." Dian Fossey (1932–1985) brought attention to mountain gorilla conservation and **highlighted** their peaceful nature compared to chimpanzees. Jane Goodall (1934-present) uncovered **complex** behaviors, tool-making abilities, and aggression in chimpanzees, connecting primate behavior and human evolution. These researchers have left an **enduring*** **legacy*** in zoology.

Controversies and Debates in the Field of Zoology

The field of zoology has several **controversies** and **debates**. One significant debate centers around the **ethics** of zoos. While some argue that zoos play a **crucial** role in conservation and **education**, others believe that keeping animals in **captivity*** is unethical and harmful to their well-being. This controversy highlights the **tension** between conservation efforts and animal rights. For instance, debates over the treatment of **orcas*** in marine parks have brought **widespread** attention to the ethics of animal captivity.

Another **major** debate **involves** the evolution of flight in birds. Scientists are divided between those who support the **gradualist*** view, suggesting that feathers evolved **initially** for insulation and later **facilitated** flight, and those **advocating** for the **punctuated equilibrium model***, proposing that feathers evolved for **display** purposes and that flight developed rapidly. This debate shows the complexity of evolutionary **processes** and varying **interpretations** of scientific **evidence**. The discovery of the feathered **Archaeopteryx*** has **fueled*** these discussions, providing critical evidence of the **link** between dinosaurs and modern birds.

Conservation **priorities** also present a significant **dilemma***. There is **ongoing** controversy over whether to **prioritize** the conservation of **charismatic*** species like pandas over less charismatic but ecologically significant species like insects. This highlights the challenges of resource allocation in conservation efforts and the need to balance public **appeal*** with ecological importance. For example, the conservation of the endangered **honeybee*** is crucial due to its role in **pollination***, impacting entire ecosystems and human agriculture.

Invasive species* management is another **area** of debate. The **cane toad*** invasion in Australia, for example, **pits*** experts who **advocate** for **aggressive*** **eradication*** measures against those who suggest allowing these species to **integrate** into the ecosystem. This controversy **illustrates** the complexities of **managing** invasive species and their impact on native ecosystems. The introduction of the **Burmese python*** in the **Florida Everglades*** is another example, where the invasive species has **disrupted*** local wildlife populations.

The question of animal **cognition*** and self-awareness continues to **intrigue*** researchers. Studies on **mirror*** self-recognition in species such as dolphins, elephants, and apes fuel debates on whether animals possess self-awareness. This ongoing research challenges our understanding of animal **intelligence** and **consciousness.** The work of scientists like Irene Pepperberg with her **African grey parrot***, Alex, has provided **compelling*** evidence of advanced cognitive abilities in birds.

Genome editing* and **de-extinction*** introduce ethical and ecological questions about the possibility of **resurrecting*** extinct species like the **woolly mammoth*** through genetic **engineering**. The **potential consequences** of **reintroducing*** these species into modern ecosystems raise significant concerns and ethical considerations. **Projects** like the **revival*** of the **passenger pigeon*** **aim** to **restore** lost species but also **prompt** questions about the feasibility and morality of such plans.

Finally, the **origins** of **zoonotic diseases***, such as **COVID-19***, highlight the complex **interactions** between humans and wildlife. Debates around human **encroachment** on animal **habitats*** and the risks associated with gain-of-function research **emphasize** the need for better understanding and management of these interactions to prevent future **pandemics***. The study of bats as carriers of numerous viruses, including coronaviruses, **underscores*** the importance of zoological research in public health.

Benefits of Zoology for Humanity

Zoology has very important advantages for **humanity*,** related to various **spheres**, such as science, **medicine**, agriculture, and education. One of the main advantages associated with zoology involves helping and treating illness. Examples include the invention of pain-killers and **anti-hypertensive agents*** inspired by certain mammals and reptiles. An example is the use of **Angiotensin-Converting Enzyme (ACE) inhibitors*** to **induce** the **relaxation** of blood vessels discovered from experiments on the **venom*** of the **Brazilian pit viper***.

The study of animal anatomy and genetics has also improved **reconstructive surgery***, the **design** of **limb prostheses***, and **organ transplantation***. Public health has also been e**nhanced** through zoological study. for instance, **disease vectors*** such as mosquitoes and ticks are studied to help control **malaria***, **Zika virus***, **Lyme disease***, among others. Control of **sleeping sickness*** was partly attributed to studying the **tsetse fly***, which is **responsible** for **transmitting** the disease.

In agriculture, animal research is important since agricultural yields depend on the behavior of **pests*** and their natural enemies. Zoological understanding also **improves** meat and **dairy*** production. For instance, in the past, **selective breeding* programs** have enabled remarkable gains in **sustainable** milk yields from dairy cows.

Another important Zoological consideration is animal conservation. Protecting ecosystems and animal species on the **verge*** of **extinction*** is **vital*** for **maintaining** biological diversity. Healthy ecosystems **promote** pollination, **seed dispersal***, and **nutrient* circulation***, which **ensure clean** water, **pure** air, and climate **stabilization**. An example of biodiversity **ensuring** clean water is the importance of the **sea otter*** in maintaining healthy **kelp forests***.

Education and public awareness of zoology allow zoologists to work with the population to promote **policies** that are **favorable*** for the conservation of natural resources. This concern may help **foster*** a greater **commitment** to conservation activities and a more nature-friendly behavior in various spheres of life. **Media**, such as wildlife documentaries, promote ethics in regard to natural ecosystems and prompt the young **generation** to care for and **defend** the biodiversity of the earth's ecosystems.

In short, Zoology benefits humanity by contributing to fields like ecology, evolutionary genetics, and ethology. In ecology, it aids in conservation efforts, such as managing endangered species and restoring habitats. Evolutionary genetics helps explain how genetic **variations** lead to adaptations, with research on antibiotic **resistance** impacting public health. Ethology, the study of animal behavior, influences **technologies*** like **navigation*** systems and **autonomous* drones***. As zoological research advances, more benefits in terms of agricultural production, public health, and cleaner environments will likely arise.

Employment Opportunities

There are many employment opportunities for those who have studied zoology. A wildlife biologist, for example, studies animals and their environments to better understand their behavior, genetics, and ecosystems. Their work **typically** involves **conducting fieldwork*, analyzing data**, and developing conservation **strategies** to protect animal species.

Key roles in animal care include zoo keepers, who **focus** on feeding, cleaning, **monitoring** health, providing **veterinary*** care, and **participating** in breeding programs to support species conservation. Conservation scientists, on the other hand, design projects to protect endangered species and their habitats. They often **coordinate** with **government** agencies to **implement** biodiversity-saving measures. Ecologists, working in **similar** conservation roles, study organisms in their environments and conduct both field and **lab*** research to develop environmental management strategies.

Marine biologists study **marine organisms*** and ecosystems, often addressing **issues** like pollution, climate change, and human impact on **ocean** biodiversity. Their goal is to **devise*** methods to protect marine life. Environmental **consultants** work with both private and public sectors to address environmental challenges, ensuring that projects **comply*** with ecological standards and **minimize adverse*** impacts.

Veterinary **technicians* assist** in veterinary medicine, **performing tasks** like behavior **modification**, preparing animals for **surgery***, conducting lab tests, and **administering*** first aid. Research scientists, another branch of zoologists, conduct investigations in various areas of animal biology such as physiology, behavior, and genetics, contributing to both scientific knowledge and **practical** applications.

In education, zoologists may become teachers or **lecturers** at high schools or universities, developing **curricula***, teaching classes, and **overseeing*** lab work to **inspire*** future scientists. Animal **psychologists** focus on animal behavior, improving **rehabilitation***, training, and understanding of animal cognition. They may work with **domestic** or wild animals, or develop animal care programs in zoos and aquariums.

Many research-related or **academic** careers **require** advanced degrees or further education. Gaining **relevant** experience through **internships*, volunteering**, or part-time work is also crucial for advancing in the field.

However, even if you don't continue your zoological studies, taking a zoology course at a liberal arts college still offers lasting benefits through its **interdisciplinary*** approach. Zoology can be **combined** with fields like environmental science or psychology, fostering a broader understanding of how different disciplines interact. This integration gives students a more **holistic* perspective** on animal biology and conservation, **equipping** them with **versatile* skills** that can be applied to various careers beyond zoology, such as environmental management, education, or **policy**-making.

James Reid
Assistant Professor and EAP Coordinator at Akita International University, Japan

Vocabulary

Words From the Second 1,000 General Service High-Frequency Word List

Aim	Consciousness
Agriculture	Critical
Argue	Defend
Astonishing	Disciplines
Attention	Disciplines
Attention	Diseases
Behaviors	Discussions
Centuries	During
Clean	Earning
Combined	Education
Compared	Education
Connect	Engineering

Entire
Explore
Feathers
Government
Harmful
Health
Health
Improved
Improves
Informed
Insects
Insects
Invention
Islands
Journey
Key
Management
Management
Managing
Medicine
Medicine
Model
Mysteries
Ocean
Origin

Origins
Pain
Parks
Performing
Practical
Preservation
Preserved
Prize
Programmes
Programs
Prompt
Pure
Rapidly
Resistance
Responsible
Risks
Roots
Seed
Skills
Threats
Tool
Treating
Treatment
Typically

Words From the Academic Word List

Academic
Adapted
Advocate
Advocating
Allocation
Analyze
Analyzing
Area
Aspects
Assist
Attributed
Author
Awareness
Benefits
Challenges
Commitment
Complex
Concept
Conducting
Consequences
Consultants

Coordinate
Crucial
Data
Debates
Design
Display
Diversity
Documented
Domestic
Distribution
Editing
Emphasize
Ensure
Ensuring
Environment
Environmental
Environments
Equipping
Ethics
Evidence
Evolution

Evolved
Expanded
Expert
Facilitated
Finally
Focus
Formulated
Foundation
Framework
Functions
Generation
Goal
Highlighted
Illustrates
Impact
Implement
Initial
Insights
Integrate
Intelligence
Interactions
Interpretations
Involves
Issues
Lecturers
Link
Major
Maintaining
Media
Methods
Minimize
Modification
Monitor
Monitoring
Ongoing
Participating
Period
Perspective
Philosopher
Policies

Policy
Potential
Precedent
Previously
Priorities
Prioritize
Processes
Projects
Promote
Psychologists
Regulation
Relaxation
Relevant
Resource
Response
Restore
Reveal
Revolutionized
Role
Roles
Selection
Selective
Significant
Similar
Spheres
Stabilization
Strategies
Structures
Sustainable
Tasks
Technological
Tension
Theory
Transmitting
Unifying
Unique
Variations
Volunteering
Widespread

Glossary

ACE Inhibitors (Noun): Medications that reduce blood pressure by inhibiting the angiotensin-converting enzyme.

Adverse (Adjective): Preventing success or development; harmful; unfavorable.

African Grey Parrot (Noun): A medium-sized parrot known for its intelligence and ability to mimic human speech.

Anti-hypertensive Agents (Noun): Drugs used to treat hypertension (high blood pressure).

Appeal (Verb): To make a serious, urgent, or heartfelt request.

Archaeopteryx (Noun): A prehistoric bird-like dinosaur from the Jurassic period, known as a transitional form between birds and reptiles.

Autonomous (Adjective): Having the freedom to act independently.

Beckons (Verb): To make a gesture with the hand, arm, or head to encourage someone to come nearer or follow.

Biodiversity (Noun): The variety of plant and animal life in the world or in a particular habitat.

Biophilia (Noun): An innate and genetically determined affinity of human beings with the natural world.

Brazilian Pit Viper (Noun): A venomous snake species native to Brazil, known for its potent venom.

Breeding (Verb): To produce offspring by reproduction.

Broadcaster (Noun): A person or organization that sends out signals or programs for television or radio broadcasting.

Burdened (Adjective): Loaded heavily with something, especially a problem or responsibility.

Burmese Python (Noun): A large nonvenomous snake native to Southeast Asia, invasive in other areas like the Florida Everglades.

Cane Toad (Noun): An invasive species of large, poisonous toad native to South and Central America.

Captivating (Adjective): Capable of attracting and holding interest or attention.

Captivity (Noun): The condition of being imprisoned or confined.

Catalogue (Verb): To make a systematic list of items.

Championed (Verb): Supported, defended, or advocated strongly.

Charismatic (Adjective): Exercising a compelling charm that inspires devotion in others.

Circulation (Noun): Movement or passage through a system, such as blood in the body or air in a room.

Cognition (Noun): The mental action or process of acquiring knowledge and understanding through thought, experience, and the senses.

Compelling (Adjective): Evoking interest, attention, or admiration in a powerfully irresistible way.

Comply (Verb): To act in accordance with a wish or command.

Comprehension (Noun): The ability to understand something fully.

Conservation Biology (Noun): The science of protecting and managing biodiversity and natural resources.

COVID-19 (Noun): The infectious disease caused by the most recently discovered coronavirus.

Curricula (Noun): The subjects comprising a course of study in a school or college.

De-extinction (Noun): The science of bringing extinct species back to life.

Devise (Verb): To plan or invent by careful thought, usually involving a new or complicated process.

Diary (Noun): A book in which one keeps a daily record of events and experiences.

Dilemma (Noun): A situation in which a difficult choice has to be made between two or more alternatives.

Dispersal (Noun): The action or process of distributing things or people over a wide area.

Disrupted (Adjective): Drastically altered or destroyed.

Documentaries (Noun): Nonfictional films or television programs that provide a factual record or report.

Drones (Noun): Remote-controlled pilotless aircraft or missile.

Ecological (Adjective): Relating to or concerned with the relation of living organisms to one another and to their physical surroundings.

Ecosystems (Noun): Biological communities of interacting organisms and their physical environment.

Encompasses (Verb): To surround or cover completely; include comprehensively.

Encroachment (Noun): Intrusion on a person's territory, rights, or lifestyle.

Endangered (Adjective): Seriously at risk of extinction.

Enduring (Adjective): Continuing or long-lasting.

Enigmas (Noun): People or things that are mysterious, puzzling, or difficult to understand.

Eradication (Noun): The complete destruction of something.

Extinction (Noun): The state or process of a species, family, or larger group being or becoming extinct.

Favorable (Adjective): Expressing approval; advantageous or beneficial.

Fieldwork (Noun): Practical work conducted by a researcher in the natural environment, rather than in a laboratory or office.

Finches (Noun): Small to medium-sized passerine birds, often with colorful plumage.

Florida Everglades (Noun): A tropical wetland located in the southern part of the US state of Florida, known for its unique ecosystem and wildlife.

Foster (Verb): To encourage the development of something (especially something desirable).

Fostering (Verb): Encouraging or promoting the development of something, typically something regarded as good.

Fueled (Verb): Powered or energized by a particular substance or factor.

Genetics (Noun): The study of heredity and the variation of inherited characteristics.

Genome Editing (Noun): A type of genetic engineering in which DNA is inserted, deleted, modified, or replaced in the genome of a living organism.

Gradualist (Noun): An advocate of the theory that evolution proceeds in small, gradual steps.

Groundbreaking (Adjective): Innovative; pioneering, especially in being the first to use a new method or approach.

Habitat (Noun): The natural home or environment of an animal, plant, or other organism.

Habitats (Noun): Plural of habitat; various natural environments where different species live.

Honeybee (Noun): A bee species known for producing honey and beeswax, critical for pollination.

Humanity (Noun): The human race; human beings collectively.

Imprinting (Noun): A phase-sensitive learning process where young animals develop attachments during a critical period.

Incredible (Adjective): Hard to believe; extraordinary or amazing.

Inspire (Verb): To fill someone with the urge or ability to do or feel something, especially something creative.

Inspired (Adjective): Of extraordinary quality, as if arising from some external creative impulse.

Interdisciplinary (Adjective): Involving two or more academic, scientific, or artistic disciplines.

Internships (Noun): Periods of work experience offered by an organization for a limited period of time.

Intriguing (Adjective) Arousing one's curiosity or interest; fascinating.

Invasive Species (Noun): Species that are not native to a specific location and that cause harm to the environment, economy, or human health.

Islamic (Adjective) Relating to the religion of Islam.

Kelp Forests (Noun): Underwater areas dominated by kelp, which are large brown algae seaweeds.

Lab (Noun): Short for laboratory; a room or building equipped for scientific experiments, research, or teaching.

Legacy (Noun): Something transmitted by or received from an ancestor or predecessor or from the past.

Limb Prostheses (Noun): Artificial limbs used to replace a missing part of the body.

Lyme Disease (Noun): An infectious disease caused by bacteria transmitted through the bite of infected ticks.

Malaria (Noun): A serious disease spread by mosquitoes in many tropical and subtropical regions, characterized by fevers, chills, and flu-like symptoms.

Malay Archipelago (Noun): A group of approximately 25,000 islands in the Pacific Ocean between mainland Southeast Asia and Australia.

Mammals (Noun): Warm-blooded vertebrate animals characterized by the presence of mammary glands, which in females produce milk for feeding their young.

Marine (Adjective): Relating to the sea; existing in or produced by the sea.

Marine Organisms (Noun): Plants, animals, and other organisms that live in salt water.

Microorganisms (Noun): Microscopic organisms, such as bacteria, viruses, and protozoa.

Mirror (Noun): A surface, typically of glass coated with a metal amalgam, which reflects a clear image.

Mythology (Noun): A collection of myths, especially one belonging to a particular religious or cultural tradition.

Naturalists (Noun): Scientists who study natural history, especially plants and animals in their natural environment.

Navigation (Noun): The process or activity of accurately ascertaining one's position and planning and following a route.

Nutrient (Noun): A substance that provides nourishment essential for the growth and maintenance of life.

Octopus (Noun): A sea animal with a soft body and eight long arms, known for its intelligence and ability to change color.

Orcas (Noun): Also known as killer whales, large and powerful marine mammals belonging to the dolphin family.

Organ Transplantation (Noun): The surgical operation of moving an organ from one human body to another or from a donor site to another location on the person's own body.

Overseeing (Verb) Supervising (a person or work), especially in an official capacity.

Passenger Pigeon (Noun): A species of pigeon that was once abundant in North America but became extinct in the early 20th century due to overhunting and habitat destruction.

Pesticides (Noun): Substances used for destroying insects or other organisms harmful to cultivated plants or animals.

Physiology (Noun): The branch of biology that deals with the normal functions of living organisms and their parts.

Pivotal (Adjective): Of crucial importance in relation to the development or success of something else.

Planet (Noun): A celestial body moving in an elliptical orbit around a star.

Pollination (Noun): The transfer of pollen from the male parts of a plant to the female parts of a plant, enabling fertilization and the production of seeds.

Profoundly (Adverb): To a profound extent; extremely.

Punctuated Equilibrium Model (Noun): A theory in evolutionary biology which proposes that most species will exhibit little net evolutionary change for most of their geological history, remaining in stasis or equilibrium.

Reconstructive Surgery (Noun): Surgery performed to restore appearance, function, or normality to a structure of the body.

Rehabilitation (Noun): The process of restoring someone to health or normal life through training and therapy after imprisonment, addiction, or illness.

Reintroducing (Verb): The act of bringing something back into use, circulation, or environment after a period of absence.

Renaissance (Noun): The period in European civilization immediately following the Middle Ages, characterized by a surge in interest in classical learning and values.

Reshaping (Verb): To give a new shape or form to something.

Resurrecting (Verb): Bringing something back into use, practice, or existence that has been forgotten or discontinued.

Revival (Noun): The process of bringing something back to life, consciousness, or strength; renewal.

Scholars (Noun): People involved in academic study, especially in the fields of science or humanities.

Sea Otter (Noun): A marine mammal native to the coasts of the northern and eastern North Pacific Ocean, known for its significant role in its ecosystem.

Seminal (Adjective): Strongly influencing later developments, especially in a particular field.

Showcasing (Verb): Presenting something in an attractive or favorable way for others to view or appreciate.

Sleeping Sickness (Noun): A disease caused by parasites transmitted by tsetse fly bites, leading to sleep disturbances, fever, headaches, and joint pains; mainly found in sub-Saharan Africa.

Species (Noun): A group of living organisms consisting of similar individuals capable of exchanging genes or interbreeding.

Superstition (Noun): Excessively credulous belief in and reverence for the supernatural, especially as a basis for decision-making or behavior.

Surgeons (Noun): Medical doctors who perform operations as a treatment method.

Surgery (Noun): The branch of medicine that deals with treating injuries, diseases, and other conditions by manual and instrumental means.

Surroundings (Noun): The environment or area around a particular place or the conditions within which someone or something exists.

Taxonomy (Noun): The branch of science concerned with classification, especially of organisms; systematics.

Technicians (Noun): Skilled workers who use technical knowledge and skills to perform specific tasks, often in a laboratory or field setting.

Texture (Noun): The feel, appearance, or consistency of a surface or substance.

The Age of Exploration (Noun): A period from the early 15th century and continuing into the early 17th century, during which Europeans explored Africa, the Americas, Asia, and Oceania.

The Renaissance (Noun): A period of cultural, artistic, political, and economic "rebirth" following the Middle Ages, generally thought to have started in Italy in the 14th century.

The Theory of Evolution by Natural Selection (Noun): A scientific theory that species evolve over time through a process where individuals with traits beneficial for survival and reproduction are more likely to pass on their genes.

The Wallace Line (Noun): A boundary that separates the ecozones of Asia and Wallacea, which is a transitional zone between Asia and Australia. Wallacea is home to a mix of species of both areas.

Tiniest (Adjective): Extremely small; minute.

Tsetse Fly (Noun): A bloodsucking African fly that transmits diseases, including sleeping sickness.

Underscores (Verb): Emphasizes or underlines.

Verge (Noun): The edge or border of something.

Veterinary (Adjective): Relating to the branch of medicine that deals with the diagnosis, treatment, and care of animals.

Vital (Adjective): Absolutely necessary; essential.

Wildlife (Noun): Wild animals collectively; the native fauna (and sometimes flora) of a region.

Woolly Mammoth (Noun): An extinct species of a large, hairy elephant that lived during the Pleistocene epoch until its extinction in the early Holocene period.

Zika Virus (Noun): A virus primarily transmitted through the bites of Aedes mosquitoes, associated with mild symptoms in adults but known to cause severe developmental issues in fetuses when mothers are infected during pregnancy.

Zoonotic Diseases (Noun): Diseases that can be transmitted from animals to humans.

www.ingramcontent.com/pod-product-compliance
Lightning Source LLC
Chambersburg PA
CBHW081329230426
43667CB00018B/2879